MORE PRAISE FOR *DARING DEMOCRACY*

"It is all too easy to fall into despair when observing what is happening in the world and contemplating the severe challenges that humans face. It is much harder, and far more important, to recognize that we need not succumb to what Frances Moore Lappé and Adam Eichen call the 'sense of futility' that 'destroys us' and can instead come together to confront the challenges, overcome them, and once again bend the arc of the moral universe toward justice and freedom. We can join the many others who are 'daring democracy' in many ways, as we learn from this instructive account of hopeful prospects."

—NOAM CHOMSKY

"Frances Moore Lappé and Adam Eichen have written a wonderfully sunny book at an exceptionally dark moment in American politics. They tell us, and I think they are right, that we are witnessing the rise of a movement of movements, and that the movement draws on reservoirs of passion and capacity embedded in our very human nature. This movement of movements that we are beginning to call 'the Resistance' may very well save our democracy. So you need to read this book, and join the movement!"

—FRANCES FOX PIVEN, professor of political science and sociology at City University of New York and coauthor of *Poor People's Movements*

"Show people that what they want is possible and they will act. This book, perhaps better than any other, shows Americans that the democracy they want is possible. Now we must act."

—LAWRENCE LESSIG, Roy L. Furman Professor of Law and Leadership at Harvard Law School and author of *Republic, Lost*

"If you're finding it tough to feel optimistic about the future of our democracy—and lately, who isn't?—then you need to read this book. Frances Moore Lappé and Adam Eichen make clear that building a positive, even joyful pro-democracy movement that restores power to ordinary Americans isn't just possible—it's already happening."

—ZACHARY ROTH, author of *The Great Suppression: Voting Rights, Corporate Cash, and the Conservative Assault on Democracy*

"It is time for a Daring Democracy. This book is a passionate call to 'transform fear into action.' We should heed this message and join the movement for democracy!"

—HEATHER BOOTH, organizer and president of the Midwest Academy

"In this cross-generational effort, Frances Moore Lappé and Adam Eichen capture and explore something very important about our moment in history. Amid the serious and intrusive challenges to our democracy, there is an energetic movement to tear down barriers, advance full participation, and create a democracy that works for everyone. And that movement is creative, is winning in many places, and is bringing new people into the fold. *Daring Democracy* is a great and uplifting read, so grab it and enjoy!"

—MILES RAPOPORT, Senior Practice Fellow in American Democracy at the Harvard Kennedy School and former president of Common Cause and Demos

"As someone who has been on the opposite side of anti-democracy forces, I can say firsthand that Lappé and Eichen speak to the problems plaguing our elections, while also offering compelling solutions. An important book for anyone who cares about democracy in America."

—ZEPHYR TEACHOUT, associate professor of law at Fordham University

DARING DEMOCRACY

FRANCES MOORE LAPPÉ
AND ADAM EICHEN

DARING
DEMOCRACY

IGNITING
POWER, MEANING,
AND CONNECTION
FOR THE AMERICA
WE WANT

BEACON PRESS | BOSTON

To our democracy heroes: the late political philosopher Benjamin Barber, for his deep insights and belief in the capacities of humankind, and Congressman John Lewis, for being our exemplar of courage in action, always inspiring and steadfast.

ı ı

BEACON PRESS
Boston, Massachusetts
www.beacon.org

Beacon Press books
are published under the auspices of
the Unitarian Universalist Association of Congregations.

20 19 18 17   8 7 6 5 4 3 2 1

This book is printed on acid-free paper that meets the uncoated paper
ANSI/NISO specifications for permanence as revised in 1992.

Text design and composition by Kim Arney

Library of Congress Cataloging-in-Publication Data
Names: Lappé, Frances Moore, author. | Eichen, Adam, author.
Title: Daring democracy : igniting power, meaning, and connection for the
America we want / Frances Moore Lappé and Adam Eichen.
Description: Boston : Beacon Press, [2017] | Includes bibliographical
References and index.
Identifiers: LCCN 2017017299 (print) | LCCN 2017032140 (ebook) |
ISBN 9780807023914 (e-book) | ISBN 9780807023815 (pbk. : acid-free paper)
Subjects: LCSH: Democracy—United States. | Political participation—United
States. | United States—Politics and government.
Classification: LCC JK1726 (ebook) | LCC JK1726 .L358 2017 (print) |
DDC 320.973—dc23
LC record available at https://lccn.loc.gov/2017017299

CONTENTS

WHY WE HAD TO WRITE THIS BOOK

WHY WOULD TWO PEOPLE, generations apart, who'd barely met commit to writing a book together about democracy in America during one of the most fraught moments in the country's history? The short answer is that we felt we had no choice.

Together, we've lived almost a century in America and never before have we experienced a moment in which so many of our compatriots are profoundly angry or near despair. At the same time, we share gratitude that our life experiences have enabled us to "taste" emerging solutions—to grasp the root causes and envision a pathway forward.

Despair is our greatest enemy in this moment. We wrote this book to meet it squarely, not with sappy bromides but with hard evidence. Let us explain by sharing a bit of our distinct journeys that brought us to a chance meeting less than two years ago in Mexico City.

Frances. The year is 1966 and the war in Vietnam is raging. I'm fresh out of college and see US military actions in Southeast Asia as evidence of something deeply amiss here at home. Determined to work for justice alongside those in our poorest communities, I head straight for a Quaker organizing school near Philadelphia.

Soon after, I find a job as part of the War on Poverty. Officially, I am hired by the city as a housing inspector, but my assignment is to help organize a chapter of the Welfare Rights Organization. I am a twenty-three-year-old white girl from the South living and working in an African American neighborhood. But as I knock on doors, I'm always welcomed inside.

In our budding chapter what proves most meaningful are the deep connections we make. I feel closest to Lilly. In her early forties, Lilly is able to remain energized and positive despite relentless struggle just to feed and clothe her children.

Then, out of the blue, I get the call: Lilly is gone. She's had a heart attack. But I am convinced that Lilly has died of the stress of poverty itself. Everything about the situation feels so fundamentally wrong.

Months later I wake up with one thought only: I don't want to do anything else to try to "save the world" until I grasp the real roots of Lilly's needless death. I have to know *how* my life is addressing root causes.

I am terrified. I know that to go deep I have to dig in somewhere specific. So why not on hunger? Everyone has to eat. So I begin, asking: are the "experts" right that hunger is caused by food scarcity? Squirreled away in the University of California, Berkeley, agriculture library, I begin what becomes *Diet for a Small Planet*, my attempt to reframe the hunger challenge.

Within less than a decade I am summing up my core message this way: hunger is not caused by a scarcity of food but by a scarcity of democracy.

To this day, I am grateful. The zeitgeist of the 1960s lifted me up, enabling me to feel part of something big, even historic—a movement across all "issues" with people who believed that together we could make the world a better place. I never felt alone. No doubt these experiences kept me motivated all these years.

So, in 2015, I land in Mexico City to attend the world's first conference on how to get money out of the control of so-called democracies. Waiting in the rain for the airport bus, I strike up a conversation with a young American named Adam.

⁝⁝⁝⁝⁝⁝

Adam. The year is 2011, and as a wide-eyed eighteen-year-old, I had just finished my third week at Vassar College and am on my way to attend the first day of the Occupy Wall Street protest.

Never having been part of a protest before, I am both excited and scared. Only a few hundred show up to the rally, which feels to me like a letdown. Yet as I head back to Vassar the next morning, I find out that we made the local news. Immediately, I feel *a part* of something.

Occupy soon explodes across the country. I become a staunch Occupy defender, debating professors who call the movement aimless, and I start avidly pursuing the study of political science.

Then, on the morning of November 17, 2011, the two-month anniversary of Occupy, I throw myself into the political maelstrom. I arrive in Zuccotti Park around 6:30 a.m. My stomach clutches, and I want to turn back and go home. Feeling an affinity with the movement and to the history that was waiting to be made, I don't.

We attempt to delay Wall Street's opening bell, rally against student debt, and take over a busy, six-lane thoroughfare with ten thousand people. The experience of collectively assembling in common purpose fills me with passion. I open myself to the voices of others—people whose lives are so different from my own—shaking the comfort of growing up in a financially stable household. The experience alters my intellectual life, too; I become fixated on why our society is incapable of alleviating suffering, of addressing the problems we collectively face.

Soon thereafter I join Democracy Matters, a national, student-based organization fighting for democracy reform as a way to supplement my learning in the classroom. I never thought about democracy policy, but after being trained by the staff my eyes are opened. I find the answer I was seeking. Until we fix our democracy, we will never be able to address the crises we face today.

After three years organizing with Democracy Matters, my commitment to democracy reform solidifies. I am invited to attend a conference in Mexico City on international money in politics. I am about to depart for a year in Paris to research this exact subject, so how could I turn it down?

Little do I know I will meet the legendary Frances Moore Lappé, beginning what will become a virtually nonstop conversation about democracy.

||||||||||||

Nine months later, in the spring of 2016, we became friends as we marched together from Philadelphia to Washington, DC, as part of Democracy Spring, a movement fighting for deep democracy reforms. We discovered remarkable similarities in our earliest political moments and spent countless hours on the march talking. Afterward we enjoyed writing short pieces about democracy reforms. But at 11 p.m. on election night 2016 our world shifted, as it did for so many. We'd been energized with hope by Democracy Spring, and suddenly all that we had marched for seemed under threat. We knew we had to tell America about the Democracy Movement that is so energizing us.

Soon we had the good fortune to be able to collaborate with Beacon Press in writing the book you now hold in your hands.

May it further the conversation, connection, and actions that are needed now more than ever.

—Frances Moore Lappé and Adam Eichen
May 2017

RETHINKING THE CRISIS

All that we are and will and do depends, in the last analysis,
upon what we believe the Nature of Things to be.

—ALDOUS HUXLEY, 1945

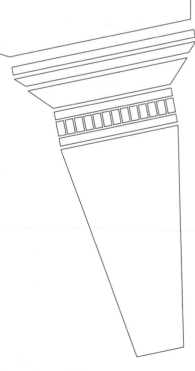

CHAPTER ONE

WHAT IT WILL TAKE

"IT'S FAR TOO LATE and things are far too bad for pessimism," wrote author Dee Hock in 1999, and we cheer in agreement.[1] Yet we also know that in this treacherous time, it's tough, really tough, to stay true to this wise insight. And that's why we wrote this book. It's our way to find focus, energy, and honest hope.

What has helped a lot is one realization: despite the repeated refrain to the contrary, Americans are not fundamentally a divided people. In the 2016 election, what drew many to Donald Trump was his pledge to side with regular folks against the elite populating "the swamp." At the same time, one thing repelling many people from him was fear that he would instead fill the swamp, accelerating the corporate takeover of our democracy.

Our point is that Americans who are typically portrayed as being far apart were actually seeking a similar change. In fact, poll after poll shows striking common ground in our values as well as our vision of the democracy we want. With one big exception. Surveys of the super-rich show a huge chasm between their hopes for our country's direction and those of the rest of us.[2]

Our book is about building on what most of us share so that we can transform fear into action together—action strong enough to get at the very roots of our historic crisis, that of the degradation and assault on democracy itself.

In our opening note we recounted a bit of our separate journeys leading to our initial encounter in 2015 at the first Global Conference on Money in Politics, in Mexico City. There we found ourselves surrounded by multitudes gathered from dozens of countries, all devoting their lives to one shared insight: democracy is not a "choice." Creating democracies truly accountable to their citizens is essential to our very survival—to the flourishing of societies supporting human life, and now, because of climate change, to the survival of the Earth as we've inherited it.

This is a colossal claim, we know. But there's one point on which human history makes us absolutely certain: it's not the magnitude of a challenge that crushes the human spirit.

At our founding, farmers, shopkeepers, laborers, and slaves defeated an empire. Since then, black Americans risked their lives to fight against the subjugation of slavery and then for their democratic rights. Women fought for seven decades to secure suffrage. In the 1930s a democratic upsurge by workers led to the New Deal, which achieved basic protections of human dignity in the workplace and in old age. For millions, though, the promise of democracy remained unfulfilled.

Soon thereafter, McCarthyism's witch-hunts again dimmed our democracy, but brave Americans fought back. And by the 1960s we began stepping up to halt an unwise war, demand civil rights protections, and embrace a War on Poverty that by the early seventies had cut the poverty rate almost in half—lightning speed compared with the pace of most social change.[3]

Confronted with that which appears to be impossible, time and again humanity has embraced the challenge with gusto, grit, and, ultimately, triumph.

No, it is not a huge challenge that kills the spirit. What most defeats us is feeling useless—that we have nothing to say, nothing to contribute, that we don't count. A sense of futility is what destroys us. And it's precisely this emotional plague that today afflicts too many Americans across all political lines.

Through our long social evolution, we humans have evolved as doers. We are problem-solvers. If we were content to be whiners and couch potatoes, no doubt we could never have accomplished any of human cultures' vast achievements. Right now, though, many of us are filled with uncertainty about what to do, just as we most need all hands on deck. So we wrote this book in part to help ourselves and others to rethink core assumptions that disempower us, specifically about the meaning and power of democracy.

THREE POWERFUL IDEAS

Often we hear that "seeing is believing," but for humans, in many ways, it's the other way around: believing is seeing. No less than Albert Einstein explained: "It is theory which decides what can be observed." If we do not believe in the possibility of genuine democracy, we will not be able to see signs of it emerging. So it's become ever clearer to us that the possibility of creating a flourishing democratic society rests on whether enough Americans believe that it's achievable. Certainly we do.

Yet, to take on any mammoth undertaking, a belief in possibility is but one ingredient. To jump in wholeheartedly, most of us also need to feel in our bones that success is essential and that there's a way for us to make a real difference. Applied to democracy, success depends therefore on whether we can embrace three simple but powerful ideas:

One. To fulfill every public need and to advance every public good, *democracy is essential.* None of our deepest needs can be served, nor our opportunities or threats met, without it.

Two. Genuine *democracy is possible*—here, we mean real democracy, accountable to the people, not to narrow, private interests.

Three. There is a rewarding, even exhilarating, role for each of us in making democracy real. As we will show in this book, a bipartisan Democracy Movement is emerging that's not about dutiful "do-gooding." It meets deep emotional needs, and maybe it's even what our founders meant by our right to "the pursuit of happiness."

These core tenets are not taken on faith. They've become real for us as we've continually tested them against our lived experiences and in our ongoing study. In this book we hope you will become a believer as well.

ESSENTIAL

When we assert that democracy is essential we mean that it's not just a "good" thing. It is the only approach to governance that brings forth the best of who we are. To really thrive, to live our possibility, we hold that beyond the physical, humans must meet at least three essential needs: for connection, meaning, and a sense of agency—that is, a sense of personal power. When these needs are met we can often accomplish what virtually no one before believed possible.

Let's begin with "connection." Most of us thrive best when we feel connected not only to our immediate loved ones but within a community in which we feel we can be ourselves and be accepted, encouraged, and protected. Next, "meaning," the need for purpose beyond our own survival—what philosopher Erich Fromm called our need to "make a dent," to believe that before we die we can feel our lives have helped bend to some tiny degree the evolutionary curve toward more life. And finally, to have meaning we must also have a sense of agency in shaping the world around us, to have a say in our wider communities' destinies.

Together the meeting of these three needs comprises, for us, the essence of human dignity. Thus, democracy, as it enables us to meet these needs, is the realization of human dignity.

Now, to aspects of our nature that are less pleasant to look at. For one, it's clear that we don't do well when power is tightly concentrated—whether in real life or in psychological experiments. And to ensure that power is fluid and dispersed, not stuck and tightly held, democracy is the only pathway.

Where power has been highly concentrated, from Nazi Germany to Stalinist Russia to Mao's China, many "good" people commit unspeakable acts. In the twentieth century alone, beyond wars, humans have likely killed more than one hundred million other humans in massive governmental assaults on civilians, including the Holocaust and the Russian Gulag.[4] And in recent years, civilians have been targeted in bloody conflicts in Syria and elsewhere.

Consider also that highly concentrated corporate power allows manufacturers to protect profits by hiding human and ecological costs—such as big firms making big money on pesticides, tobacco, sugar-laden products, and fossil fuels. If current trends persist, tobacco alone could take one billion lives during this century, the World Health Organization predicts.[5] And this pales in comparison with the devastating impact on our planet of unaddressed climate change.

Evidence of our capacity for behaving brutally when power is tightly held also comes from what became known as the "Stanford Prison experiment." In 1971, Stanford professor Philip Zimbardo put young people who'd tested normal into a mock prison setting and divided them into prisoners and guards, dressed for their roles. The experiment was planned for two weeks, but on the sixth day Zimbardo abruptly called it off. He had to. Using techniques eerily similar to those shown in photos of US soldiers in Iraq's Abu Ghraib prison more than three decades later, the experiment's "guards" had begun brutalizing their "prisoners" to the point of severe emotional breakdown.[6]

All of this, and so much more, offers inescapable proof that decent people do horrific things when power is too concentrated.

More broadly, concentrated power measured by economic inequality—typically translating into political power—saps the life out of a society. UK social epidemiologists found that economic inequality strongly correlates with higher rate of a vast range of social and physical ills, from homicide to imprisonment to mental illness.[7]

Democracy, by definition, is the opposite. It lives in the dispersion of power. It flourishes to the degree that all of us have a real voice, one that meaningfully helps to shape society's big decisions.

But concentrated power is only one condition virtually certain to elicit the worst in us. A second condition is secrecy—the lack of transparency, whether in government, on Wall Street, or in our personal lives. Before the 2008 financial collapse that wrecked lives and whole economies, bankers were busily creating highly risky financial "products" and feverishly pushing them on unwitting customers. Among their creators, a favorite slogan was I.B.G. Y.B.G.: "I'll be gone, you'll be gone." Its meaning? The traders creating the financial nightmare harming billions knew they would be gone from their companies by the time their schemes went south, running off unscathed with bonuses in tow.[8] And they were right. When we humans believe no one's watching, we're vastly more likely to cheat. Democracy requires transparency.

A third condition that puts us at risk has less to do with economic and political rules than with social norms. A "culture of blame" is what we call it—a culture in which people jump to finger-pointing before exploring shared responsibility. Ongoing conflict is certain, and time spent pointing fingers is time lost from actually solving a problem. In this political moment, for example, time and resources devoted to blaming and expelling immigrants is time and resources lost from generating new jobs, rebuilding infrastructure, and curing diseases, or, for that matter, creating the fair and rewarding society that can help to undercut the appeal of extremists' ideologies threatening us in the first place.

For humans, blaming is a really tricky piece. While we come equipped with deep capacities for caring, empathy, and cooperation, we also reveal—unfortunately—even in our earliest years, a tendency to "other"—to dislike those who seem different from us.[9] From there, it's easy to imagine how cultures of blame arise.

Our tendency to prefer those like us and distance ourselves from those perceived as "the other" has huge downsides. For one, it brings very real harm, including the limiting of democratic rights, as we note later in the selective targeting of people of color by those seeking to suppress voting rights. Second, othering diminishes the lives of all of us, as the gifts of those perceived as "other" are denied their full flourishing. Imagine how many potential scientists, artists, teachers, and presidents were never allowed to arise in our society because of othering. Othering is the opposite of valuing diversity, which enhances creativity, innovation, and our overall capacity to solve problems, social science research shows.[10]

As we permit othering, so too do we make ourselves vulnerable to its being used against our own interests. When Donald Trump falsely portrays immigrants as criminals, for example, he's diverting attention from his policies that are already threatening us as they deepen inequality and diminish public health and safety protections.

What's also clear, however, is that humanity doesn't have to stay in this dreadful trap. Vast differences in cultures on this point prove that, indeed, we humans are malleable. The Democracy Movement at the heart of this book offers endless opportunities for realizing common ground and shedding imagined differences as we engage shoulder to shoulder to bring about the America we want.

In all of this we can learn to accept the truth that, since we're all connected, we're all implicated. Both for better and for worse. On first thought, this realization can be uncomfortable. It means, for example, that we citizens can't just blame Wall Street bankers for the Great Recession. We also have to ask, Where were *we* as the banking industry was deregulated, enabling the disaster?

As discomfiting as it might at first seem, the insight that we're *mutually* accountable, that we each carry some share of responsibility for our society's predicaments or progress, is good news. It means we each do have real power. We are not simply victims. We realize that, even if in minor ways, every choice we make does ripple out. Then, as we harness this power and experience working together in democratic problem-solving, we can reduce our tendency to "other" and to blame.

To sum up our argument: democracy depends on the active creation and protection of these three conditions—dispersion of power, transparency, and a cultural norm of accepting mutual accountability among citizens. These conditions protect us from the worst tendencies in our nature and are also essential for meeting the three emotional needs identified above that humans need to thrive: for connection, meaning, and power.

Understood this way, democracy is essential both to protect us from the worst in our nature and to realize the best. On this ground, we reject Winston Churchill's snarky comment that "democracy is the worst form of government except all those other forms that have been tried from time to time." Democracy is not just essential. It is noble, and in fact, worthy of our devotion.

POSSIBLE

When we assert that *democracy is possible*, of course, we do not mean a perfect democracy—one fully transparent and accountable to all citizens. We agree with William Hastie, America's first African American federal appellate judge, who noted that democracy is "becoming, rather than being. It can easily be lost, but never is fully won. Its essence is eternal struggle."[11]

So the real question for each generation is whether America's democracy is still "becoming" or is instead stymied or even in decline. To believe that democracy is "possible" suggests both that we believe humans are theoretically equipped for it and that history offers proof that we've shown ourselves capable of manifesting at least some of its key elements, if imperfectly.

What's the proof of our capacity?

Democracy requires our species, or at least the vast majority of its members, to share a deep sensitivity to fairness, along with capacities for empathy and cooperation. Fortunately, a vast and growing body of social and neural science shows that all three are fundamental human qualities.[12]

About our potential for empathy, we now know, for example, that what are called "mirror neurons" in our brains fire as if we were taking an action even when we're only observing it.[13] Some amusing evidence of our cooperative spirit came from researchers using MRI scans to observe the brains of subjects competing and cooperating. Cooperating, they found, lights up the brain's reward-processing system in ways comparable to eating chocolate.[14]

On our innate sense of fairness, even the supposed godfather of greed, Adam Smith, wrote more than two centuries ago that humans feel "in a peculiar manner tied, bound and obliged to the observation of justice."[15] Even Capuchin monkeys demonstrate a measurable sense of fairness. In one experiment they happily accepted a snack of cucumbers as long as their nearby buddies were getting the same, but when they saw a neighbor monkey being given grapes while they had to settle for cucumbers, some said, effectively, "hell, no," throwing their cucumber treat right back at the caretaker.[16] So monkeys know inequitable distribution when they see it, too.

Now, what's the proof that those capacities can create democratic progress through elected government responsive to the needs of the majority?

Here at home, from 1933 to 1938, our federal government created fairness rules—including Social Security, the right of workers to organize, and a legal minimum wage, dramatically narrowing the gap between most of us and a tiny minority at the top. For decades this approach fostered broad-based economic prosperity. From 1947 to 1973 median family income in the United States doubled. Every economic class gained, with the poorest gaining the most.[17]

Other examples of democratic progress abound outside of the United States. As George Lakey notes in his book *Viking Economics*, some Nordic countries were among Europe's most unequal a century ago, but citizen "movements . . . challenged a thousand years of poverty and oppression, took the offensive, and built democracy."[18] Today, most Nordic democracies, for example, boast voter turnout of 77 percent or more, compared with about 56 percent in the United States.[19]

Note that Americans often dismiss evidence of Scandinavia's social goods, including superior education and health care, because we absorb the notion that such gains come at the expense of economic dynamism. If you've let this notion deprive you of inspiration, consider that in the 2016 *Global Innovation Index*, Sweden ranked second, surpassing the fourth-placed United States; three Scandinavian countries were among the top ten.[20]

Germany is also proof of possibility. Since the 1940s, it has gone from fascist global pariah to paragon of fair elections, with an economy in which workers have a significant voice. Its elections are not gripped by the influence of private wealth, and income distribution in Germany is about a third more equal than in the United States.[21]

Our point here is simple: to jump into the good fight for democracy, we need confidence in its possibility, and a goal of our book is to show that grounds for that confidence are all around us.

A ROLE FOR EACH OF US

Our final premise is that right now, in the budding movement we call the Democracy Movement, there's an exhilarating role for each of us—one that fills deep emotional needs. In part III we strive to capture this emerging "movement of movements," focused on democracy system reforms, perhaps the first of its kind in our nation's history.

By this, we mean that Americans embodying the broadest array of issue passions are embracing an additional commitment—to work for democracy itself. They are not abandoning their specific concerns. They are creating a "canopy of hope" across all of them by coming together to create a transparent and accountable democracy, one that is essential to success in addressing any of them.

Stopping many Americans from imagining such a movement's growing power is the oft-repeated refrain that we are a "divided people," and we know divided people can accomplish little. Yet, as we've stressed, there is strong unity in the widespread anger at and sense of betrayal by a "rigged system." Eighty-four percent of Americans, for example, believe that money has too much influence in our elections.[22]

Even on specific issues there's much more common ground than typically appreciated. One study, covering 388 questions, compared views of people living in red congressional districts or states with those of people living in blue congressional districts or states. It found "no statistical differences" in two out of three cases.[23] Also note that though President Trump calls climate change a hoax, 74 percent of Americans, including half of Republicans, agreed in 2015 that the government should be doing "a substantial amount" to combat it.[24]

Our book is about naming such unity and building on it. Just as important as recognizing our common ground is grasping how we got to this place, to the election of a president who immediately began disappointing many of his supporters while scaring the daylights out of the rest of us.

So there's a lot of digging to do. This book is about that—digging for the deepest roots of this historic crisis so that we can choose the most powerful steps we can each take right now, knowing that real democracy is a daring and noble calling and that it is achievable.

CHAPTER TWO

BRINGING DOWN THE THOUGHT BARRIERS

LET'S START WITH THE TAP ROOT, the power of ideas—those often-unspoken assumptions that shape an entire culture. We've long been fascinated by how many differences among societies worldwide—from murder rates to assumptions about how children best learn to the legitimacy of inherited gender roles—can be explained by such ideas, often called "frames," that shape our behavior.

Take the highly charged issue of immigration. Canadians frame immigration as an opportunity, and as a result so many Canadians want to sponsor Syrian refugees that there's a waiting list. Many are even willing to pay for the privilege of helping. But here, Americans are encouraged to frame immigration as a threat, and thus to expect strict limits. So we've admitted one-third as many Syrian refugees as has Canada, even though our population is ten times bigger.[1]

Frames have power.

As suggested in chapter 1, our ideas even shape what we can and cannot see. Applied to our national crisis today, we argue that if we don't believe in an accountable, vital democracy engaging citizens, we won't see it anywhere—neither the movement to create it nor the signs of its emergence.

An amusing experiment illustrates the point. Psychologists instructed subjects observing a basketball game to count passes among players. During the game, a woman dressed in a gorilla costume entered and pounded her chest in the middle of the action. Yet half the subjects did not see this most obvious anomaly. They were focused on counting passes.[2] We're reminded of George Orwell's observation: "To see what is in front of one's nose needs a constant struggle." If we are not expecting something or are focused elsewhere, too often we just don't see it. Thus, a challenge we tackle in this book is shifting our expectations and focus so that we can see democracy arising.

The first step, though, is checking our mental frames antithetical to democracy. So here we probe more deeply the big ideas that have led to our democracy's crisis—focusing on several commonly held ideas about the market, freedom, and democracy itself that hold us back.

Ultimately, we believe this exploration can help answer the biggest question we can think of: *why are we together creating a society full of suffering that as individuals none of us really wants?* We don't know a single person who gets up in the morning thinking, It's great that one in five American children lives in poverty.[3] Or that babies die here at twice the rate of many other industrial countries.[4] Not to mention that even before our 2016 election, America ranked fifty-second in a "perceptions of electoral integrity" index among 153 countries.[5] Since on these and other basics our society is far from what we want, *why don't we do more to change it?*

It can't be that we really don't care. There's no reason Americans would care less than others do about their country's well-being. For us, the most obvious answer is simply that *most of us feel powerless*, for otherwise wouldn't we go for what we really want? But that answer only raises the *why* question again. Why do we feel so powerless?

Here we suggest several big ideas robbing us of power, ideas now trapping us in a self-reinforcing spiral of powerlessness from which we can free ourselves.

HOW A ONE-RULE MARKET BREEDS BRUTAL CAPITALISM

Markets are really handy. They have served human culture for eons. After all, trading our sweet potatoes for your clay bowls made a lot of sense. Markets, historian Karl Polanyi explained in his classic 1944 book *The Great Transformation*, were long embedded in webs of mutuality shaped by each culture's traditions.

But once the notion of an infallible market—one called "magic" by Ronald Reagan—took off, the long-held understanding of a market embedded in community was left in the dust. By the 1960s the simple idea of a market largely working on its own was put forth most starkly by Milton Friedman. Building on the theories of Austrian economist Friedrich August von Hayek, the influential Chicago School of Economics, led by Friedman, argued that a "free market" operating with only the most minimal role for government is the bulwark against communism.[6]

These thinkers claimed Adam Smith, the eighteenth-century author of *The Wealth of Nations*, as their own, appropriating his image of a market in which an "invisible hand" guides individual self-interest to serve society's needs. (Adam Smith neckties were popular in the Ronald Reagan White House, we understand.) Yet this worldview has led to what we call a "one-rule market," a market whose single driving premise is to bring the highest return to existing wealth. Thus, wealth—and the power it brings—inexorably concentrates in ever fewer hands, and widespread impoverishment follows.

Smith would likely be appalled by how his metaphor has been made to serve this outcome. He wrote tenderly of our "moral sentiments," saying that though "man may supposed" to be selfish, "there are evidently some principles in his nature, which interest him in the fortune of others, and render their happiness necessary to him, though he derives nothing from it except the pleasure of seeing it."[7] Nonetheless, Friedman's narrow market logic, a vulgarization of Smith's sophisticated views, is beloved by those who believe it makes us "free to choose."

In the 1980s, I, Frances, was excited to be invited to debate Milton Friedman at the University of California, Berkeley. But having long worried about how his concept of "freedom" had been used in our culture, I was nervous, too. In a big auditorium on campus, Friedman reinforced his thesis that the market serves freedom by enabling people to make choices based on their values. When my turn came, I was brief. If that's true, I said, the market serves human freedom *only on one condition*: that people have purchasing power to express their values in the market. Thus, freedom, using Friedman's definition, actually expands as societies set rules to ensure that wealth is widely and fairly spread. A market operating without rules to keep wealth circulating widely and fairly actually denies individuals freedom. Needless to say, the Nobel laureate didn't agree with me.

Since that night, further evidence has amassed that in our "one-rule"—highest return to existing wealth—market, more and more of us end up with fewer and fewer choices: of jobs paying enough to live in dignity, of neighborhoods in which we can afford a home, of higher education that won't lock us into lifetime debt.

Because our culture has embraced the Friedman worldview with particular vigor, it's not surprising that the United States has become more economically unequal than any country in western Europe.[8] In the first three years after the financial meltdown, almost all the gains in wealth in the United States went to the top 1 percent.[9] Thus, too many Americans face multiple indignities, from poor schools and food insecurity to a lack of access to health care. Note that inequality in America doesn't just mean tougher lives for those at the bottom; it means shorter lives. The gap in the lifespan, for example, between men in the bottom 10 percent economically and those in the top 10 percent grew from five years for men born in 1920 to twelve years for men born in 1940. In others words, over this period, poverty has come to rob American men living in poverty of seven years of life.[10] Such outcomes are one reason we call this form of a market system "brutal capitalism."

Defenders of the one-rule market gospel rave about its efficiency while failing to acknowledge hidden, uncounted costs. Such downsides get dubbed "externalities" but they are in fact our "realities." Take coal. We hear about its contribution to heating the planet, true. But in counting other costs, including to health, and additional environmental impacts, the total burden each year comes to as much as half a trillion dollars.[11] Or consider the celebrated success of US agriculture, where the "free market" efficiency myth is dispelled by one stunning fact: per acre, US agriculture feeds fewer people than does Indian or Chinese.[12]

Plus, we're made to believe that the market's success depends on shifting everything possible from a community benefit, created by all for the use of all—even health care and education—to something very different: a dollar exchange among consumers. From this stance, human beings coming together, deliberating, setting standards, and choosing the rules governing the market—in other words, democracy—is increasingly viewed as downright dangerous. Yet it is, of course, the only safeguard of basic fairness, healthy communities, and our irreplaceable commons.

Another outcome? Narrow market logic magnifies whatever sells—and sex and violence sell. So entertainment, advertising, fashion, and now even newscasts become increasingly sensational and sexualized. In fact, as will be shown, market reductionism destroys the whole model of "news," understood as reasonable people attempting to share knowledge of world events. Narrow market logic gone amok had by 2016 given rise to an oxymoron incompatible with democracy: "fake news."

Finally, and most profoundly, is this negative consequence of our supposedly no-rules market: if we believe an unerring market rewards those who work like the devil to succeed, logically it follows that those who fail to achieve the "American dream" are at fault. They are not deserving of help. From that frame, Mitt Romney probably really believed his claim that half of Americans are "takers," as he privately told supporters in 2012.[13] Plus, because of the aura of infallibility surrounding the market, we're convinced that interfering to assist the "laggards" would only throw the market out of equilibrium, and we'd all suffer.

So, we come to see ourselves in a "dog eat dog" world—once called "social Darwinism," an idea scientists discredited long ago but unfortunately failed to dislodge from our culture. Sadly, rather than spotting the system problem—the notion of an infallible market—we're caught in rampant shaming and blaming that divides us, undermining our power to come together to shape solutions.

WHAT "WE DECIDE TO DO TOGETHER"

And, there's another big downside to a narrow, market dogma. Viewing our prized market economy as operating in opposition to government leads us to disdain government, and that means disdain for ourselves; for as Barney Frank, with three decades in the House of Representatives under his belt, once reminded us: government is simply what "we decide to do together."

That's a start, but it hardly captures government's essential roles in creating a prosperous society. In their provocative book, *American Amnesia*, professors Jacob S. Hacker and Paul Pierson brilliantly remind us that in the twentieth century: "It is hard to find a major innovation that did not significantly owe its birth to public support." Among the many breakthroughs they attribute to public investment are key medicines, GPS, radar, microwave, as well as the computer and the internet that then catalyzed ongoing private-sector innovations.[14]

Anti-government dogma today tells us that virtually all "regulation" undercuts prosperity. So, of course, Americans don't appreciate that, to pick just one example, since the Clean Air Act passed in 1970 our economy has grown three-fold, yet, simultaneously, we've cut levels of six major air pollutants by more than 70 percent. Anti-government zealots tell us only that "regulations" are too costly, so we don't learn that, for example, according to an EPA peer-reviewed estimate, by 2020 the annual benefit of Clean Air Act protections will come to $2 trillion, exceeding their costs by a ratio of more than thirty to one.[15] Neither do we learn that just two simple federal safety measures—those requiring air bags and seat belts—save many more lives each year that are taken in homicides.[16]

Appreciating government's essential roles and contributions changes how we view taxes, too. Note that in the World War II era, a Gallup poll found that 85 to 90 percent of Americans thought the taxes they paid were fair. (By 2017, 61 percent shared this view, which is still more favorable than many would guess.)[17]

Bringing down the market-is-all-we-need thought barrier means taking off the blinders and appreciating that accountable government and a market economy are essential allies, not enemies. Certainly, without accountable government enforcing antimonopoly rules, concentration takes over and the very virtues we most associate with a market—competition, for one—are out the window.

FREEDOM VS. ECONOMIC SECURITY?

There's yet another big thought barrier in the path of vital and accountable democracy. It's about how we understand freedom. Americans prize freedom—"Live free or die" has been New Hampshire's motto since 1945. But seldom do we pause to define it. That's too bad because differences in how we define freedom move us in very different political directions.

For example, if freedom means defense against government, all rules that government sets are perceived as evil interference. But if freedom is the opportunity to participate in exercising power with others, including creating rules that ensure economic opportunity for all and protect our communities, then government is neither inherently evil nor benign. Its impact depends on what we citizens do or fail to do.

Simple free-market ideology teaches us that there's always a trade-off between basic economic security assured by the government and a nation's economic growth and innovation. We've got to choose: do we want security or economic dynamism?

But this dichotomy is false, because as we've seen, countries that achieve stronger measures of well-being than we do also do fine economically.[18] The Nordic countries, emphasizing basic security via strong, publicly supported childcare, health care, higher education, and income for elders, rank high in economic competitiveness as well as in longevity and happiness.[19] Might we want to add "being free to live a long and happy life" to our freedom equation?

As we Americans envision the future we want and ponder the meaning of freedom, we could come to see basic security not as a threat to freedom but its foundation. Such is the understanding of freedom at the heart of President Franklin Delano Roosevelt's commitment to what he called the "four freedoms": freedom of speech and religion, and freedom from want and fear. He gave soldiers returning home after World War II a medal with those words emblazoned on it. A strong positive link between freedom and security (the end of "want") is our national heritage.

THE SPIRAL OF POWERLESSNESS

The dogma of an infallible market, the crusade against government, and a narrow view of freedom result in a brutal form of capitalism that denies many of us a sense of agency—personal power in our lives—as well as community, as it rips our society apart.

Moreover, we see the logic of brutal capitalism working hand in glove with another widely held assumption: a dim view of human nature as essentially self-centered and competitive. Much of Western philosophy, after all, draws on Thomas Hobbes's dark view of our origins. In *Leviathan*, he wrote in 1651 that "during the time men live without a common power to keep them all in awe, they are in that condition called war . . . of every man, against every man."[20]

And, way before Hobbes, a second-century-BCE proverb translates to "Man is a wolf to his fellow man." Such bleak assessments of human nature, as selfish with no regard for others' well-being, have obviously been with us for a very long time. And "rational self-interest" remains the foundational premise of standard economics. One telling result is that economics students, imbibing this premise in their course work, show up as more self-centered in psychological testing.[21]

So our culture carries in it the dreary view that our selfish and competitive traits trump our more cooperative selves. From there it's hard to trust each other. In 1972, almost half of Americans felt they could trust others; however, by 2016, as brutal capitalism tightened its grip, only about a third felt that same trust.[22] Because democracy depends on an assumption that humans can come together for the common good, distrust itself helps to sink democracy's chances. Viewing our nature as essentially self-interested, we come to doubt our own and others' capacities to deliberate, learn, and compromise for the good of all.

This cultural frame teaching us to distrust others and just fend for ourselves leads us down a self-reinforcing *spiral of powerlessness* that goes like this: given our flawed nature, a market that works on its own to sort things out for us looks really attractive; in fact turning over our fate to an infallible "free market" makes perfect sense. But, as noted, a one-rule economy—highest return to existing wealth—makes it virtually inevitable that wealth, and with it, political power, becomes ever more tightly held. Economic elites dominate political contests through massive campaign contributions, as the following chapters lay out. Understandably, our representatives in Washington and in our statehouses come to accept—no doubt partly unconsciously—that their decisions must favor their wealthy funders' interests, not ours. Our favorite label for this sad outcome is "privately held government."

Then what happens? Distrust deepens still further, as we see those at the economic pinnacle behave callously. Millionaire Wall

Street bankers daily walk by a growing number of homeless people. CEOs reap huge profits from selling sugar-laden drinks implicated in twenty-five thousand US deaths annually; and fossil-fuel magnates help to heat our planet and destroy life while raking in more than $20 billion a year from US taxpayers via subsidies.[23]

In this awful cycle we're affirmed in our starting assumption: humans really are heartless materialists, looking out only for themselves, with the most powerful inevitably screwing the rest of us. So, we disengage further, believing that trying to have a real voice is futile.

But nothing in this spiral of powerlessness is inevitable.

On this we want to add a surprising note we find, oddly, encouraging. Americans typically dismiss Scandinavia as either too "socialist"—"its taxes are too high"—or so different from us as to offer no useful lessons. All Americans want to be millionaires, the story line goes, so we'd never accept the "leveling" they tolerate in "those" countries. But what if the concentration of wealth in say, Sweden, were comparable to that in the United States? At the same time, though, what if it had achieved vastly greater freedom of opportunity in higher education, health care, retirement, childcare, and more, all covered with public support? Plus, in politics, what if Swedes had kept private money's grip at bay and their voter turnout was one-third higher than ours?

In fact, all this is true.[24]

So, the lesson for us could be that when citizens stand up strongly, as Swedish workers did in the 1930s and onward, they can achieve a greater voice in political decisions, much fairer income distribution, and a quality of life freer of fear and richer in opportunity.[25] And they can do so, *even though* they have not yet achieved a fair distribution of wealth. One reason might be that Sweden's modern economic "guru" was a different Noble laureate, not Milton Friedman but Gunnar Myrdal, who rejected Friedman's rigid market dogmatism. Myrdal believed economic dynamism and prosperity flowed from investing in people.

Our point is multilayered. The dogmatic beliefs that have created economic and political rules tightly concentrating income, wealth, and political power in our country are those proven over our long social evolution typically to bring forth the worst in people, as we laid out in the previous chapter. No wonder we're in trouble.

At the same time, nothing is as fixed as it seems.

To create the America we want we can reject the premises fueling the spiral of powerlessness and reverse its deadly momentum. To do so, we can rethink core ideas about democracy itself that stand in our way.

DITCHING DEMOCRACY'S SORRY RAP

In the previous chapter we declared that hope for real progress depends in part on the degree to which we believe that *democracy is essential*—that none of our deepest needs or values can be served, nor opportunities seized and threats faced, without it. That's quite a claim.

It's also a challenge. Believing that democracy is essential depends a lot on our emotional attachment to it. Yet, as we lamented in chapter 1, democracy is too commonly viewed as kind of shabby, simply the best we flawed humans can do—which hardly inspires devotion. So it's critical that we dig up and reexamine additional "thought barriers" that dim our confidence in democracy and thus help to deprive us of the America most of us desire. The first we've already touched upon.

Democracy is out of reach because it depends on humans overcoming our self-centered nature. But our species evolved in tightly knit tribes in which we became by far the most social of primates. As noted, most humans have an innate sense of fairness, have a capacity for empathy, and take pleasure in cooperating.[26] Confirming these findings is research suggesting that humans are happier when giving rather than receiving and happier when outcomes for others are not extremely different from one's own.[27] Of course, we're also capable of extreme brutality; thus, to repeat our key point: what shows up is largely shaped by the social rules we together create and uphold.

Also very practically, we can shake off the deadly generalization about human beings' incapacity for democracy by observing how our species is doing in societies where citizens are standing up for democracy more than we Americans are today. Europeans' embrace of public financing of elections is one example.

Democracy is a dull, burdensome duty—the spinach we must eat to get our dessert of personal freedoms. Once we realize that protecting individual freedom from interference is only the beginning, our eyes open to a very exciting dimension of democracy: citizens' *freedom to participate in power.* As we move from the narrow, negative freedom of "Get out of my way" to the positive freedom of "I have a real say," much changes. With this understanding we grasp that while rights and privileges protect us, it is in our duties and responsibilities that much of our power lies. We come to see that fixing our democracy deficits—with avenues for each of us—is all about realizing our power.

As we hope you'll discover in later chapters, instead of being a boring, annoying "you should," the practice of "living democracy" becomes an exhilarating calling, perhaps unlocking parts of ourselves that we didn't even know existed. There, in stories of democratic engagement, we emphasize democracy's inherent passion, dignity, and promise.

Democracy is losing favor almost everywhere because it's failing. Worldwide, positive sentiment about democracy's capacity to solve society's problems is indeed waning.[28] In this country, one in six Americans is now so disillusioned as to approve of the idea of military rule, up from one in fifteen in 1995.[29] But it is not democracy that is failing. It is the lack of democracy that's taking us down—primarily, the growing crisis of concentrated wealth controlling our political system. So the big threat we can take on is citizens' lost hope for real democracy.

And we are not alone; millions across the world are also fighting to claim and reclaim democracy in their respective countries. In recent years, movements for democracy have emerged in Spain, France, Turkey, Iceland, and many other places.

OUR CHANGING MINDS

We've stressed in this chapter that the first avenue for finding direction in these tough times is in recognizing the ideas that have held us back. The great news is that neuroscientists now assure us that our brains—producing these frames—evolve moment to moment. New thoughts and experiences create new synapses in our brains, and with them, the potential to see new possibilities.[30] "When the brain thinks that something is possible, it will sketch out the route for achieving it," Harvard's Srinivasan Pillay explains.[31]

In other words, hope has power.

And a big, big shock can help, too. It can shake us up enough to reconsider assumptions. The election of Donald Trump and many of the steps he is taking—such as filling his cabinet with the very corporate chiefs from which he promised to wrest control—are causing disorientation for some. Many of us are living in a national "moment of psychic dissonance"—a time when long-held assumptions about our country no longer hold. But, as in a frightening storm, the biggest tree can topple and for the first time we're able to see its roots; so in our nation's storm, we hope our book will help to identify some of the deepest roots that lie in our own faulty or incomplete assumptions.

This storm is thus a great time for asking, how, specifically, did we get here and what are the lessons we must glean? So, before turning to solutions, let's explore how over the past forty years, in particular, some of the most dangerous ideas we've just covered have been brilliantly, actively, and dangerously spread.

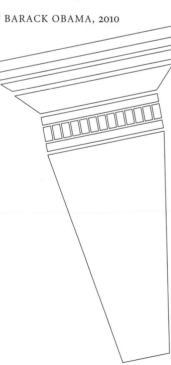

EXPOSING
THE ROOTS

Millions of Americans are struggling to get by, and their voices shouldn't be drowned out by millions of dollars in secret, special interest advertising. The American people's voices should be heard.

—PRESIDENT BARACK OBAMA, 2010

CHAPTER THREE

MANIPULATING THE MINDSET

SO FAR, WE'VE SOUGHT to bring to light deep patterns of thought—the "big ideas"—that have created the economic and political rules taking us to a place most of us do not want to go. But we worry that we might have left an impression that these democracy-killing ideas have evolved and diffused themselves spontaneously through our cultural ether. They have not.

Here we lay out strong evidence that America's peculiarly extreme, market-directing-all ideology has taken hold through largely invisible and highly effective anti-democracy organizing efforts led by a few Americans of enormous wealth. We try to capture the mindset, goals, and strategies of this movement, based on the public record.

As you learn about the Anti-Democracy Movement, please keep in mind what we're *not* saying. We are not simply blaming a handful of ultrarich people and their allies. They've been able to move our nation in a destructive direction because of rules and attitudes in which virtually all of us are complicit, if only by our inaction. Blaming "bad people" can be a dangerous diversion from the real task of remaking our society's rules and norms, ensuring that power is always widely distributed, transparent, and accountable.

Neither do we want to leave the impression that being among the ultrarich means you share an anti-democratic mindset. We know people of great means devoting their lives to making our society more democratic. Take the Patriotic Millionaires, who are working for democracy reforms and even asking to be more heavily taxed.

So let's get started, noting that while the set of ideas tackled in the previous chapter has in some form been around for centuries, in the 1970s something new took off.

ORIGINS OF THE ANTI-DEMOCRACY UPRISING

America had just completed the 1960s, a decade some found really disturbing. It had brought most Americans freedom-enhancing gains. The War on Poverty helped to slash the rate of poverty. Civil rights and voting rights laws had helped to free African Americans from life-stunting oppressions. And the women's liberation movement had started to release women from historical constraints.

In 1963, the Clean Air Act expanded our freedom to breathe healthy air. And early in the decade, a gutsy young Ralph Nader triggered what soon became a movement to save us from unseen hazards in the products we buy. By 1966, he had helped spur the passage of the National Traffic and Motor Vehicle Safety Act, empowering the federal government to set new vehicle and road safety standards. In 1970, twenty million Americans turned out for the first Earth Day and Richard Nixon signed an executive order to launch the Environmental Protection Agency. And in that year, the vibrant labor movement ensured a voice and protection for one in every four workers.[1]

None of this sat well with some key players in the world of American big business. They saw not enhancement of Americans' freedom from fear and harm but a threat to the heart of what made America great: what they called a "free enterprise system" and we refer to as brutal capitalism, a market economy detached from democratic values.

And in the early 1970s those fearing threats to the capitalist market launched a well-funded, well-orchestrated Anti-Democracy Movement. It's likely, of course, that many key players perceived their defense of our "free enterprise system" as a moral crusade to protect what's best for all. The fact is, however, it laid the groundwork for the crisis of democracy we face in this moment.

LEWIS POWELL'S BIG WORRY

We mark the birth year of today's Anti-Democracy Movement as 1971. On the 23rd of August, soon-to-be Supreme Court Justice Lewis Powell—a former head of the American Bar Association and at the time serving on eleven corporate boards—wrote a thirty-four-page "confidential" memo commissioned by the US Chamber of Commerce.

Its purpose was to outline the strongest possible response to what Powell perceived as a growing attack on corporations and "the free enterprise system" itself. It is in "deep trouble, and the hour is late," Powell warns. The "time has come—indeed, it is long overdue—for the wisdom, ingenuity and resources of American business to be marshaled against those who would destroy it." His dismay seemed rooted in a perception that corporations were being unfairly treated, as he writes that "few elements of American society today have as little influence in government as the American businessman, the corporation, or even the millions of corporate stockholders."[2]

Justice Powell, a Democrat and a decorated officer during World War II, seems to have been a decent enough guy. As head of the Bar Association he ensured it supported federal legal services for the poor.[3] After Powell's death, in 1998, President Bill Clinton praised him for approaching "each case without an ideological agenda."[4] And former Supreme Court justice Sandra Day O'Connor, a moderate Republican, described him as a "model of human kindness, decency, exemplary behavior, and integrity."[5]

What appears indisputable, however, is that his memo served as the playbook for the ensuing campaign to elevate private power and to undermine public voices, a multifaceted effort ultimately funded and guided by some of the wealthiest families in America.

MARCHING ORDERS TO SAVE "FREE ENTERPRISE"

That "the American economic system is under broad attack . . . no thoughtful person can question," the Powell memo begins. What had been sporadic attacks on our system are now "broadly based" and "gaining momentum and converts."[6]

As Powell expressed near panic about threats to our economic system, ironically, the US economy had shown amazing health in the previous decades. From the late forties to the early seventies, real median family income had doubled.[7] True, just a few years before Powell sat down to write his historic memo, US corporations' profit rate had dropped sharply, due in part to increased global competition. But this big dip in profits followed a huge late-1960s spike, and corporations were still enjoying a profit rate often approaching that of the prosperous 1950s.[8]

Nonetheless, Powell saw imminent disaster.

Early in the memo, he amps up his readers' blood pressure by quoting the *New York Times*, reminding them that "'Since February 1970, branches (of Bank of America) have been attacked 39 times, 22 times with explosive devices and 17 times with fire bombs or by arsonists.'"[9] What Powell doesn't mention, but must also have been on his mind, was a Vietnam War protest just months earlier that had almost shut down the capital. It had even forced three members of Congress to canoe across the Potomac to get to work. Seven thousand protesters had been locked up, likely a record.[10]

Moreover, what seemed to really get to Powell was that criticism of the "enterprise system" was coming from throughout our culture, from "the college campus, the pulpit, the media, the intellectual and literary journals, the arts and sciences, and from politicians." He appears particularly outraged that some attacks came from institutions supported by public dollars.

Obviously upset by Ralph Nader's instant acclaim, Powell writes of Nader's "hatred" of "corporate power." As evidence he offers *Fortune* magazine's report that Nader believes "a great many corporate executives belong in prison—for defrauding the consumer with shoddy merchandise, poisoning the food supply with chemical additives, and willfully manufacturing unsafe products that will maim or kill the buyer."[11] As a Philip Morris board member, Powell no doubt felt personally threatened.

He fought back by discrediting critiques of free enterprise as "Marxist doctrine," in part because they assert that "'capitalist' countries are controlled by big business." Interestingly, today many Americans can relate, as a Gallup poll in 2016 found that nearly two-thirds of us were dissatisfied with the size and influence of major corporations.[12]

As an important aside, Powell avoids the label "capitalism" for the system he is defending. Instead, he uses only "free enterprise," for who doesn't want to be "free"? But for us, it's important to use the term capitalism. Doing so reminds us that the market economy Powell is talking about is only one type, that controlled by capital. It's a very limited view, for markets can operate well when businesses owned by the public, workers, consumers, and communities—not just capitalists—are major contributors. In most states, for example, public utilities provide lower-cost electricity than do those privately held.[13] And, in a particularly prosperous region of Europe, Italy's Emilia-Romagna, co-ops owned by workers and consumers generate 40 percent of its GDP.[14]

In Powell's mind, fighting back against the assault on free enterprise was a matter of life and death. To a beleaguered corporate America, Powell calls out, "If our system is to survive, top management must be equally concerned with protecting and preserving the system itself." Very specifically, he directs corporations to appoint "an executive vice president" to counter the attacks.

More broadly, Powell calls for action on fronts ranging from education to the media to political action and the courts.

Under the heading "What Can Be Done About the Campus," he advises the Chamber of Commerce to establish a "Speakers Bureau" from the "top echelons of American business." And he goes much further, calling on the chamber to sponsor an "Evaluation of textbooks . . . toward restoring the balance essential to genuine academic freedom." His overall goal is "equal time" for what he's convinced is the maligned business point of view. He advocates for "a panel of independent scholars . . . [to] evaluate social science textbooks, especially in economics, political science and sociology," and he urges the chamber not to forget high school texts.

Powell proceeds to stress the role of the media in shaping the public mind, recommending that "national television networks should be monitored." The Chamber of Commerce could also help ensure that "complaints [about media coverage are] made promptly and strongly." And don't ignore the "news stands," he states, "at airports, drugstores, and elsewhere," as well as paid advertisements.

Powell then advocates for businesses to start directly engaging in politics, and presses the business community to step up with "more direct political action . . . used aggressively." Yet another "neglected opportunity," he writes, lies "in the Courts [where business can] engage, to appear as counsel amicus in the Supreme Court." In all, business must be "far more aggressive than in the past," he advises. "There should not be the slightest hesitation to press vigorously in all political arenas for support of the enterprise system. Nor should there be reluctance to penalize politically those who oppose it."

In all, Powell calls for "careful long-range planning and implementation, in consistency of action over an indefinite period of years, in the scale of financing available only through joint effort, and in the political power available only through united action."[15] By the end of his memorandum a reader probably isn't surprised by Powell's judgment that the campaign for which he calls is "not one for the fainthearted."

Soon we'll explore how Powell's alarm was received, but to understand its impact, it is critically important to grasp a complementary and also powerful narrative that reinforced his framing. It came to be called the Southern Strategy and had begun to take shape a few years earlier, as Richard Nixon in 1968 "premised his own campaign almost entirely on winning the white backlash vote," Ari Berman writes in his insightful book *Give Us the Ballot*. Nixon linked communities of color with civil unrest, and promised to return "law and order."[16]

The strategy was to stoke racial resentment during the civil rights era to shift white southern Democratic voters to the Republican Party. A tactic in the pernicious narrative, especially in the ensuing decades, was the use of "dog whistles," i.e., coded political messages that convey specific meaning to selective audiences, in this case, whites. One notorious example is the term "welfare queen," meant to stir white resentment by suggesting that "big government" is helping minorities to live luxuriously while the struggling white voter is paying for it. The tactic helped to divert voters' attention from the real root of their difficulties, the anti-democracy policies Powell and his followers were promoting. The impact of the strategy continues today as some whites—encouraged to believe falsely that government has been helping people of color but not them—feel resentful, a sentiment abetting the election of Donald Trump.[17]

DID THE CHAMBER AND ITS ALLIES LISTEN TO POWELL?

The answer is a strong and certain "yes."

The Chamber of Commerce's budget tripled in just six years, from 1974 to 1980, and its membership jumped more than fourfold between the late 1960s and 1980.[18] Then, in 1997, when Thomas J. Donohue rose to its helm, the chamber turned fully "into a free-enterprise research outfit [and] Supreme Court advocacy group," according to the *New York Times.*[19] The chamber soon became the nation's largest lobbying force. In almost every year since 2001, it has devoted two to three times more to lobbyists than the next-biggest spender.[20]

In 1998, Donohue boasted of the chamber's new muscle. In the past, if a "couple of party leaders didn't want you to do your deal, you were dead in the water," he lamented, according to *Newsday.* "That's not true anymore. . . . You can roll a [committee] chairman now. Or other chairmen will help you roll 'em."[21]

In line with the Powell persuasion, Donohue defined his purpose as not only to advance the interests of the chamber's members but also to engage ideologically—to "'defend and advance a free-enterprise system' whenever it 'comes under attack.'"[22] As it's taken this framing to heart, the chamber has become solidly pro-Republican. Once viewed as a bipartisan business advocacy organization, by 2016 its independent expenditures in political races had hit almost $30 million, none of it going to Democrats.[23]

The chamber now reflects only the biggest players, especially the tobacco, banking, and fossil-fuel industries. In "some respects, if not most, the positions taken by the Chamber are well to the right of how most small business owners think," *US News & World Report* noted in 2015.[24] In 2009, rejecting climate-change science, the chamber even proposed putting global warming "on trial" as a way to defeat policies to cut emissions.[25] But small business seems to have a different view. A 2014 poll found almost two-thirds of owners of small businesses (those with up to one hundred employees) agreeing that government regulation is needed to limit power-plant carbon emissions.

Eighty-seven percent identified at least one climate-change consequence as being "potentially harmful to their businesses."[26]

As will be explored later in this chapter, the rest of corporate
America has largely followed the Chamber of Commerce's lead.

BIG-FORTUNE FAMILIES FUEL MARKET EXTREMISM

Starting in the 1970s some of America's wealthiest families took up
Powell's call, as well. Politically passionate families came to see their
enormous fortunes as tools to shape our nation's belief system and
remake how we govern ourselves. They have used a range of strategies to turn more and more of society's direction over to a power-
concentrating market, no matter who is hurt.

In helping us understand this grave development, our special appreciation goes to Jane Mayer, whose widely acclaimed 2016 book *Dark
Money* offers an exhaustive exploration. Her analysis challenges those
who portray the rightward movement in political thought since the
Reagan presidency as a spontaneous "backlash against liberal spending programs." This view, she stresses, misses the "less-examined . . .
impact of [a] small circle of billionaire donors."[27]

Astonishingly, much of the leadership of the Anti-Democracy
Movement rests in the hands of a mere handful of families, including
the Olin, DeVos, and Koch clans.

Olin? The name might ring a bell for environmentalists because
the Olin corporation produced one-fifth of the DDT used in the
United States before the deadly pesticide was banned in 1972.[28] And,
during the fifties and sixties, the company itself estimates that an Olin
factory "spilled about a hundred pounds of mercury every day" into
public waterways, Mayer reports.[29]

From a few years after Powell's 1971 memo until 2009, when the
Olin Foundation closed, it was part of what progressive political strategist Rob Stein called "the most potent machinery ever assembled in a
democracy to promote a set of beliefs and to control the reins of government," Mayer notes.[30]

John M. Olin showered money on conservative culture warriors,
transforming them into significant public players. He spread his support to a wide range of figures, from right-wing standard-bearer William F. Buckley Jr., to feisty ideologue Dinesh D'Souza, to prominent

academics such as *Closing of the American Mind* author Allan Bloom, to professor Samuel Huntington, who for years led Harvard's John M. Olin Institute for Strategic Studies and in 1975 would famously complain of America's "excess of democracy."[31] Olin also backed conservative policy journals and the Federalist Society, known for incubating court cases to overturn the Affordable Care Act and favoring the elimination of unions.[32]

Another anti-democracy force, with a name now familiar to many Americans, is the family of billionaire Richard DeVos, founder of the Michigan marketing colossus Amway. When Donald Trump picked Richard's daughter-in-law Betsy to be Secretary of Education, few knew that years before the DeVos family had been key in orchestrating the *Citizens United* lawsuit. It ultimately reached the Supreme Court and culminated in the widely disliked 2010 ruling that led to a vast increase in independent and nondisclosed election spending.[33]

In the late 1990s the DeVos family was criticized for being the largest contributor of less-regulated "soft money" to the national Republican Party, and Betsy DeVos responded, "I have decided . . . to stop taking offense at the suggestion that we are buying influence. . . . They are right. We do expect some things in return."[34]

For some time, though, the champions of the Anti-Democracy Movement have been Charles and David Koch—fossil-fuel magnates—known as the Koch brothers. They have built a radical right-wing political apparatus that rivals those of the two major parties. In 1974, citing Powell's memo, Charles called for "radical new efforts to overcome the prevalent anti-capitalist mentality" in a speech to Dallas businessmen.[35] One root of the family's fortune enabling the Koch brothers' influence today was their father Fred's lucrative business dealings in Stalin's Soviet Union and in Nazi Germany.[36]

Mayer strives to help us understand the Kochs' worldview, suggesting that brutal treatment by Charles's first caregiver and his father led to a bitterness toward authority. Perhaps Charles Koch "was driven by some deeper urge to smash the one thing left in the world that could discipline him: the government," a researcher with access to the family's history surmised.[37]

Another key force in Charles's political formation was the Freedom School that he discovered through the John Birch Society, a radical group of which his father, Fred, had been an original member. (The society's founder, Robert Welch, was so extreme that he called Republican president Eisenhower "an agent of the communist conspiracy.")[38] The Freedom School was, frankly, bizarre. Mayer describes its founder, Robert LeFevre, as a "radical thinker with a checkered past" who declared government "a disease." In the school's version of American history, "robber barons were heroes, not villains," the Gilded Age was the "country's golden era," and "taxes were denigrated as a form of theft." Students in its program reported being taught that our Bill of Rights should be trimmed down to one, "the right to own property." By 1966, Charles Koch both supported the school financially and served as a trustee.[39]

Beyond the Olins, DeVos, and Koch families, in the second half of the twentieth century other wealthy leaders in the Anti-Democracy Movement included Richard Mellon Scaife, heir to the Mellon banking and Gulf Oil fortunes; brothers Harry and Lynde Bradley, whose wealth came from defense contracts; and Joseph Coors, of the brewing company. Together, all have been "bent on using billions of dollars from their private foundations to alter the direction of American politics," Mayer explains.[40]

The new kids on the billionaire block, and now rivaling the Kochs in influence, are the solitary Robert Mercer and his outspoken daughter Rebekah. Unlike the Kochs, they hit mega-wealth status only in the 1990s. Then in midlife, Mercer was hired by Renaissance Technologies, where his mathematical and computer prowess produced astonishingly lucrative hedge-fund investment strategies. Mercer's political views are extreme, bordering on the inexplicable. For example, Mayer reports, he has argued that the Civil Rights Act of 1964 was a "major mistake" and believes that after the US atomic-bomb attacks in 1945, those Japanese citizens "outside the immediate blast zones" were "healthier" for it.[41]

After giving millions to right-wing groups in the 2000s, the Mercers found their calling in 2012. Frustrated by the Koch network's failure to defeat Barack Obama, the Mercer family geared up to "erect an alternative media ecosystem," with the encouragement of Steve Bannon, a self-described promoter of the "alt-right" and later chosen by President Trump as his chief strategist. The Mercers have worked with

Bannon on five "ventures" for "sowing distrust of big government and eroding the dominance of the major news media," the *Washington Post* reports.[42] Rebekah Mercer was also instrumental in bringing Steve Bannon and Kellyanne Conway into the Trump campaign inner circle.[43] In all, the Mercers have become "arguably the most influential financiers of the Trump era," according to the *Washington Post*.[44] Nick Patterson, a former colleague of Robert Mercer, summed up his effect on the 2016 election: "In my view Trump wouldn't be President if not for Bob."[45]

FOUR STRATEGIES OF HIGHLY EFFECTIVE BILLIONAIRES

"Despite what most Americans say they prefer," Harvard's Theda Skocpol and Columbia's Alexander Hertel-Fernandez argue, when "the Kochs, the national Chamber of Commerce, and an array of other ideological and corporate groups call in one loud voice for government cut backs, tax cuts, and anti-union measures, virtually all of today's Republicans, and quite a few Democrats, too, do their bidding."[46] So, how have these super-rich anti-democracy activists been so effective in encouraging Americans to share their strongly anti-government, pro-big-business views? Here, we identify four strategies for shaping the culture's mindset. In the following chapter, we turn to an additional set of four strategies used to rig the rules of our democracy. All are key to understanding today's democracy crisis.

Strategy 1: Command the Narrative

Think tanks pump out anti-government and pro-market gospel
A think tank's job is to shape the way the public interprets the world and to push policy according to its interpretation. Those who believe that freedom is always enhanced when markets reign and government retreats have used think tanks to get their big ideas to "catch on." We highlight three:

> *American Enterprise Institute.* In the 1960s, a former Chamber of Commerce staffer reconfigured the American Enterprise Institute—founded in 1943 as a business lobby—into a think tank to counter the centrist Brookings Institution.[47] Its board draws from

business and finance, including billionaires Peter H. Coors and Richard DeVos, as well as former vice president Dick Cheney. The Koch brothers, the Bradley family, and John M. Olin have also been major backers.[48] One of the institute's big hits in shaping the public mind was Charles Murray's 1984 book *Losing Ground*, which framed welfare as a key cause of poverty, and later his even-more-controversial *The Bell Curve*, which linked social inequality to our genes.

Heritage Foundation. For billionaire sponsors such as Olin, who expected "their" think tanks to promulgate pet-policy preferences, the emergence of hyper-partisan alternatives such as the Heritage Foundation must have seemed like a godsend. Founded in 1970, Heritage was the brainchild of Paul Weyrich and Edwin Feulner Jr., two congressional aides who, Mayer notes, had "become exasperated by [American Enterprise Institute's] refusal" to proactively "weigh in on legislative fights until after they were settled" for fear of losing tax-exempt status.[49]

In Mayer's account, Joseph Coors was key to the birth of the Heritage Foundation. He gave $250,000 to Weyrich and Feulner's fledgling organization, which then became Heritage, to help fulfill their vision of an "action-oriented think tank that would actively lobby members of Congress before decisions were made, take sides in fights, and in every way not just 'think' but 'do.'"[50] Fellow right-wing billionaires got on board too. By 1998, the Scaife family accounted for a "vastly disproportionate share" of Heritage's "overall funding," with donations reaching a total of some $23 million.[51] By the early 1980s, the Heritage Foundation's sponsors ran the gamut of Fortune 500 companies.[52]

In a tell-all book, *Blinded by the Right*, covering in part his experience at Heritage, David Brock writes, "I saw how right-wing ideology was manufactured and controlled by a small group of powerful foundations."[53]

The size and influence of the Heritage Foundation soon soared. By the early 1980s its budget equaled those of the American Enterprise Institute and the Brookings Institution combined.[54] With Ronald Reagan's election in 1980, it soon supplanted the American Enterprise Institute as the premier right-wing policy organization.

President Reagan even gave Heritage's "phone-book-sized policy playbook" to every member of Congress, Mayer recounts, and his administration ended up adopting 61 percent of its 1,270 proposed policies. [55]

How Heritage spent its larger budget is telling. While Brookings devoted less than a twentieth of its budget to public relations and outreach, Heritage allocated about four times that share, reflecting its mission "to persuade rather than investigate," observe Jacob Hacker and Paul Pierson in *Winner-Take-All Politics*. [56]

Cato Institute. A third market-fundamentalist think tank is the distinctly libertarian Cato Institute, established in 1977 by Charles Koch. [57] In its first three years alone, Koch injected an estimated $10 million to $20 million in tax-deductible donations. [58] And at least in its early years, Koch controlled the institute. Early Cato employee Ronald Hamowy recalled, "Whatever Charles said, went." [59] The Cato Institute helped bring the formerly fringe ideology of libertarianism into the political mainstream, setting the stage for doctrinaire libertarian politicians such as Ross Perot, Ron Paul, and his son, Rand Paul.

By the late 1980s, its new president, Richard Fink, inspired a vision strongly echoing Powell's memo. His practical blueprint envisioned "a three-phase takeover of American politics." [60] First: invest in intellectuals "whose ideas would serve as the 'raw products.'" Second: finance "think tanks that would turn the ideas into marketable policies." Third: subsidize "citizens' groups that would, along with 'special interests,' pressure elected officials to implement the policies." The plan was "in essence," Mayer notes, "a libertarian production line, waiting only to be bought, assembled, and switched on." [61]

Think tanks influence us when government acts on their recommendations, but we're also influenced when the media spread their works. And in this respect, right-wing efforts have paid off. In a study of the twenty-five top think tanks, reporting a ten-year average of how often their work makes it into the news, right-leaning think tanks including Heritage and Cato did very well. They garnered 51 percent of the total media hits, while centrists such as Brookings got 36 percent. And progressives? Only 14 percent. [62]

Shape what's taught, from grade school to grad school

Since worldviews typically take shape early in life, those seeking to shift the American mindset wisely set their minds on education. The "Koch brothers' spending on higher education is now a critical part of their broader campaign to infuse politics and government with free-market principles," according to the Center for Public Integrity.[63] In 2013 two Charles Koch charitable foundations spread more than $19 million across 210 college campuses touching almost every state.[64]

The Kochs have kept a "laser-like focus" on furthering a market system they call "free"; so while bits of the Koch fortune are indeed spread widely in academia, the vast majority of Koch higher education funds goes to two centers at George Mason University.[65] The largest is the Mercatus Center, whose core program is inspired by Milton Friedman's intellectual forbearer, the Austrian economist Friedrich August von Hayek. Koch wealth also supports George Mason University's Institute for Humane Studies, where the goal is spreading the Hayek-inspired Koch version of "freedom" to other countries. Hayek's worldview is at least partly captured in one clear warning: "Even the striving for equality by means of a directed economy can only result in an officially enforced inequality."[66] Here Hayek implies that progressives seek to equalize social outcomes, conjuring up scary notions of a forced flattening of differences. But progressives typically seek fairness as a key to a healthy society, and argue that fairness requires equalizing opportunities through democratic rules that keep wealth circulating.

Another big-donor impact on shaping the public mind is the Olin Foundation's success in moving what Mayer calls "a fringe theory," known as law and economics, into mainstream academia. Critics argue that the approach applies "free market" economics to the legal field, simplistically assuming, for example, that people are narrowly motivated by their own, largely financial, self-interest and that social goods can be reduced to commodities, from education to health care.[67] Mayer likens the Olin Foundation to "an academic Johnny Appleseed," as it covered "83 percent of the costs for all Law and Economics programs in American law schools between the years of 1985 and 1989." In all, the foundation scattered millions to these programs, from Harvard to Yale to the University of Chicago.[68]

The Anti-Democracy Movement's efforts likely even shaped the work of one of the twentieth century's most influential economists, Nobel laureate Paul Samuelson. In the postwar era, his bestselling textbook emphasized the virtues of a "mixed economy" in which government and the market work together. By the 1980s, however, in new editions, government and the market had become "polar opposites," notes historian Daniel Rodgers.[69]

Most recently, with support from the Sarah Scaife Foundation, a report by a conservative group innocuously named the National Association of Scholars derides the so-called new civics being taught on college campuses. Schools are usurping the title of civics to teach progressive activism, the report charges.[70] It singles out Public Achievement, based at Augsburg College, in Minnesota, saying it "reduces politics to the use of force to defeat hostile opponents." Public Achievement's projects involve young people in community problem solving, including turning a neglected lot into a playground, protecting urban wildlife, and "supporting our troops," as featured on its website. (Scary, right?)

Beyond the classroom, the Anti-Democracy Movement also infuses its mindset on campuses by funding "Astroturf" activism—right-wing student groups that appear to organize spontaneously but are "propped up by a handful of . . . conservative funders," according to the progressive watchdog group Media Matters. An example is Young Americans for Liberty, which claims nine hundred chapters on campuses nationwide. Appearing to be funded largely by the Koch brothers, its agenda is strongly anti-government and in favor of allowing firearms on campuses. Similarly, the DeVos family funds Young Americans for Freedom, encouraging students to speak out against what it sees as the liberal agenda.[71]

Command the narrative via media

As far back as 1835, perhaps our nation's earliest and most astute observer, Alexis de Tocqueville, understood the power of the media. He described the press as "the chief democratic instrument of freedom." But today our "instrument of freedom" seems to mean the freedom to enrich oneself privately, whatever it takes. How did we get to this sad state?

In 1969 the US Supreme Court unanimously upheld the public-good understanding of the press, stating, "The First Amendment is relevant to public broadcasting, but it is the right of the viewing and listening public, and not the right of broadcasters, which is paramount."[72] In the 1960s, for example, media broadcasting gas-guzzling car advertisements had to pay for rebuttal airtime by public interest groups.[73] But soon dramatic changes undermined this frame, as market ideology tightened its grip during the 1980s. "Television is just another appliance. It's a toaster with pictures," quipped Mark Fowler, the chair of the Federal Communications Commission (FCC) during Ronald Reagan's presidency, as he mocked the very notion of media as a public good.[74]

Appointed by Reagan, a market dogmatist, FCC commissioners started in the 1980s to take away the commission's role in protecting the public good, which had been its founding mandate in 1934.[75] Soon thereafter the Fairness Doctrine—which had required the airing of a range of views on TV and radio since 1949—was abolished.[76]

This nail in the coffin came in 1987 in Syracuse, New York, when the Syracuse Peace Council filed a complaint against a local TV station that had denied it airtime while simultaneously broadcasting nine paid ads advocating building a nuclear plant. The FCC upheld the TV station's actions and eliminated the Fairness Doctrine. Prior to that year, Congress had passed a law to codify the doctrine, but Reagan vetoed the attempt.[77]

Then, after lobbying by major telecom companies, the hammer dropped. The Telecommunications Act of 1996 eliminated the cap on the number of radio stations one company could own and increased the nationwide share of households one corporation could reach via its local television stations from 25 to 35 percent.[78] Key in its passage was the Heritage Foundation, with help from the Koch-funded Citizens for a Sound Economy.[79] Further, lobbying by the media industry convinced Congress to give digital frequencies to existing TV stations—a $70 billion giveaway.[80] Then FCC chairman Reed Hundt labeled the gift "Beachfront property on the cybersea."[81] Both the 1996 Act and this giveaway encouraged media consolidation.

The 1990s' deregulation of media illustrates the effectiveness of the Anti-Democracy Movement in convincing Republicans and Democrats alike that a narrow, market-driven, anti-government approach was imperative even if it led to oligopoly.

As the media became a multibillion-dollar industry, a frenzy of mergers continued, wiping out hundreds of competitors. So today most of what Americans watch and see is controlled by just a handful of companies—all preoccupied with their shareholders' wealth, not our society's health. The result is a downward spiral of programming. One telling narrative? By 2000 the average length of presidential candidates' sound bites on the network nightly news had shrunk to seven seconds, less than a fifth of their length in the 1968 presidential election.[82]

As Craig Aaron, president and CEO of the media-focused public interest group Free Press, explained to us, "Years of rubber-stamping merger deals plus the removal of and raising of ownership limits in the 1996 Act did tremendous damage to the media landscape."

The undermining of media as a public good and its parallel con-solidation helped take us to the election of Donald Trump. A narrow focus on profitability led to this shocking finding by longtime news analyst Andrew Tyndall: in 2016, from the first of January through October 26, the three major television networks' evening newscasts together "devoted just 32 minutes to issues coverage."[83] That's roughly one-seventh of what it was in 2008.[84] What did they cover instead? Heading into the primary season, sensational Trump stories were all but ubiquitous. By March of 2016 he had received nearly $2 billion in free media coverage.[85] But virtually none of it touched on the serious issues our country faces.

Moreover, our hunch is that many of Trump's lies were never se-riously challenged simply because digging might have interrupted the "excitement" of the election, dimming media's profits from political advertising. In 2012 such profits accounted for about 20 percent of TV station revenues, as much as four times the share of ten years earlier.[86] Another reason: as online news outlets and social media have taken off, newspaper journalism—long entrusted with investigating in the public interest—has taken a big hit, with its workforce shrinking by 39 percent in twenty years.[87] So even if many outlets wanted to expose Trump's lies, they had little staff to investigate.

Concurrently, more Americans are choosing self-reinforcing news sources, from blogs to websites—creating an echo chamber that alternative narratives can't penetrate.[88] As *Wired* warned, "we develop tunnel vision [and] eventually become victims to our own biases."[89] So too has talk radio become increasingly polarized, insular, and narrow-minded, and abetted, unsurprisingly, by essential players in the Anti-Democracy Movement. From 2008 to 2012, the Heritage Foundation, the Kochs' Americans for Prosperity, and related groups provided approximately $22 million in sponsorships to extreme right-wing talking heads including Sean Hannity, Glenn Beck, Rush Limbaugh, and Mark Levin.[90] Many of these radio figures, especially Beck—and the local radio hosts they inspire—were critical in stirring up resentment and providing guidance to Tea Party activists from 2009 onward, as chronicled by journalist Will Bunch in his book *The Backlash*.[91]

Moreover, Facebook exacerbated self-reinforcing media bubbles and allowed "fake news" to become a significant force in 2016. An investigation by *BuzzFeed* concluded, "In the final three months of the US presidential campaign, the top-performing fake election news stories on Facebook generated more engagement than the top stories from major news outlets."[92] What's more, all but three of the top-twenty-performing fake news stories were "overtly pro–Donald Trump or anti–Hillary Clinton."[93]

It is in this perilous media environment that billionaire Robert Mercer stepped up with a media-and-messaging strategy to influence elections. It involved three prongs, according to Carole Cadwalladr of the *Guardian*.[94]

The first was creating media outlets to host extreme, far-right viewpoints. In 2011, Mercer put at least $10 million into *Breitbart News*.[95] Not only are its stories narrowly anti-government, but they also mock and denigrate women and people of color, carrying headlines that include, for example, "Hoist It High and Proud: The Confederate Flag Proclaims a Glorious Heritage" and "Birth Control Makes Women Unattractive and Crazy." Mercer also funded the Media Research Center, which "documents and exposes liberal media bias," according to its newsletter.

The big problem for democracy is that these outlets lack professional journalism's commitment to evidence-based reporting. The Media Research Center owns *CNS News*, whose coverage, for example, prominently features crimes by immigrants, supporting Trump's blame-the-other worldview; in fact, immigrants, both legal and undocumented, commit proportionally fewer crimes than do native-born citizens.[96]

Mercer's second prong is creating front-page stories via "investigative journalism," a profession once paid for by subscribers. The Mercer-funded Government Accountability Institute, founded by Steve Bannon, is one such attempt; it published *Clinton Cash*, a screed against Hillary Clinton, in 2015. *Clinton Cash* made the front page of the *New York Times*, debuted at number two on the *Times'* Best Sellers list, and was later made into a film by Bannon and Rebekah Mercer.[97] An *ABC News* independent review of the book found errors, which the author said he would correct.[98] In any case, we're confident that journalism "commissioned" by and for the interests of the wealthy is not what de Tocqueville had in mind for our "instrument of freedom."

The third prong of the Mercer strategy has been to abet a massive data collection on voters, largely through online sources, enabling far-right candidates to micro-target their online messages to voters. Toward this goal, Mercer reportedly invested $10 million in Cambridge Analytica, an American affiliate of a UK firm, which would eventually partner with the Trump campaign.[99]

Cambridge Analytica "claims to have built psychological profiles using 5,000 separate pieces of data on 220 million American voters. It knows their quirks and nuances and daily habits and can target them individually," Cadwalladr reports. The firm conducted tens of thousands of polls for the Trump campaign to help with messaging.[100]

Speaking anonymously, Cambridge Analytica insiders have told news organizations that the company's claims are greatly overstated.[101] Nevertheless, according to Cambridge University professor John Rust, with the proper data, "a computer can actually do psychology, it can predict and potentially control human behavior. It's what the scientologists try to do but much more powerful. It's how you brainwash someone. It's incredibly dangerous."[102] Moreover, "the ways this data is processed and applied to affect our decision-making is withheld by companies like Cambridge Analytica and their marketing partners, as it is considered, in most cases, proprietary," communications professor Jonathan Albright, of Elon University, explained to us. So no one knows how sophisticated these tools are or what exactly Cambridge Analytica did to help to elect Trump.

What is clear is that these secretive and potentially intrusive, manipulative techniques are anathema to democracy. As Tim Berners-Lee, founder of the World Wide Web, said in 2017, "Targeted advertising allows a campaign to say completely different, possibly conflicting things to different groups. Is that democratic?"[103] Our answer is a resounding no, for democracy depends on citizens trusting that they are in one conversation with shared facts.

Strategy 2: Delegitimize Democracy's Norms and Institutions

Especially since the 1970s, anti-democracy forces have sought to delegitimize government itself. Ronald Reagan, in his 1981 inaugural address, declared, "government is not the solution to our problem; government is the problem." But by then, ongoing anti-government rhetoric was already eroding the postwar consensus around government's essential role. One telling measure is a contrast in the State of the Union addresses of two presidents, four decades apart. In 1953, Dwight Eisenhower's first State of the Union mentioned "government" almost forty times, and "the overwhelming majority . . . were positive." But by 1993, Bill Clinton's address of comparable length mentioned government "around half as often, and the majority of his references were negative," professors Jacob Hacker and Paul Pierson observe.[104]

Beyond the ongoing rhetorical attack on government, the Anti-Democracy Movement also set out to undermine an effective culture of governance.

In civics class American youngsters once learned that democracy requires good-faith negotiation and compromise, rewarding skills of evidence-based persuasion. But beginning in the 1990s the cutthroat approach to politics of minority whip and soon-to-be Republican Speaker of the House Newt Gingrich—who was first elected in 1978 in part abetted by anti-government think-tank messaging—normalized a different M.O.

Norman Ornstein of the right-leaning American Enterprise Institute teamed up with Brookings' Thomas Mann to critique the Gingrich effect in their book *It's Even Worse Than It Looks*. Gingrich's influence on congressional politics "deserves a dubious kind of credit" for much of "the current state of politics," they conclude. "By moving to paint with a broad brush his own institution as elitist, corrupt, and arrogant, he [Gingrich] undermined basic public trust in Congress and government, reducing the institution's credibility over a long period." They blame his take-no-prisoners attacks on partisan adversaries for creating a "norm in which colleagues with different views became mortal enemies." Gingrich "helped invent the modern permanent campaign, allowing electoral goals to dominate policy ones," they charge.[105]

Gingrich himself confirmed these scholars' dire assessment, declaring in a speech to the Heritage Foundation in the 1980s that this political "war has to be fought with a scale and a duration and a savagery that is only true of civil wars."[106]

In a similar spirit, in the early 2000s House Majority Whip Tom DeLay of Texas disseminated among his GOP colleagues *The Art of Political War*, by radical right-winger David Horowitz. The Heritage Foundation did the same with key activists.[107] The pamphlet, true to its name, urged Republicans to treat politics as warfare. In this worldview, one's opposition is not a legitimate contributor to democratic problem-solving but a force to be wiped out. So when Democrats took control of Congress, what better way to bring them down and simultaneously destroy faith in government than to make the institution dysfunctional?

During the Obama years Republicans used the filibuster in unprecedented frequency to bring Congress to a halt. They filibustered Obama's legislation and his judicial and executive-branch nominees more than twice as frequently as Democrats had during George W. Bush's presidency (judging by the number of times voting was called to end debate), journalist Zachary Roth reports.[108] "[E]very nominee for Senate confirmation and every routine procedural motion is now subject to a Republican filibuster," veteran Republican Congressional staffer Mike Lofgren wrote in 2011. It's "no wonder that Washington is gridlocked," he added.[109] Policies enjoying broad public support that were blocked in this manner ranged from expanded background checks on gun purchasers to increased disclosure of political spending to strengthened collective-bargaining rights for firefighters.[110]

To further discredit Congress the GOP forced the shutdown of government. In 2013, a group of Republican congressmen refused to support any budget resolution that did not defund the Affordable Care Act. No resolution was reached by the October 1 deadline, so the government shut down. The result? Hardship—including disruption of veterans' benefits and many furloughed federal workers.[111] In all, this act of malfeasance costs taxpayers about $24 billion, according to Standard & Poor's.[112]

Americans were so angry that almost half believed we'd be better off if nearly all members of Congress lost their jobs.[113] A majority of Americans also lacked confidence another shutdown could be avoided once the agreed-on budget deal ran out.[114] Their pessimistic prediction turned out not to be far off, as government came close to shutting down during each of the next three years.

As frustrating as these obstructionist tactics were to Democrats, they also upset a lot of Republicans. In 2011 the longtime congressional staffer we quoted above, Mike Lofgren, announced his retirement in a long statement with the strongest rebuke: "Legislating has now become war minus the shooting, something one could have observed eighty years ago in the Reichstag of the Weimar Republic." He then offered historian Hannah Arendt's insight on the rise of Nazism: "A disciplined minority of totalitarians can use the instruments of democratic government to undermine democracy itself."[115]

Remember, Lofgren was no angry Democrat. He was describing the practices of his own party. *

Then, in 2016, Republicans tossed aside another longstanding norm, that concerning confirmation of Supreme Court appointments. After the death of Justice Antonin Scalia in February, Senate Majority Leader Mitch McConnell made an unprecedented declaration: "This vacancy should not be filled until we have a new president."[116] This position ignored the view of nearly 70 percent of Americans, who believed President Obama's nominee, moderate Merrick Garland, should receive a Senate hearing and an up-or-down vote.[117] Before this unilateral abrogation of norms of fair play, the longest a Supreme Court nominee had ever had to wait for an up-or-down Senate vote was 125 days. But the GOP blocked a hearing on Garland's nomination for almost a year, through the end of Obama's term.

As Congress and "dysfunction" became synonymous in the minds of many Americans, the congressional approval rating hit 13 percent in 2016.[118] Disgust with government's failures, we believe, stemming from decades of delegitimizing its institutions, helped to open the door for a bombastic self-promoter who claimed the mantle of bold outsider eager to shake up a gridlocked, corrupt system.

Strategy 3: Quietly Create a Parallel Political Operation Pushing the Anti-Democracy Message, with Hundreds of Front Groups, Community By Community

As we've seen, the Anti-Democracy Movement is learning to work all angles, and that's especially true of the Koch brothers. "The most resourceful new political organizations built on the right in recent years are tied to David and Charles Koch and their close political associates," Harvard's Theda Skocpol and Columbia's Alexander Hertel-Fernandez write. Their website, *Research on the Shifting US Political Terrain*, tracks, among other trends, the Kochs' far-right movement. Koch-controlled groups, they note, accounted for three-fourths of the budgets of all GOP and conservative organizations created since 2002.[119]

Americans think of politics as the turf of political parties, but increasingly, funding for political organizations on the right comes from nonparty groups, such as Karl Rove's American Crossroads political action committee and the Koch brothers' Americans for Prosperity. By 2013–14, nonparty groups had risen to 70 percent of the right's total organizational resources.[120]

More and more political money operating outside of political parties, encouraged by court rulings dating back 1976, compounds our democracy's accountability crisis. Albeit imperfectly, our political parties at least declare what they stand for and directly engage with us, the public; whereas those behind independent expenditures are beyond our reach and thus essentially unaccountable.

The Koch network has expanded into a "nationally federated, full-service, ideologically focused parallel" to the GOP. It "operates on the scale of a national U.S. political party," Skocpol and Hertel-Fernandez underscore.[121] In the 2016 cycle, it pledged "more than twice what the Republican national committee spent in the previous presidential election."[122]

With 107 offices around the country, this "Koch machine" involves 1,200 staff, working full-time, year-round. Even by late 2015, those employed in the Koch network already outnumbered the Republican National Committee and its "congressional campaign arms" by three and a half times, Kenneth Vogel, chief investigative reporter at *Politico*, reports.[123] While the local groups of the Koch brothers' Americans for Prosperity are dubbed "chapters," they have no autonomy. Regionally appointed managers operate from Virginia headquarters.[124] Top leaders channel funds "into big advertising buys during key Senate election battles or into hot campaigns to block Medicaid expansion in particular states," Skocpol and Hertel-Fernandez explain.[125]

To push its priorities, Americans for Prosperity combines advertising, lobbying, and remarkably fast-growing community-by-community organizing. Its budget grew five-and-a-half-fold in just six years, from 2009 to 2015, all to propagate one clear idea: limited government plus a pro-big-business market equals "liberty," the primary thought barrier we explored in the previous chapter.[126]

What's so scary is that this top-down network can deploy Astroturf campaigns, which create the appearance of a grassroots effort while being largely funded and manipulated by big-money interests. FreedomWorks, which Mayer calls an "estranged sibling of Americans for Prosperity," was a large player in the Tea Party movement, coordinating, funding, and providing resources for rallies and town halls that were supposedly driven by local grassroots groups.[127] FreedomWorks went so far as to pay talk-show host and Tea Party driver and promoter Glenn Beck an annual sum that climbed to more than $1 million to embed the group's messaging in his program, perpetuating the perception of its popularity.[128]

Since 2010, the Koch brothers have launched three new, targeted, constituency-mobilizing organizations, focusing on youth, Latinos, and veterans. Plus, a key operative in their network, Jeff Crank, went on to create Aegis Strategic, which grooms political talent and develops campaign strategies for candidates capable of pushing the far-right ideology.[129]

Unlike other right-wing advocacy groups, the Koch network is "intertwined with (although not subordinated to) the institutional

GOP," Skocpol and Hertel-Fernandez observe.[130] Staff flows back and forth between the GOP and the Koch network, as it "operates as a force field to the right of the Republican Party, exerting a strong gravitational pull on many GOP candidates and officeholders."[131] Confirming that "pull," by 2015, 88 percent of the time GOP members of Congress voted with Americans for Prosperity.[132]

As we take in the impact of the Anti-Democracy Movement, it is important to remind ourselves how profoundly the views of the Kochs, for example, differ from those of most of us. More than seven in ten Americans polled support, for example, raising the minimum wage, expanding Social Security benefits, and regulating carbon dioxide emissions, while the Kochs are dead set against all three.[133]

Simply put, the central goal of the Anti-Democracy Movement is to overwhelm the views of a majority of Americans.

Strategy 4: Build Big Donors' Common Purpose and Coordinate Their Efforts to Achieve the Three Strategies Above

Justice Powell's call to action made clear that success depended on a "scale of financing" that could become "available only through joint effort." Clearly, the Koch brothers got that message, as they "pull many like-minded donors into supporting a comprehensive political strategy carried through by an interlocking network of tightly controlled organizations," Skocpol and Hertel-Fernandez write.[134]

Since 2002, the strategy has translated into twice-yearly Koch donor "seminars," growing from a dozen or so to five hundred people, all willing to pay a minimum of $100,000 to hobnob with others of great wealth.[135] These gatherings are organized to encourage a common agenda and "foster . . . camaraderie among conservative millionaires and billionaires."[136] Their programs, the names of attendees, and the activities are supposed to be kept secret, but Skocpol and Hertel-Fernandez could ascertain through leaks that one clear goal was to facilitate one-on-one meetings between Koch network staff and major donors.[137]

This strategy has paid off handsomely, as on inauguration day in January 2009 these donors did not sit at home and mope. Instead they all gathered and immediately began plotting their revenge on an electorate that would elect a liberal like Barack Obama. From these gatherings came coordinated schemes to win back Congress in 2010 and obstruct Obama by any means necessary.[138]

Ultimately, it doesn't take too many people to make these summits a success. Mayer explains that "[n]o fewer than eighteen billionaires would be among the 'doers' joining the Kochs' clandestine opposition movement during the first term of Obama's presidency." The combined fortunes of these eighteen alone topped $214 billion in 2015.[139]

WHERE A MANIPULATED MINDSET HAS LED US

So here we are. Numerous, powerful Americans, many of whom have likely never heard of Justice Powell, have been promulgating his worldview; and the result has been disaster for most of us. Take just one measure. Since just after Powell wrote his memo, American workers over almost half a century have seen only a paltry 9 percent gain in their real wages.[140]

The mindset Powell embodied failed America because it leaves out something big. It ignores the need for transparent public decision-making that reflects and is ultimately accountable to the will and well-being of the people. In other words, it leaves out democracy.

His framing of the problem, taken up by some of the wealthiest among us, intensified the power of a narrow market logic that increasingly concentrates wealth at the very top, also anathema to democracy. Thus, while workers have hardly gained, CEO compensation has soared sixteen-fold since the Powell memo.[141] And even by the 1980s, corporations had managed to reduce their share of taxes from a fifth of federal receipts in the 1960s to a mere 7 percent.[142]

The frame's anti-government stance has helped to turn Americans against the key institution that could have been used to help them—their government. In the mid-1960s, more than two-thirds of us believed that government was "run for the benefit of all the people." But by 2008, 70 percent saw government as "pretty much run by a few big interests looking out for themselves." Distrust, leading people to disengage, had fed more distrust, creating a self-reinforcing cycle.[143]

Moreover, this anti-democratic frame has been reinforced by those deliberately pitting whites against communities of color. Understandably, anger and feelings of betrayal have deepened.

Decades of discounting democracy and government set us up for an even more direct attack. Disgusted and feeling voiceless, in 2016 many voters chose to throw a brick through the Beltway glass. The result is a disturbed, impulsive, self-aggrandizing personality in the White House. Lacking a coherent ideology or moral grounding himself, Donald Trump turns to his chief strategist, Steve Bannon, and together, they proceed directly to undercut democracy and government further.

Blaming is the primary strategy of authoritarians; and for America's ills, Trump and his advisors blame international elites, foreign governments, immigrants, people of color, and those not within the Judeo-Christian tradition. They even point fingers at the Washington, DC, "swamp" and at "crony capitalism," knowing that this framing of the blame has great appeal. Simultaneously they place standard-bearers of crony capitalism in the highest government posts and propose cutting taxes on the wealthiest, along with drastically cutting agencies that protect citizens' health as well as their rights.

Moreover, Trump and his advisors employ lies and threats to get their way. Such actions harm us all, as democracy lives only with truth-telling and honest negotiation. Powell himself would likely be appalled by how his worldview has been corrupted and by what it has produced.

Fortunately, the rising Democracy Movement we chronicle in part III is actively countering these dangerous trends. But to be effective in reversing them, we need first to grasp four additional strategies the Anti-Democracy Movement is using to subvert rules we need for democracy to succeed.

CHAPTER FOUR

ııııııııııııııı

RIGGING THE RULES

LEWIS POWELL'S 1971 advice to the Chamber of Commerce to "marshal" resources against those setting out to "destroy" American business got quite specific. Beyond changing minds, business interests were told they must also pour resources into changing laws. The Anti-Democracy Movement's influence grew way beyond think tanks, schools, and media. It has gotten its hands dirty, even helping to draft laws that define our electoral process and determine who can vote and when. In this chapter, we explore four of these strategies effectively eroding democracy, from enabling more private wealth to influence elections, to suppressing the vote, to instances of abolishing local democracy altogether.

Strategy 1: Open Doors Ever Wider to Big-Money Influence In Our Political System

Instinctively, Americans get it: fully 84 percent agree that "money has too much influence" on elections.[1] We're told that "our" democracy is about fairness and equal voices but instead many see pay-to-play politics, with an ever-rising entry fee, making a mockery of this basic value.

How much money is in our elections? The total cost of all federal elections hit nearly $6.5 billion in 2016. In some races, the fund-raising required seems almost impossible. Pity Pennsylvania GOP senator Pat Toomey, who, for his 2016 reelection bid, had to raise an average of $89,000 a week for the entire six years of his Senate term.[2]

Some Americans don't see a problem because they think money on the "right" and on the "left" cancels each other out. Not really. Republicans have outspent Democrats in seven of the past ten election cycles.[3] But even if big bucks spent by opposing political elites were to balance out, would anyone call it democracy?

Amid all the bad news about big money in our political system, it is critical to keep in mind that there's nothing unchangeable here. Since 1900, Democratic Party platforms have regularly decried the influence of big money in politics, and in 1974, Watergate finally spurred Congress to act. It passed new rules that enabled qualifying presidential candidates to run for office using public funds—conditioned on accepting modest spending limits—and in 1976, such funds fueled most of Jimmy Carter's successful run for president.[4] So we can learn from our own past as well as from other countries that have made significant advances in reducing the power of private wealth in politics.

First, let's get a handle on why big money in politics hurts us all. It happens in at least five ways.

Determining who holds office. Money, not the people's will, decides who can run for office and—more often than not—win.

Narrowing the debate. A disproportionately wealthy, white, and male donor class decides which issues get attention and which policies are enacted.

Diverting legislators' focus. Legislators' time and energy go heavily toward raising money rather than serving constituents, which also discourages many highly qualified people from running in the first place.

Keeping us in the dark. Big-money donors thrive in anonymity. Citizens can't evaluate donors' self-interest when disclosure is not required in political spending and big-money donors use their deep pockets to keep it that way.

Diminishing trust in democracy. Turned off by what feels like a rigged, insider system, Americans are less inclined to participate, and trust—the heart of democracy—declines.

Let's go a bit deeper into this sad picture.

First, money's domination of our political process creates what's been dubbed the "money primary." Americans scoff at authoritarian regimes that pick a couple of trusted cronies to run and then inform voters they have "a choice." Our primary system has become distressingly close to this sham. In the money primary, it's how much money you can raise, not your experience or leadership qualities, that counts the most. Those without access to networks of wealthy donors, disproportionately women and people of color, are often blocked from running for office.

In Wisconsin, Kelly Westlund got up the courage to run for Congress and approached the Democratic Party. "[I] told them I wanted to jump in, [and] their representative asked me if I could raise a quarter of a million dollars in three weeks. I laughed at him," she explained. When she told him it was impossible, he responded, "Then, you're not viable."[5] The person who brushed off Westlund was in the money trap too, aware that candidates who raise the most money have a high probability of victory. In 2012, congressional candidates with a fund-raising advantage were nine times more likely to win their race.[6] Likewise for state-level races: nationwide, 84 percent of state candidates who had raised the most money won in the 2013–2014 cycle. Among incumbents who outraised their opponents, 94 percent won.[7]

Whether we want to admit it or not, money matters, a lot.

Second, a tiny minority of Americans actually funds campaigns. In the 2016 election, less than 1 percent of American adults contributed $200 or more, but together these Americans provided two-thirds of the money going to all federal candidates, political action committees (PACs), and parties.[8] For House races, donations under $200 consistently make up only 10 percent of overall funds.[9] This big-donor class is overwhelmingly white, wealthy, and male.[10]

Because big-money contributors are the key to electoral success, their views get heard while the rest of us are largely ignored. A data-driven study covering 1981 to 2002 shocked even those who thought they knew something about the political power of elites. The majority of Americans had "near zero" influence on public policies, while economic elites had strong influence, according to a 2014 study

by professors Martin Gilens and Benjamin Page.[11] And the elite's policies often directly endanger our well-being, as examples at the end of
this chapter illustrate.

Third, money-driven politics robs us of our legislators' attention.
Imagine: each winning senator in the 2012 election raised on average
more than $14,000 *each day* of the election cycle.[12] Party leadership
calls on members of Congress to spend four hours each day in "call
time" to potential donors and one more hour in "strategic outreach,"
which also involves fund-raising. And time assigned to doing the
work that voters put them in office to do? Just three to four hours.[13]

Most go along, but some get fed up. No longer able to stomach
the endless begging for bucks, New York Democratic representative
Steve Israel announced his resignation in 2016. He told a money-
out-of-politics gathering that he survived the relentless fund-raising
only by pleading for frequent bathroom breaks—so frequent that his
staff let him know they were worried he'd developed prostate cancer!
The environment is one in which only those who can withstand the
pain run for office.

Fourth, loopholes in reporting requirements created and main-
tained by big money allow donors to remain secret, heightening distrust, and leaving donors unaccountable. From 2010 to 2016, excluding
party committees, about one-quarter of the $3.3 billion in outside
spending in federal elections was undisclosed. Big money from secret
donors outside of electoral districts makes voters doubt whether their
elected officials represent them; 80 percent of us see secret corporate
money as bad for democracy.[14]

Finally and perhaps most pernicious, when Americans see only a
nasty, rigged system, we simply tune out, feeling our voices mean little. So trust, essential to democracy, erodes.

Nothing accidental

The crisis of our democracy did not arise spontaneously from the
changing views of the people. In addition to the deliberate tactics already noted, Supreme Court decisions, mostly by a majority of one,
have played a critical role in its creation. Those pursuing their idea of
justice in a contentious area—whether conservative or liberal—often

choose to push a particular case forward in hopes of reaching the highest Court, believing it will rule in their favor.

The DeVos family of Amway wealth, mentioned in the previous chapter, has taken this tactic to a new level. They have long sought to eliminate restraints on political spending. Toward that end, the family has funded legal challenges to campaign finance laws, specifically through the James Madison Center for Free Speech, which Jane Mayer calls "ground zero" in the family's money-in-politics fight. Its single purpose, according to Mayer, is to wipe out all legal restrictions on money in politics. In 1997, Betsy DeVos became a founding member of its board. The work of DeVos and the Madison Center ultimately led to the *Citizens United* ruling.[15]

For more than fifteen years, attorney James Bopp Jr. has led the James Madison Center's fight in the courts, and it turns out that Bopp himself pretty much *is* the Madison Center. In addition to the DeVos family, its early donors include several of the most powerful groups on the right, such as the Christian Coalition and the National Rifle Association.[16] In apparent violation of its IRS "nonprofit" status, virtually all the center's resources—$2.6 million during the years 2005 to 2010—went to one law firm, that of Bopp.[17] About the arrangement, Washington lawyer Marcus Owens, formerly the overseer of tax-exempt groups for the IRS, commented: "I've never heard of this sort of captive charity/foundation funding of a particular law firm before."[18]

In 2008 Bopp seized on the film *Hillary: The Movie*, which attacked then presidential candidate Hillary Clinton. Its producer was a small, right-wing group, Citizens United, then known for making vicious campaign ads. The Federal Election Commission ruled that airing the film was illegal, based on a 2002 law, which barred the airing of corporate-funded "electioneering communications" within thirty days of a primary. Bopp and company sued, arguing the ruling was an abridgment of their First Amendment rights. The question, as the Supreme Court interpreted it after ordering a second round of oral arguments, was whether the ban on corporate spending on elections was constitutional. In the *Citizens United* decision, the Court held that corporate spending on electioneering communications such as

Hillary: The Movie was protected speech, which could not be barred on the basis of the "speaker's" corporate identity.[19]

The ruling "was really Jim [Bopp]'s brainchild," election-law expert Richard L. Hasen told the *New York Times*. "He has manufactured these cases to present certain questions to the Supreme Court in a certain order and achieve a certain result," said Hasen. "He is a litigation machine."[20] And one oiled by the DeVos family.

The upshot? Corporations and certain other associations can now pour unlimited sums directly from their treasuries into elections—so long as they are independent from candidates or parties.

Many Americans are aware of *Citizens United*. But few know of the case right on its heels: a lesser-known federal court ruling, *Speech Now.Org v. FEC*, which made it easy to make unlimited independent-campaign expenditures. It opened the door to the now infamous super PACs (independent-expenditure-only PACs). The "Bopp-equivalent" pushing this case along was David Keating, a longtime warrior for unlimited political spending and the director of the Center for Competitive Politics.[21] *Citizens United* and SpeechNow.org were major factors in making 2016 the first year in which outside groups in ten competitive US Senate races outspent the parties and candidates themselves.[22]

And some top GOP leaders cheered on these and related efforts to rid America of campaign spending rules. "In a Senate debate on proposed campaign-finance restrictions, [Kentucky senator Mitch] McConnell reportedly told colleagues, 'If we stop this thing [limits on spending], we can control the institution [Congress] for the next twenty years,'" reports Mayer.[23]

Before Citizens United

The *Citizens United* ruling inflamed a lot of people. Roughly 80 percent of Americans now want this decision overturned.[24] While citizen outrage is mostly directed at this case, it was the much earlier 1976 *Buckley v. Valeo* ruling that allowed the voices of the wealthy to drown out the voices of virtually everyone else. "Make no mistake," Adam Lioz, a lawyer and policy advocate at the pro-democracy think tank Demos, told us, "the *Buckley* decision has damaged our democracy more than any other money-in-politics case."

In *Buckley*, the Supreme Court struck down many checks that would have prevented the distortion of our democracy. It prohibited limits on so-called "independent expenditures" by individuals—political communications such as television and newspaper advertisements that are not made in coordination with the candidate's official campaign. The ruling also prohibited limits on total campaign spending and spending by a candidate using out-of-pocket funds. The *Buckley* Court insisted that the government could regulate money in politics only to prevent corruption or its appearance. Any attempt to level the playing field was disallowed.

Since then—with a brief exception at the end of the twentieth century, which allowed for more regulation of campaign finance—the Court's decisions have opened the door ever further to money in politics.

The effect of it all? Just from 2000 to 2016, the total amount spent on races for Congress and the presidency, adjusted for inflation, jumped from more than $4 billion to almost $6.5 billion.[25] Further, almost half of all spending in the federal races of 2016 (more than $3 billion) was made possible by Supreme Court decisions. The share is even bigger for competitive congressional races, reaching almost 80 percent. And of this money, the 1976 *Buckley* decision had the greatest impact, a 2017 study by Demos concludes.[26] "When the Supreme Court opens the door, big donors take advantage," Lioz explained.

Reversing court rulings will require the Democracy Movement to build pressure for change, and, interestingly, for those arguing in front of the Supreme Court, there's a ray of hope in the language of the *Buckley* decision itself. There, the Court bases its case for removing spending limits in part on the First Amendment, which requires protections "to assure [the] unfettered interchange of ideas from diverse and antagonistic sources for the bringing about of political and social changes desired by the people."

We see poignant irony here, for notice the Court's emphasis is on a *public purpose* within First Amendment protections. That purpose is bringing about changes "the people" desire via "unfettered interchange" among "diverse sources." However, it is precisely the Court's stance allowing unlimited spending in campaign messaging that defeats this vital purpose. Citizens can't participate in, or even witness, "unfettered interchange" if those who can afford to dominate the media drown out the rest of us. Thus, within the Court's own argument against limits, we believe, is a more profound argument *for* limits.

How this played out in 2016

National attention to big, and often undisclosed, money in politics is typically riveted on a presidential race. But in many ways such money is even more decisive and dangerous in House and Senate races, and this was especially true in 2016.

Take Wisconsin, for example, where the Kochs' Americans for Prosperity spent more than a million dollars in the last week of the campaign to push incumbent GOP senator Ron Johnson over the top against his opponent, democracy-champion Russ Feingold.[27] The Senate Leadership Fund spent \$2.2 million "to paint Feingold as anti-veteran," and the Chamber of Commerce spent more than half a million dollars to attack him as well, the Center for Media and Democracy reported.[28] *OpenSecrets* showed that outside groups attacking Feingold spent almost twice as much as those opposing Johnson.[29] Republican Senate candidates also benefited from more outside spending than did their Democratic opponents in Florida, Nevada, Ohio, Indiana, Missouri, and Arizona—almost all won their races.[30]

Big money also crushed congressional candidates seeking democracy reform, such as Zephyr Teachout in New York. Billionaires Robert Mercer and Paul Singer collectively dropped over a million dollars to fund a super PAC opposing her. In total, outside groups spent almost \$2 million more attacking Teachout rather than her opponent—a stunning sum for a congressional race.[31]

Of course, money matters in a presidential race too, though unlike in congressional races, presidential candidates benefit from extraordinary media attention. As Nick Nyhart, president and CEO of Every Voice Center, explained to us, "The national spotlight with endless, day-in, day-out free media coverage acts almost like hundreds of millions of dollars in free advertising, in a way that isn't true for down-ballot races." This advantage can allow a media-savvy "outsider" like Trump to win using less money. As we saw in the previous chapter, though, media coverage can be highly focused on the sensational, not the issues that shape our lives.

Strategy 2: Expand an army of lobbyists and usher anti-democracy forces into government

Lobbying has been with us since the nineteenth century, when the term referred to those paid to hang out in lobbies of legislative chambers to chat up lawmakers. But before the 1970s lobbying was "a sporadic, tinpot, and largely reactive activity," Lee Drutman observes in *The Business of America Is Lobbying*, and few corporations placed lobbyists in Washington.[32] Trade associations, not individual corporate lobbyists, were the primary political players on behalf of business.

But when public concern about the environment and product safety awakened in the 1970s, and trust in corporate power began to fade, lobbying began to change. Corporate America entered politics, big time. In 1972 a group of leading CEOs created the Business Roundtable, with lobbying as its explicit purpose. The Chamber of Commerce moved from the political outside to become a major player. The number of firms with lobbyists in Washington exploded fourteenfold, from 175 in the year of Powell's memo to 2,445 in 1982. The result? Corporations succeeded in stemming the pro-consumer and prolabor tide of American politics as they blocked many new government safety rules.[33]

After achieving these victories in the late 1970s, corporations set their sights higher. In line with Powell's directives, they established government-affairs offices and firms that "began to lobby more for their own narrow interests," Drutman notes. By the 1990s, "corporate leaders increasingly came to see public policy as a way to improve their profits."[34] Many corporate lobbyists began moving from the "lobby" into legislative offices, even helping to craft and implement policy for their benefit.

Annual inflation-adjusted corporate spending on lobbyists almost doubled, to more than $2 billion, between 1998 and 2010. Corporations now seem to view lobbying as their best investment in Washington—putting almost thirteen times more money into lobbying than into political action committees.[35] On lobbying alone in 2016, they spent a total of more than $3 billion.[36]

But what about unions? Aren't they big players too? Combining union and public-interest groups' spending on lobbying, together they are still outspent thirty-four to one by corporations. Public-interest groups make up only 1 percent of total lobbying spending, while business makes up more than 75 percent.[37]

"Corporations," Drutman suggests, "have now fit their way into almost every process of American democratic policymaking."[38] The chemical industry's success in evading safety rules is a particularly potent example of the power of lobbying. Due to a complex legal process, the EPA has tested about two hundred of approximately eighty-four thousand chemicals used in the United States, and has banned or restricted the use of only nine, even though many others have been banned in Europe.[39]

Plus, ongoing denigration of government by the Anti-Democracy Movement has led to the undervaluing of public-service jobs, so their salaries can't keep up with private-sector lobbying jobs. One consequence is that underpaid congressional staffers have an incentive to aspire to future jobs as lobbyists, potentially making them less likely to challenge corporations with authority over such prospects.[40] This threat to objective legislating was made worse by former House majority leader Tom DeLay, who—seeing no conflict of interest—created the K Street project to help Republican staffers land lobbying jobs after their government jobs ended.[41] Of course, the "revolving door" is not confined to staffers and K Street. In 2012, about half of retiring members of Congress became lobbyists, up dramatically from 3 percent in the early 1970s.[42]

Perhaps the most efficient way for corporations to get what they want is to bypass the middleman and enter government directly. Trump's cabinet—whose total wealth equals that of a third of American households combined—draws heavily on a vast network of donors and corporate interests.[43] The most egregious of these include Secretary of State and former CEO of Exxon Mobil Rex Tillerson and Treasury Secretary and longtime Goldman Sachs executive Steven Mnuchin.

This phenomenon is not unique to Trump. Henry Paulsen, the Treasury secretary during the George W. Bush administration and the leader of the response to the financial collapse of 2008, for example, had previously served as CEO of Goldman Sachs. He was criticized for failing to enact regulations that could have prevented the Great

Recession and for presiding over a recovery effort greatly benefiting his former employer.[44]

Neither are Republicans the only party guilty of appointing a "fox to guard the hen house." Democrat Bill Clinton, for example, appointed the co-chairman of Goldman Sachs, Robert Rubin, to lead the Treasury. In this capacity he helped prevent the regulation of risky derivative trading, a scheme that would play a key role in the 2008 financial collapse.[45] After Rubin left the Treasury, he joined Citigroup, a bank that would greatly benefit from derivatives, eventually becoming chairman of the firm's executive committee.[46]

No longer in the lobby

Lobbying becomes more effective the closer you get to the drafting board, and the American Legislative Exchange Council (ALEC) understands this well. Founded in 1973, just two years after the Powell memo, ALEC operates behind the scenes, turning representatives of business interests into direct collaborators with state legislators.

ALEC was launched by an Illinois state senate staffer, Mark Rhoads, upset by Richard Nixon's "big government" policies such as creating the EPA, writes Bill Bishop in *The Big Sort*.[47] For Jane Mayer, though, ALEC was the "brainchild" of Heritage Foundation founder Paul Weyrich, with Richard Mellon Scaife providing "most of its start-up funding." Also among ALEC's "financial angels" were the Kochs, and a Koch Industries' representative served on ALEC's "board for nearly two decades," she notes.[48]

Defining itself as an "educational organization," ALEC enjoys tax-exempt status, but it is "in many ways indistinguishable from a corporate lobbying operation," Mayer writes.[49] ALEC gets a lot more up close and personal than an ordinary lobbyist group, though. It convenes lawmakers and corporate representatives, as they mingle and vote (with equal voting power) on legislative goals behind closed doors.[50] ALEC creates model legislation and distributes to its lawmaking members on a range of hot-button issues, from cutting corporate taxes to gutting environmental protections to tightening voter-identification rules.[51] Given that many lawmakers, especially on the state level, have limited staff, pre-drafted bills are enticing.

A 2011 ALEC membership brochure bragged that each year more than one thousand bills based on ALEC's model legislation are introduced, and a remarkable 17 percent passed.[52] On average, that's between three and four bills adopted for every state each year. In 2015, 172 ALEC-sponsored bills to privatize public education appeared in forty-two states.[53] ALEC also spread "Stand Your Ground" laws, which provided the justification in the killing of Trayvon Martin and other innocent men and women.[54] The group also specializes in voter-suppression laws. Of "sixty-two voter ID bills introduced in thirty-seven states in 2011 and 2012, more than half were sponsored by members of ALEC," according to journalist Ari Berman.[55]

ALEC founder Weyrich does not hide his views on democracy. In a speech to the Religious Roundtable in Dallas in 1980, he proclaimed: "I don't want everybody to vote. Elections are not won by a majority of people. They never have been from the beginning of our country, and they are not now . . . our leverage in the elections quite candidly goes up as the voting populace goes down."[56]

Strategy 3: Reduce the Voting Power of Those Most Likely to Be Hurt By, and Therefore Opposed to, the Anti-Democracy Agenda

Before and after his victory, Donald Trump loved to shout "voter fraud!" claiming, without evidence, that millions of undocumented immigrants had voted illegally.[57] In his first nationally televised interview as president, he called for an investigation into voter fraud.

The most comprehensive study on the subject, conducted by the Justice Department in 2006, confirmed a voter-fraud rate of 0.00000013 percent, which makes the incidence of voter fraud less frequent than humans being struck by lightning.[58] And, as the Brennan Center for Justice explained to us, there is no evidence to suggest things have changed. Nonetheless, for decades Republican Party leaders have repeated the claim. However false, it has served anti-democracy ends quite well. Such falsehoods are believed, feeding distrust among citizens. In 2016, 68 percent of Americans polled agreed that voter fraud is a problem, with more than half of Republicans saying it was a "major problem."[59] These charges and the misconceptions they create have very real impacts. They help to justify actions that end up restricting voting rights while diverting eyes from the consequences of these assaults.

Sneak attacks on voting rights began almost as soon as the 1965 Voting Rights Act was passed.[60] And today, voting rights are denied and diminished in many ways: requiring identification that members of minority groups are less likely to possess, limiting early voting, reducing polling places and limiting voting hours, making voter registration more difficult, and depriving anyone convicted of a felony of the right to vote.

These strategies have been disastrous for democracy. Here we share examples of their impact, and also explain how our power as citizens is diminished by virtue of jiggering congressional districts to lock in one party's power.

Insidious assaults on the right to vote

After the 2010 wave of GOP victories the passage of these anti-voter laws really picked up steam. "From 2011 to 2015, legislators introduced 395 new voting restrictions in 49 states," a Democracy Initiative report explains.[61] And in just the first three months of 2017, according to the Brennan Center, "at least 87 bills to restrict access to registration and voting have been introduced in 29 states."[62]

Perhaps most devastating for democracy are voter ID laws. As of spring 2017, thirty-two states had some form of voter ID provision.[63] The Brennan Center underscores that more than twenty-one million citizens lack necessary identification.[64] And getting the correct ID can be difficult, if not impossible. In Mississippi, for example, the voter ID law "requires that a birth certificate be presented in order to get a photo ID." The catch-22? You've got to have a photo ID to get a copy of a birth certificate.[65]

Cost can also be a voting barrier for lower-income Americans because, even if the voter ID itself is free, some states charge for the birth certificates and passports needed to get them.[66] Such fees remind us of the vile "poll tax" that kept blacks from voting in the South for decades. Choice of what counts as a valid voter ID can also be discriminatory. In Texas, for example, gun licenses are acceptable, whereas student IDs aren't.[67]

ID laws disproportionately hurt people of color. A 2016 study by political scientists showed that in general elections "Latinos are 10 percent less likely to turn out in states with strict ID laws" than in those states without, and similar effects show up in Latino, black, and Asian American turnout in primaries.[68] And American voters have now learned that small margins can have huge consequences.

It seems that those behind these measures know what they are doing. According to the Brennan Center, during a 2016 trial on Wisconsin's voting restrictions, "former Republican staffer Todd Allbaugh testified that some Wisconsin legislative leaders were 'giddy' that the state's strict photo ID law could keep minority and young voters from the polls."[69]

These laws also selectively "diminish the participation of Democrats and those on the left," which is a "clear partisan distortion," another study concludes.[70] Jim DeMint, a former US senator from South Carolina and now president of the Heritage Foundation, admitted as much, stating that he's been promoting ID laws "all over the country, because in the states where they do have voter-ID laws you've seen, actually, elections begin to change towards more conservative candidates."[71]

Another Supreme Court strike against democracy

A huge setback for voting rights came in the 2013 *Shelby County v. Holder* ruling that effectively ended the Voting Rights Act's requirement that jurisdictions with long records of racial bias get approval from the federal government before altering voting rules. Before *Shelby*, when a new law or rule could potentially harm the voting power of minorities, such as the 2011 Texas voter ID law, the federal government could block it before it went into effect.

Since the *Shelby* ruling, it's much harder for the federal government to block discriminatory voting laws. Within a few hours of the ruling, Alabama and Texas put ID laws into effect.[72] Once federal oversight ended, "Republican legislatures in some seventeen states adopted new laws that civil rights groups said were targeted at suppressing the minority vote," NPR reported in 2016.[73] State legislatures have similarly cut back on early voting, same-day registration, and pre-registration for minors. These laws had significantly increased voter participation, and their gutting was "concentrated in communities with diverse electorates."[74] Some states have even reduced the number of polling sites.[75]

Certain states have also gone out of their way to make registering to vote more difficult, as well. In Texas, it's now a crime to register people and submit their ballots to the elections office unless you are officially deputized. But there are few classes to become deputized, and one must be re-deputized at the end of each even-numbered year. Moreover, a person is deputized only for a single county, making it tough to organize volunteers for statewide voter-registration drives.[76] Alabama, Kansas, and Georgia all attempted to go further, mandating proof of citizenship to register, which would have all but killed citizen-led, public voter-registration efforts. (Who brings their passport to the mall?) Luckily, in 2016, a federal appeals court blocked such attempts, which were described by the nonpartisan League of Women Voters as "thinly veiled discrimination."[77]

How did this play out in the election of Donald Trump?

Fourteen states initiated voter ID laws for the 2016 election, including critical swing states such as Wisconsin.[78] As voting-rights expert Ari Berman stresses, while it's impossible to quantify their precise impact, these laws obviously had an effect on the number of people casting ballots in 2016. In critical Wisconsin, Donald Trump's margin of victory was just twenty-seven thousand votes, while a federal court confirmed that three hundred thousand registered voters lacked required voter IDs.[79] In other words, in a key swing state the number of people blocked from voting by the lack of newly required IDs was *eleven times* greater than the number of voters supplying Trump's margin of victory. Given that voter ID laws are proven to disenfranchise primarily Democratic votes, this change undoubtedly contributed to Trump's victory in the state.

Moreover, in 2016, compared with the previous presidential election, Berman reports, "there were 868 fewer polling places in states with a long history of voting discrimination, like Arizona, Texas, and North Carolina." He estimates that "hundreds of thousands of voters" were affected.[80] Moreover, in Ohio, some counties dismissed provisional ballots for what seem like fishy reasons, including "names written in cursive rather than print."[81]

A felon, still a citizen?

All but two states deprive those convicted of felonies of the right to vote while in prison. Some return the right upon release, while ten states may never do so. In those states, the former convict's only hope may be an individually granted clemency.[82] And in a variety of states, law professor Michelle Alexander adds, even when felons are granted the right to vote, the process to regain it is "so cumbersome, confusing, and onerous," often requiring payment of debts and legal costs, that many don't even attempt it.[83]

The United States stands almost alone on the global stage in this respect. Only Armenia, Chile, and Belgium (in rare cases) never return the right to vote after incarceration.[84] The impact is significant. But the psychological harm of being treated as less than a citizen can be eased when it is returned: the likelihood of being rearrested is cut in half among formerly incarcerated people who vote.[85]

"Felon disenfranchisement" is a big deal both as a matter of human rights and because of its practical impact on our biggest political choices. Both are amplified by the size of the prison population. Since the 1980s, it has multiplied six-fold, from three hundred thousand to more than two million.[86] As Alexander explains, "The United States now has the highest rate of incarceration in the world . . . even surpassing those in repressive regimes like Russia, China, and Iran."[87] And this massive increase has little to do with violent crimes. More Americans are in prison today because of drug crimes than the total number of people in jail in 1980.[88]

These laws also reflect racial biases. African Americans make up 40 percent of the felon population, despite being only 13 percent of the population. Black men, in some states, are between twenty to fifty times more likely to be admitted to prison for drug charges than white men—despite using drugs at virtually the same rate.[89] More than two million African Americans cannot vote because of these laws, according to journalist and election-data expert Harry Enten.[90] Predictably, felon disenfranchisement also disproportionately affects Latinos.[91]

Not surprisingly, it was ALEC that provided the language for bills responsible for the staggering increase in incarceration, such as mandatory minimums, three-strikes laws, and "truth in sentencing" bills, which seek to abolish or curb parole.[92]

In 2010 approximately 2.5 percent of the voting-age population was barred from voting due to felon disenfranchisement.[93] Since then, its impact has worsened in some states, including Florida. There, in 2011, the newly elected Tea Party governor, Rick Scott, and the state clemency board repealed previous progress and created additional restrictions on felons.[94] Florida bars an estimated 1.5 million people from voting—that's three thousand times the vote margin that decided the 2000 election in the state.[95]

African Americans and Latinos tend to vote Democratic, so it's hard not to see these restrictions as a political maneuver. In 2016, the number disenfranchised because of felon status exceeded Trump's margin of victory in five states, according to the United States Elections Project.[96]

How bad is this systematic disenfranchisement? Please take a moment to absorb this damning judgment on the state of American democracy: the United Nations Human Rights Committee deemed these laws to be "discriminatory and [to] violate international law."[97]

Rigging district lines

When money and voter suppression aren't enough, cleverly drawing the boundaries of congressional and state political districts can help preserve one party's political power. And it can be easy. With some exceptions, state legislatures set district lines, and they can draw them to ensure the (re)election of fellow party members. Because lines are typically redrawn when a new census is released every ten years, manipulating district lines can effectively shut out opposition for an entire decade.

The trick is called "gerrymandering"—dating back at least to 1812. Its two basic tactics are "packing"—squeezing like-minded voters into one district so they won't dilute others; and the opposite, "cracking"—spreading out other like-minded voters to ensure they don't comprise a majority anywhere. "Gerry" derives from the offending governor of Massachusetts, Elbridge Gerry; and "mander" comes from "salamander," since that's what one of his rigged Senate districts looked like, at least in the eyes of a popular cartoonist. The term stuck, and so did the practice. In 2010, almost two hundred years later, the Anti-Democracy Movement aggressively harnessed the power of gerrymandering, and in a version more dangerous than ever before.

Why more dangerous? Partly, the answer lies in the vastly more sophisticated technology developed in recent decades. The massive data trails we each leave online can be used to draw district maps to fit precise political aims. Former *Salon* editor in chief David Daley explains that, using the data, "you can create an index that bounds enough of the right people, in the right way, to guarantee a result throughout the decade." With increasingly sophisticated data analysis, partisan map makers are "rewiring our democracy."[98]

Another part of the story lies in the historic campaign Republicans waged in 2010 to take back statehouses across the country. The Republican State Leadership Committee, under new chairman Ed Gillespie, shifted its focus from lobbying statehouses in the interests of corporate donors and launched the Redistricting Majority Program, or RED-MAP.[99] It raised $30 million to gain control of state legislatures and was one reason Republicans ended up winning 680 state legislature seats nationwide, the "biggest rout in modern history."[100] In eleven state legislatures across the country, including Pennsylvania, North Carolina, Ohio, Michigan, and Wisconsin, they took control of both houses.

The Republican State Leadership Committee then offered, without charge, to assist officials involved in redistricting.[101] The goal was to draw lines to ensure a Republican majority in the House and in state legislatures for the rest of the decade. It worked. In 2012 Republicans won thirteen of eighteen congressional seats in Pennsylvania even though they received one hundred thousand fewer votes than their Democratic competition.[102] In Ohio, the GOP won a staggering twelve of sixteen congressional seats even though they only received 52 percent of the votes for Congress.[103] Moreover, Democrats won more votes in House races in four states—Michigan, North Carolina, Pennsylvania, and Wisconsin—but still lost the majority of seats.[104]

And in some state-level races, the outcome was even more undemocratic. In Ohio, Republicans won sixty of ninety-nine state House seats even though overall more people voted for Democrats.[105] In the three cycles since redistricting, Michigan Democrats have won more votes but lost the majority of seats.[106]

Overall, the distortion caused by gerrymandering is clear. In 2012 Democrats won almost 1.6 million more votes than Republicans in House races but lost the majority of seats.[107] In all, a 2016 report from the Campaign Legal Center concludes, "Partisan gerrymandering has never been worse in modern American history than it is today."[108]

It's clear that at least some Republicans who engaged in manipulating district boundaries knew just how unsavory their actions were. In North Carolina, Daley describes two redistricting processes, "one very public," the other "behind closed doors."[109] In Ohio, the redistricting team, moving away from curious legislators' eyes, "rented a room at the Columbus Doubletree hotel from July 17 through October 15, moved out the furniture, and dubbed it 'the Bunker.'"[110] In Florida, those intent on rigging district lines used imposters pretending to be ordinary citizens. Allies submitted "amateur" maps as public comments to committees gathering public opinion when they were actually created by the GOP itself.[111]

Unfortunately for democracy, so far the Supreme Court has rejected challenges to gerrymandering on political grounds.[112] In 2004 the Court said it lacked a "neutral" standard by which to judge whether gerrymandering infringed on equal representation.[113] But there is hope. Academics, legal scholars, and good-government groups such as Common Cause and the Campaign Legal Center have been working to develop a usable standard. Plus, in early 2017, Wisconsin appealed a federal court decision striking down its district map on partisan grounds, so the Supreme Court might just revisit the question.[114] Perhaps the Court could finally rule that gerrymandering does indeed deprive citizens of equal representation.

Less a result of the Anti-Democracy Movement, but nevertheless deleterious to our democracy, is "prison gerrymandering." The US Census counts incarcerated Americans as residents of the district in which they're imprisoned, despite the fact they cannot vote there. A few small communities with prisons gain outsized political power and, simultaneously, the power of the communities from which the prisoners hail shrinks, as well as the power of any voter not living near a prison: an obvious violation of one-person, one-vote. In a 2005 election in the second ward of Anamosa, Iowa, 96 percent of the population lived in the state's largest prison and was thus ineligible to vote. The voting pool was thus so small that only two write-in votes decided the winner.[115]

Prison gerrymandering is "inherently unfair," says Susan Lerner, president of Common Cause New York. And it is particularly harmful in her state. There, two-thirds of prisoners are from New York City, but 91 percent are incarcerated upstate.[116] So, for example, Senate district 45 in upstate New York boosted its power by including almost thirteen thousand incarcerated people.[117] Republican state senator Dale Volker "boasted that he was glad the almost 9,000 people confined in his district couldn't vote, because 'they would never vote for [him].'"[118] Given that mass incarceration disproportionately affects communities of color, prison gerrymandering has a strong racial bias. (Fortunately, Lerner and her fellow New Yorkers stepped up with a solution, which we celebrate in the next chapter.)

Strategy 4: Where Possible, Wipe Out Local Democracy Altogether!

In a maneuver called "preemption," states can prevent local governments from enacting a range of laws—from prohibiting a raise in the minimum wage to disallowing new restrictions on tobacco to blocking environmental protections, such as bans on fracking. Its use picked up in the 1980s, now with ALEC as one of its chief advocates. One of the rationales offered for these provisions by an ALEC executive was the "danger of too much local democracy."[119]

Even more draconian is displacing local democracy altogether, as egregiously implemented in the state of Michigan. In 2011, Michigan's governor, Rick Snyder, promising to run the state "like a business," signed Public Act 4.[120] Building on a 1990 law, the act greatly expanded the power of managers assigned to municipalities and schools deemed to be in "financial emergency." The new statute proclaimed that an emergency manager's power "'shall be superior to and supersede the power' of other officers and entities."[121] Behind the approach were the same anti-democracy think tanks and billionaires described earlier, including the DeVos family and the Kochs.[122]

Since 2011, eleven Michigan schools and municipalities, including Flint and Detroit, have been assigned emergency managers.[123] And, what has since unfolded in Flint, a largely African American city seventy miles from Detroit, is nothing less than tragic.

In the spring of 2013, negotiations over the price of water broke down and Detroit gave Flint notice that in one year it would stop supplying water to the city. So, in 2014 Flint, under the control of emergency managers, switched its drinking-water source to the Flint River.[124] The problem? It is highly corrosive, in fact, nineteen times more so than Detroit's water, as Virginia Tech researchers later determined.[125] Because Flint failed to treat the water, the city's old pipes soon began leaching lead at poisonous levels into its water supply.[126] While city government denied the problem, residents continued drinking the water unaware that it could bring both immediate and severe, long-term harm.[127] In fact, lead exposure may increase the "risk of Parkinson's and prostate cancer," Detroit neurologist Peter LeWitt warns, or even the "health of a person's unborn children."[128] For children, exposure carries risk of lifetime intellectual disability.[129] An outbreak of the fatal Legionnaires' disease was also linked to Flint water.[130]

For months, residents reported not only foul-smelling water but rashes, hair loss, and stomach pain; yet the city's managers only acted after Virginia Tech researchers found problems. So, a full year and a half elapsed after the menace began before the water system was finally returned to the safer source, the Detroit system, in the fall of 2015.[131] As our book goes to press, the tragedy of anti-democracy—authority with no accountability—continues to play out in Flint. In late 2016, the state's "prosecutors . . . charged four former government officials in Flint, including two city emergency managers, with conspiring to violate safety rules," according to Reuters reporter Steve Friess.[132] In 2017, a class-action lawsuit charged the EPA with failure to follow agency protocol and take emergency action for several months after issues with the Flint River water came to light.[133]

Flint's poisoning tragedy is the outcome of decades of economic decline, flowing from a worldview denigrating democracy and promoting a brutal form of capitalism. Without accountable democracy to deal with the city's declining economy, over decades, even the essential infrastructure of life—from water to education—was undone. "In Flint, there's little to no tax base to speak of . . . no one trusts anyone from government," Flint native Stephen Arellano tells us. Replacing local democracy with unelected managers was not the root problem in this small Michigan city. It was the culmination of decades of anti-democracy steps.

WEAKENING THE RULES PROTECTING WORKERS

In this chapter, we've focused on efforts to "rig the rules" in our political life, but let's not forget the rules of our work life—also essential for democracy—including those that enable workers to have a voice through union representation. Since the 1970s, government has increasingly failed to enforce labor law protecting workers against union-busting tactics by employers.[134] Furthermore, systematic efforts, largely led by ALEC's aggressive lobbying, have succeeded in passing laws in twenty-eight states that eliminate the requirement that those who benefit from union representation must pay union dues to sustain that protection.[135]

Workers are hurt directly by these laws, but so is our democracy, as studies find that members of unions are more likely to vote, to hold less authoritarian views, and to be more appreciative of cultural and racial differences.[136] Thus, citizens standing for labor rights are also standing for democracy.

TOUCHING US ALL

The Anti-Democracy Movement undermines basic fairness and assaults our dignity as citizens, bringing painful, real-life consequences affecting just about all of us. Examples of the impact of concentrated, unaccountable power are countless. Here are just a few to suggest their range:

As in Flint's tragedy, the Anti-Democracy Movement's denigration of government's role leads to neglect of essential public goods. Nationwide, for example, civil engineers give our drinking water a grade of "D." More than eighteen million Americans depend on community water systems with lead violations.[137]

Financially, we are also endangered. In just four years following the financial meltdown, from 2007 to 2011, a quarter of "American families lost at least 75 percent of their wealth."[138] Yet, resistance, largely from the financial sector—number one in political contributors—means that we're still unprotected against another such crisis.[139]

Our health is at greater risk as prices of essential medicine soar out of reach of many. In just over a decade, the cost of a year's cancer treatment shot up more than ten-fold, from $5,000 to $10,000 before 2000 to an average of $120,000 in 2012. Seventy-eight percent of Americans favor allowing the government to limit the price of high-cost drugs for serious illnesses like cancer or hepatitis.[140] Yet no progress has been made. Why? Because the power of the drug lobby blocks congressional action.

Another example of great harm is inaction on climate change. Almost two-thirds of Americans want government to do more to address the causes of global warming.[141] Why isn't government acting? A strong clue lies in one fact: between 1990 and 2016, fossil-fuel industry political contributions leaped eight-fold, mainly going to Republicans.[142]

Finally, trust is also a victim of the Anti-Democracy Movement. Americans are losing trust that their democracy is really theirs. By 2014, only 11 percent of Democrats and 15 percent of Republicans reported trusting that members of Congress are "significantly" influenced by their constituents.[143] From the early seventies, when Lewis Powell sat down to write his infamous memo, to 2016, confidence in Congress has crashed from 42 percent to a mere 9 percent.[144]

NOW WHAT?

For us, understanding *why* our nation has been moving in a dangerous direction has been essential in deciding what is most needed in changing course. We want to contribute to removing big money's grip on our democracy and igniting citizens' engagement in everyday democracy. Thus, we hope that these sobering revelations don't smother our readers with hopelessness, but clarify and motivate.

The saying "knowledge is power" is a cliché, but it's also true. With knowledge, we won't waste time on palliatives. Instead we can embrace solutions that cut to these deep system roots of our crisis. *Democracy is calling all of us*, so let's get started.

PART III

CREATING SOLUTIONS TOGETHER

"Democracy is not just a counting up of votes, it is a counting up of actions."

—HOWARD ZINN, 1968

CHAPTER FIVE

DEMOCRACY'S CALLING

HAVING EXPLORED KEY STRATEGIES of the Anti-Democracy Movement robbing Americans of democracy's promise, we now turn to democracy's champions—those who step by bold step are moving us toward a real democracy—one that's responsive, inclusive, fair, and enlivening.

You'll see that their vision is broad and it is deep. For some, tackling the power of big money in our political system is the "mother of all issues." For others, voting rights and racial justice are the key points of leverage. How citizens arrive at their focus is itself intriguing. Here's a dramatic, to say the least, story of how one leader in the Democracy Movement came to his.

In 1997, Josh Silver, in his early twenties, was hiking the Peruvian Amazon when his travel buddy was killed in an ambush. Josh escaped wounded, and after a harrowing, multiday trek to safety, he finally made it home. Hearing his tale, of course our jaws hit the floor. Then we scratched our heads, wondering what on earth this experience has to do with democracy in America. So we asked, "Josh, how did a nightmare in the jungle lead you to money-out-of-politics?"

"Simple," he said. "I realized life is short, no time to waste, better focus on what makes the most difference . . . the most change. The leverage point? It's getting money out of politics." He heard about a campaign for clean elections in Arizona and jumped at the chance to work on it, though it paid next to nothing, and eventually to lead the effort. In 2012, Josh founded Represent.Us, an innovator in grassroots organizing against political corruption.

Largely unknown to most of us, Josh and many other courageous Americans have been fomenting reforms that are already proving to make a big difference.

BIG MONEY OUT, CITIZENS IN

Some say the way our nation finances elections produces plutocracy. Others, including a beloved former president, are even more direct. "[I]f the people tolerate the growth of private power to a point where it becomes stronger than the democratic state itself, that in its essence is fascism," Franklin Delano Roosevelt warned in 1938.

So how do we replace big-donor power with people power—with the voices and views of everyday citizens? To find answers, lovers of democracy would do well to check out what's happened in Maine over the past two decades.

Twenty years ago Mainers had a pretty dim view of their state government. And understandably so. Before big votes, Andrew Bossie, executive director of Maine Citizens for Clean Elections from 2011 to 2017, tells us that many believed Maine lobbyists literally handed checks to lawmakers. The last straw for many Mainers came on October 10, 1993, when a sleepy trucker hit and killed four teenagers.[1] Grieving friends and family believed stronger rules governing the legal maximum length of a trucker's shift could have prevented the tragedy, so they pushed the legislature to act. They were furious when trucking industry lobbyists convinced the legislature not to strengthen the rules.

At the time, few believed change was possible. But not everyone. By 1995 some Mainers were finally ready to shake things up. Their simple goal? Enabling candidates to run for office without becoming beholden to big donors.

Environmental, labor, and religious groups all banded together to create a bill.

"We sat around; twenty drafts went around the table. We tried to shoot holes in it . . . We tried to stand it up and knock it down and redraft it again," recalls David Donnelly, who later led the ballot-initiative campaign.[2]

Their goal was freeing candidates from having to beg for contributions from wealthy donors. Under the clean-elections law they came up with, candidates who commit to using only public money receive a block sum to fund their campaigns. To qualify, they would also have to prove sufficient public support by collecting $5 each from fifty supporters within their district in a House race, and $5 each from 150 residents for a Senate race.

At only twenty-six, Donnelly was hired to lead the effort. Earlier, he'd quit state politics because he saw the system turning candidates into telemarketers. He was willing to go anywhere in the country to make reform happen when he got wind of Maine's effort. He landed a research position, and within six months had risen to head the campaign.

Its strategy was clear: bypass lawmakers and go straight to voters via a state ballot initiative. In 1995, to get on the ballot, the campaign needed approximately fifty-five thousand Mainers to sign petitions of support, a lot in a state with just under a million people of voting age. And convincing Mainers that some of their tax dollars should go toward campaign finance seemed like a hard sell—so hard that some pollsters said they could not ethically justify being paid to poll the question because they were sure its chances were zilch.

The biggest opposition was the "seed of cynicism . . . [the] doubt in peoples' heads that the system is so bad that we actually can't do anything to fix it," Donnelly later told the *New York Times*.[3] But doubt did not quell determination, as Donnelly and other Maine civic leaders masterminded what he called a "high stakes, high reward" signature-collecting strategy. A big turnout was expected on election day 1995 because a gay-rights measure was on the ballot, so the campaign turned it into an opportunity to inform voters and collect signatures. And did they ever. With 1,100 volunteers in polling stations all over the state, in a mere thirteen hours they'd gathered a staggering sixty-five thousand signatures, way over what was needed.

Clearly, many Mainers were hungry for reform.

In the summer before election day 1996, polls didn't look good, though, and by July 4, the campaign's bank account had sunk to around $2,500. But excitement was growing about the campaign, around the state, and even nationally, so Donnelly and company were gradually able to raise enough money to recruit volunteers, print yard signs, distribute literature, and even air limited television ads. On the final weekend, hundreds went door to door for the cause. Sure enough, they pushed the Clean Election Act through by a margin of 12 percent.[4]

In 2000, the first election cycle under clean elections, about one in three candidates seized the opportunity for public financing—a share that by 2006 had hit 81 percent.[5]

Clean elections made possible public health and environmental protections many believe wouldn't have stood a chance if big money had still dominated elections, Andrew Bossie told us. One phases out a flame retardant, long banned in the European Union and associated with a range of health concerns.[6] Another, the Kids Safe Products Act, led to the ban of the harmful additive BPA from products sold in the state.[7] Many also link clean elections to Maine's becoming the second state to pass the 2004 electronics "takeback" law that holds manufacturers responsible for the full life cycle of their products. It's kept lead and other pollutants out of Maine's gorgeous landscape.[8] Bossie put it to us simply: "Many lawmakers credit clean elections with allowing them to vote their conscience without the threat of withheld campaign money."

Maine's experience is just one story that proves Americans are not starting from scratch in shaping effective pro-democracy policies. But like any good story, Maine's 1996 public-financing launch has a sequel.

In the 2000s, the Anti-Democracy Movement amped up its efforts, and corporate and other big-and-often-secret money flooded elections nationwide. Unlike other states, for a while Maine's reform largely withstood the assault because its law provided clean-elections candidates with additional funds if outspent by a certain margin by big-money opponents. This "trigger" mechanism made it viable to run as a clean-elections candidate.

Unfortunately, though, secret money could still infiltrate the system. A clean-elections legislator we admire, the former small-town waitress and five-term Maine legislator Deborah Simpson, was wiped out by a nasty, race-baiting, xenophobic attack in 2010—carried out with unaccountable, outside money. Still, clean elections stood strong.

Then, in June 2011, the Supreme Court struck again. It overturned a triggering mechanism in Arizona that was similar to Maine's, and suddenly Maine's clean elections seemed like it could soon be history, for who would want to run on public financing if you couldn't compete against big-money attacks? [9]

But Mainers were fortunate. Volunteers with the Maine Citizens for Clean Elections had great foresight. Worried that the Supreme Court might make their system unviable, they were prepared with a plan to come up with a "fix" if the Court ruled adversely. Before the 2011 decision, advocates had convinced the legislature to agree on a timely public process to respond to the ruling.[10] When the ruling did come down, the state ethics commission was prepared to enter a process bringing together stakeholders and the general public to come up with ways to deal with the ruling and keep clean elections strong.

Plus, just two weeks before the troubling Supreme Court ruling, the clean-elections organization had hired a new, energized executive director, Andrew Bossie. Immediately after the negative Court ruling, Andrew and his team leapt into action. They developed an innovative solution that complied with the Court's ruling while keeping their beloved law strong: a change in the Clean Elections Act allowing candidates to seek additional funds if greatly outspent by private money. They had only to collect an additional set of $5 donations from different Maine residents. Within the next few legislative sessions, they'd built enough pressure to pass their fix with bipartisan support.

But that victory wasn't enough. Maine requires a bill to go through two rounds of approval—one to pass the law, the other to fund it. The fix never made it through the second round, and it slowly sank into the political abyss. As a result, participation in the clean-elections program continued to drop, and by 2014, the share of candidates using public finance had fallen to just over half.[11] "It was just really sad, watching this thing deteriorate before your eyes," Andrew recalls.

But he and his allies didn't give up. They decided to develop and bring to the ballot a new clean-elections initiative that included the "fix," plus strengthened disclosure rules, exactly what had been missing when Deb Simpson was defeated by secret money's nasty attack.

Then, not unlike the original effort twenty years earlier, they got busy going directly to the people, explaining how important public financing is.

David Donnelly, now leading the national democracy-defending organization Every Voice, rejoined the fight. Together, his organization and Maine Citizens for Clean Elections built a campaign called Mainers for Accountable Elections, in which community groups and everyday people collected signatures, wrote letters to the editor, coordinated house parties, and went door to door to inform voters.

In November 2015, these democracy diehards celebrated a well-deserved victory. And by 2016, the share of candidates using public financing had risen again, to nearly two-thirds of the state legislature.[12]

For Donnelly, this experience is more proof that "we are 'a more perfect union,' not a perfect one. We always have to be making it more perfect." Citizens must be prepared to create "deep power," Donnelly explains. "We're literally talking about changing the way politics and economics intersect. If we are going to dismantle that . . . we have to go much deeper."

PROGRESS BEYOND MAINE

Eighty-five percent of us want big changes in how elections are funded, with almost half of us agreeing that a complete rebuild is needed.[13] Yet some roll their eyes and say that big money, legal or not, *always* finds its way into a political system. Perhaps, but what's certain is that we can do vastly better. The proof is in, as we've just seen. Even without perfection, people's lives and democracy itself can be improved with straightforward solutions.

The Supreme Court, mostly by only a one-vote majority, has blocked progress on campaign finance reform. Yet for the most part, it's given a green light to the approach we've just featured in Maine: public financing of elections, arguably the most important money-in-politics reform. Although still uncommon in the United States, it's used in the vast majority of democracies worldwide, where elections are commonly viewed as a public good. About two-thirds of countries make public funding available to political parties. In Europe, almost 90 percent do.[14]

In the United States, support for public financing at the highest level goes way back. In 1907, then-President Theodore Roosevelt proposed public financing to Congress, declaring:

> The need for collecting large campaign funds would vanish if Congress provided an appropriation for the proper and legitimate expenses of each of the great national parties, an appropriation ample enough to meet the necessity for thorough organization and machinery, which requires a large sum of money.[15]

And, as noted, after Watergate, Americans wanted to clean up our politics and acted—adopting partial public financing for primaries and full public funding for the general election in presidential campaigns. The impact was immediate. The system was set up in 1974, and in the spring of 1976, when Jimmy Carter's campaign was in debt, "public money saved his candidacy," Marilyn Thompson writes in the *Atlantic*. In that same year, Ronald Reagan had fifteen times less money than his opponent in the Republican primary, but public funding kept him "viable" and "paved the way" for his victory in 1980.[16]

Unfortunately, citizen pressure for public financing flagged, while private-campaign contributions ballooned. So in 2008 candidate Barack Obama, apparently judging the spending limits would handicap him, became the first presidential candidate since 1976 to forgo public financing.[17] And today public financing for presidential elections is all but irrelevant. In early 2017 the House GOP began moves to abolish it.[18]

The year 1976 was also significant for public financing on the state level, as Minnesota became the first to use it, though in a limited fashion. Public financing even helped elect a third-party governor, Jesse Ventura, in 1998.[19] Then, in 2000, Maine and Arizona shared the honor of becoming the first states to implement full public financing for all statewide and legislative offices. In 2008 Connecticut joined the crew.

Most recently, in 2016 South Dakota voters approved a ballot measure that would have provided each voter with $100 in "democracy credits" to donate to any candidate for state offices, along with other anticorruption provisions. But cleaning up elections was too much for sitting legislators.

Using emergency measures, Republicans in the legislature overrode voters and repealed the law before it took effect.[20] Nevertheless, the fact that South Dakota—where Republicans throughout the state's history have been victorious in more than 80 percent of statewide elections—passed this measure proves common-sense democracy reform is not partisan.

In response to their legislators' hubris in defying the will of the people, in early 2017 South Dakotans across the state began calling them and protesting their anti-democratic action. And soon reformers announced a campaign for a state constitutional amendment—which the legislature can't reverse—to be placed on the 2018 ballot. It would include a modified version of the anticorruption act. While citizen-allocated credits will not be included in the amendment, such widespread citizen engagement tells us this is not the end of the trail for public financing in South Dakota.

In all, thirteen states (including those listed above) have some form of partial public funding.[21] Way back in 1990, New York City implemented public financing for city council and mayoral races, too. A range of cities has since enacted their own versions, including Albuquerque, New Mexico; New Haven, Connecticut; and Tallahassee, Florida. Counties have followed suit, as well. In 2014, for example, Montgomery County, Maryland, enacted public financing.

In 2014, US representative John Sarbanes of Maryland introduced the Government by the People Act, modeled after New York City's system, which would mean public financing for congressional elections. Eligible candidates opting into the system receive public funds to match small-donor constituent contributions, and citizens are entitled to vouchers and tax credits to support candidates of their choice.

"Right now, Americans are spectators in the bleachers of their democracy," Sarbanes told us. "To create a fair game, they can try putting a referee on the field—making the big-money players stick to some rules. But Americans still aren't players with real power. To uproot deep cynicism, [we need] Americans to get down on that field." That's the heart of the Government by the People Act because voters' small donations get supplemented by public dollars. "Plus," Sarbanes added, "Congress can pass it without getting tangled up in opposition from the courts."

Clean Elections, Big Impacts

Candidates seem to really appreciate the public funding option. In Connecticut, 85 percent of candidates in the 2014 general election relied on public financing. In Arizona 64 percent of candidates used public funds in 2008 before the rate fell heavily in response to the Supreme Court's 2011 decision, weakening the viability of publicly financed candidates.[22] And as stated, in Maine in 2016, almost two-thirds used the program.

Public financing "not only leveled the playing field, it completely upended the playing field," says Connecticut state senator Gary Winfield, a beneficiary of the program.[23] Two years out of college, Winfield was elected to the state's General Assembly in 2008, and then to its Senate in 2014.[24] It was public financing, Winfield notes, that enabled him to defeat a candidate endorsed by the Connecticut Democratic Party.[25]

Voters like public financing, too.

In 2015, when local investigative journalists revealed Connecticut's legislature was considering temporarily suspending public financing to meet a budget crisis, hundreds called state legislators and thousands more sent e-mails in protest. A few days after the revelation, those who'd used public finance to seek office held an emergency press conference to denounce the suspension. Just as he got up to speak, Evan Preston, then the director of Connecticut PIRG, was handed a piece of paper. On it, he told us, the Senate president and the speaker of the House had repented. They'd promised not kill public financing. A bold display of citizen power had saved Connecticut's publicly funded elections, and they continue to stand strong.

What differences do we see when big-money donors are put on the sidelines and citizens in the center? Here are a few:

Candidates are motivated to meet with their constituents. Candidates in states with full public funding spend less time fund-raising and more time in the field talking to voters.[26] As political scientist Michael Miller explains, spending more time with voters under a full public financing system correlates with higher voting rates in state elections—those that are often less publicized and seen as less significant.[27]

Diversity increases among those running for and being elected to office. The number of Latino and Native American candidates in Arizona nearly tripled between the first and second election cycles of Arizona's public finance program.[28] Diversity has also increased in Connecticut.[29] In New York City in 2009, after twenty years of publicly financed elections, people of color had become the majority on the city council.[30] Moreover, in 2006 seven out of ten women candidates for Maine's state legislature using Clean Elections funding reported that the program was "very important" in their decision to run.[31] Clean Elections has also given Maine a state legislature with the highest percentage of working-class people in the country.[32]

More citizens feel like "players" on the field of politics and donor diversity increases. When small donations are multiplied by public funds, the power of voters without a lot of money gets multiplied, and the incentive to contribute increases. Matching-funds systems also diversify the donor pool, which has long been overwhelmingly white, rich, and male.[33] In 2009, "twenty-four times more small donors from the poor and predominately black Bedford-Stuyvesant neighborhood and the surrounding communities gave money to candidates for the [New York] City Council," where contributions are matched, "than for the State Assembly," where they are not matched.[34] In Arizona, the public financing system increased "the number of contributors as well as their geographic, economic and ethnic diversity," a Clean Elections Institute study found.[35] Therefore public financing encourages politicians to listen to more diverse demographics. Being a "player" in elections might also encourage citizens to engage in other ways on vital public choices affecting us all.

More campaigns are powered by small-money contributors, not big donors. Public financing enabled participating New York City Council candidates in 2009 to raise 37 percent of their private contributions from donors giving $250 or less, two and a half times as much as nonparticipating candidates—a remarkable contrast to the state as a whole, where these smaller contributions made up just 6 percent of funding in 2010.[36]

The number of people running for office increases.[37] In Maine, the number of candidates for state legislature general elections increased more than 10 percent in the six years after the implementation of publicly funded elections in 2000.[38]

Public financing decreases the advantages of incumbents. In New York in 2009, after the public-funding matching ratio for small-dollar contributions was raised from 4–1 to 6–1, the incumbent reelection rate went down 10 percentage points. While the reelection rate remained high, at 87 percent, at least incumbents became aware that they will have to work harder to win, and that's a good thing.[39]

Is all this a pipe dream? We don't think so. In 2015, 72 percent of Americans polled favor small-money matching funds and this support bridges ideological lines.[40]

THE RIGHT TO KNOW

Just as the right to be heard is foundational to democracy, so too is the right to be informed. Secrecy is anathema to democracy. Whether it's knowledge of campaign financing or a candidate's coordination with foreign governments, citizens cannot make sound decisions without access to necessary information.

Remember, 80 percent of Americans find secret money in politics to be a problem, and even the late Justice Antonin Scalia believed transparency is critical. Yet, *Citizens United* made the problem of nondisclosed money much worse.

In 2010 we were oh-so close to significant national reform. The DISCLOSE Act, which would have required super PACs to disclose donors, fell just one vote short of the sixty needed to break a Senate filibuster. In 2012, when the act was reintroduced and subject to another filibuster, Rhode Island senator Sheldon Whitehouse and a group of Democrats led a midnight vigil to bring attention to the act.

Progress has been made across several states, though. A 2009 Massachusetts law required funders of political ads to take credit for the message.[41] Later, the rule was strengthened to require ads and mailers to include a list of the top five donors to the message.

We can't stop at passive transparency, though. "Full disclosure at every level of government is only useful if it is not tucked away somewhere in a state or city office or even on the FEC website," Joan Mandle, the executive director of Democracy Matters, tells us. "We need to make sure the data is clear and easy for the average voter to access. Moreover, any transparency measure should be bolstered with publicly funded efforts to distribute the information and make it meaningful to the public."

REFORM THE ENFORCERS

The Federal Elections Commission was established in 1974 to inform the public about campaign finance; to enforce rules governing limits, prohibitions, and transparency; and, when it functioned, to oversee public funding of presidential campaigns. But in 2015 "worse than dysfunctional" is how Ann Ravel, an FEC commissioner, described this critical institution.

Ravel, appointed in 2013, had long been a democracy defender, previously serving as head of the Fair Political Practices Commission in California. She resigned from the FEC in early 2017 and explained the crisis in a *New York Times* op-ed. "Unfortunately, a controlling bloc of three Republican commissioners . . . are ideologically opposed to the FEC's purpose. . . . The resulting paralysis has allowed over $800 million in 'dark money' to infect our elections since *Citizens United*. . . . This breakdown has been purposeful," she said. We've ended up with "an agency mandated to ensure transparency and disclosure that is actually working to keep the public in the dark.

"By law, no more than three of [the agency's] six members can be from the same party. Four must agree to begin an investigation," she continued. Presumably, the arrangement could work if all members were committed to its goals.[42]

Ravel explained to us, "I believe that reform starts with the appointment of commissioners who understand their role under the law which established the FEC—to ensure disclosure of campaign finance transactions to prevent corruption and provide transparency to the voters, and to fairly enforce the law." That could happen, she believes, if the commissioners were selected from a list provided by an independent blue-ribbon commission. Other reformers suggest that the makeup of the commission should always be an unequal number so that it could not be made ineffective by partisan deadlock.

LIMIT THE LOBBYISTS, LISTEN TO US

"Congress has about a third fewer committee staff than it had in 1980. And the staff it does have are younger and less experienced," Lee Drutman notes. "If you wanted a legislative branch run by K Street lobbyists and 25-year-old staffers, mission accomplished," one congressional staff member lamented.[43]

Reducing lobbyists' power requires revaluing government work, creating competitive salaries for congressional staff, and increasing the budget of the nonpartisan, respected Government Accountability Office and Congressional Research Service. Boosting unbiased policy research, on which congressional staff depends, would reinforce a counterweight to the flood of private, special-interest information sources.[44]

Addressing what's become known as the "revolving door" is another key to limiting lobbyists' influence. Today, members of Congress can assume that a lucrative corporate job awaits in the very industries they oversee, and this revolving door from Congress to business compromises objectivity. Presently, the legally required gap between the two careers is one year for the House of Representatives and two years for the Senate.[45]

In early 2017 President Trump weakened rules governing the revolving door for the executive branch.[46] To reduce incentives to cater to corporate interests, the Democracy Movement can push to widen the gap between public-interest and corporate careers, as well as to better regulate lobbyists, now allowed, for example, to hold $100,000 fund-raising bashes for members of Congress.[47]

Simple and immediate transparency could help a lot too, Drutman says. Every lobbying interaction could be made instantaneously visible on a public website, including information about the issue on both sides, with opportunity for public comment. Citizen-watchdog groups could then expose under-the-radar corporate influence.[48]

Of course, lobbying is not all about private gain. More and more citizens are realizing they too can "lobby" their legislators. Because regular citizens lack corporate lobbyists' resources, Drutman proposes for democracy reformers additional innovations: federal subsidies for grassroots lobbying efforts, provided they meet a certain level of support, and the creation of what he calls an Office of Public Lobbying to provide expertise for public-interest advocates.[49]

OUR SUPREME COURT, A BARRIER TO DEMOCRACY?

The Supreme Court ruling in *Citizens United* outraged Americans—and understandably so. In response, many in the Democracy Movement have been pressing for city and state resolutions calling on Congress to begin the process of amending the constitution to allow limits on money in politics.

For some, a goal is to clarify that the Bill of Rights applies only to natural persons, not corporations, enabling the Court to permit limits on corporate political spending. We're aware, though, that killing once and for all the concept of "corporate personhood" as it relates to political expenditures would not end or even greatly reduce the current assault on political equality—that is, each citizen having an equal voice in elections. What's often overlooked is that it is not corporations but largely extremely wealthy individuals who flood the coffers of super PACs, entities triggered by a federal court ruling on the heels of *Citizens United*. Super PACs are handy channels for contributions going to support campaign expenditures that are, at least ostensibly, independent of the campaign. In the 2012 election, individuals provided more than 70 percent of super PAC funds.[50]

Among several proposed constitutional amendments, New Mexico senator Tom Udall's seems to have the most support. It would effectively reverse the 1976 *Buckley* ruling by giving Congress and states the power to regulate the raising and spending of money in federal and state elections, respectively. Certainly a step in the right direction.

Amending the constitution is, however, a lengthy and uncertain process. It goes like this: two-thirds of Congress must first approve an amendment, *or* two-thirds of states must call for a constitutional convention (an avenue that's yet to succeed). Then, *in either case*, three-fourths of state legislatures must also approve it. Bottom line: thirteen state legislatures can block the amendment process indefinitely.

So, we choose to focus on legislative actions—local and national reforms proven to work, and work now. Why? Legislative reforms require only a majority vote. And, of course, the legislative reforms featured in this chapter—from public financing to all dimensions of voting rights—also lay the foundation essential for an amendment to succeed. In other words, amending the constitution to address money in politics requires the Democracy Movement to become powerful enough to elect majorities in Congress and in state legislatures who would vote for the amendment as well as for the necessary campaign-finance reforms it would permit.

So legislative and Supreme Court approaches aren't in competition. Quite the contrary. The Democracy Movement must make progress simultaneously on many fronts.

More Voters, More Democracy

Today, voting rights require strong action, both defensive and offensive. As we've shown, unfounded charges of "voter fraud" have long been used by the GOP and now by the Trump White House as a ploy to limit voting and to undermine proven strategies to increase voter turnout.

At the heart of progress is restoring the 1965 Voting Rights Act, reinstating the requirement that states or counties that historically disenfranchised people of color must get clearance from the Justice Department *before* changing voting rules. Supreme Court Justice Ruth Bader Ginsburg said it best in her dissent in the *Shelby County* decision: "Just as buildings in California have a greater need to be earthquake-proofed, places where there is greater racial polarization in voting have a greater need for prophylactic measures to prevent purposeful race discrimination."[51]

Repealing voter ID laws and expanding early voting, same-day registration, and government-sponsored get-out-the-vote campaigns also help move America closer to a democracy of one person, one vote.

Thirty-seven states, and Washington, DC, have early voting. Fourteen states, and Washington, DC, have implemented same-day voter registration, and one more, Hawaii, will offer it in 2018. Ten states (and DC) allow preregistration for sixteen- and seventeen-year-olds, five for seventeen-year-olds.

And these measures work.

Early voting, according to the Brennan Center, can make election day go more smoothly, with shorter lines and fewer errors—improving the experience of voters and poll workers.[52] One study demonstrates that preregistration for sixteen- and seventeen-year-olds can boost youth turnout by up to 13 percent.[53] And in states that offer same-day registration, voter turnout is more than 10 percent higher than in those that don't.[54]

Same-day registration has especially gotten reformers excited. "Allowing people to register during early voting and on election day, which also allows them to fix problems with their registrations, consistently increases voting in every state where it operates," reports Miles Rapoport, a senior practice fellow in American democracy at the Harvard Kennedy School.

Automatic voter registration is another key. Registration and voting have become easier over the decades—especially as more states enact online voter registration—but it is still not nearly easy enough, especially for many low-income families or anyone working long hours with limited transportation. Americans in the lowest socioeconomic bracket are registered at a rate 20 percent below that of those in the highest bracket.[55] The implication is huge: "If low-income people voted at the same rate as those earning over $100,000 a year, the electorate would grow by 11.5 million voters," according to Project Vote.[56] That's more than twice the victory margin for Obama in 2012.

A straightforward way to help close our democracy deficit is to put the obligation to register voters on government. After all, voting is a *public good.* The Department of Motor Vehicles can, in coordination with the appropriate board of elections, easily register or update the registration of people automatically as they get or renew a license or register a car. (Anyone can opt out by checking a box on the provided forms.) And this applies to any governmental agency.

Called automatic voter registration, this time- and money-saving convenience for citizens and government significantly decreases chances for error in the voter registration process.

And the impact?

In March 2015 Oregon took the lead, becoming the first automatic-registration state. During the first few months in use, three times more people registered to vote per month compared with 2012.[57] By election day 2016, the new system had registered over a quarter of a million people, and nearly one hundred thousand of them had voted—a remarkable success.[58]

One of those whose lives were touched is Charles, a disabled veteran of both the Korean and Vietnam wars who had never registered because a superior in the military had told him not to. Unfortunately, the advice had stuck. But then he met the Bus Project, and something got unstuck. The Oregon-based group takes its name from its M.O.—piling young volunteers on buses to go out to small towns to knock on doors, chat, register people to vote, and now, to let people know they'd been registered automatically. When a Bus Project volunteer knocked on Charles's door, she could tell he was surprised to learn he was registered to vote and he seemed lukewarm about actually voting. The volunteer gave him her number and encouraged him to call with any questions.

Two days later, the volunteer picked up her phone and it was Charles, recounts Nikki Fisher, executive director of the Bus Project. He wanted to vote, but his disability prevented him from dropping off his ballot. Delighted to help, a volunteer drove to his home, picked up his ballot, and got it to the polling station. (Oregon has drop-off voting.) In 2016, Charles joined ninety-eight thousand Oregonians who voted for the first time.[59]

Within a little over two years of automatic voter registration in Oregon, seven more states—California, Vermont, West Virginia, Connecticut, Alaska, Georgia, Colorado, and DC—had jumped on board. If every state followed suit, twenty-seven million Americans would immediately be added to the voter rolls, estimates Demos.[60]

Voting would rise also if voting day were on a Saturday, and better yet, if it were made a national holiday, as Senator Bernie Sanders has proposed.[61] Or, to avoid religious conflicts, political scholars

Thomas Mann and Norman Ornstein suggest a twenty-four-hour voting period, from noon Saturday to noon Sunday.[62] In Costa Rica, which enjoys publicly funded elections and weekend voting, Election Day is the first Sunday in February. It feels like "one big party," as voters head to the polls with sounds of honking horns and displays of party flags, according to one observer. Voter turnout approaches 70 percent.[63]

Debt to Society Paid, Still a Citizen with Rights

In 2016 Virginia governor Terry McAuliffe did a gutsy thing. Believing it was profoundly wrong to deny hundreds of thousands of Virginians the right to vote because of a past crime, and one for which they'd paid their debt to society, he restored by executive order the voting rights of all the state's former convicts (around two hundred thousand of them). But the Virginia Supreme Court said no, he couldn't unilaterally restore the right to vote all at once. McAuliffe, though, was undeterred. He simply signed—one by one—each order restoring the franchise, ultimately making more than sixty-seven thousand released felons eligible to vote.[64]

Withholding the right to vote is not in the public interest. As stated previously, studies show that those who vote after being released are half as likely to reenter prison. Moreover, when felons regain the right to vote, they "describe a feeling of validation, even pride," Michelle Alexander reports.[65] "I have a vote now," a former offender explains. "It's a feeling of relief from where I came from—that I'm actually somebody."[66]

And, over the past two decades, sixteen states have passed laws making it easier for ex-felons to vote, so far enfranchising more than seven hundred thousand citizens.[67] The movement for reform also picked up a powerful ally in President Obama, who voiced support to end felon disenfranchisement in 2015, and then, two years later, wrote a *Harvard Law Review* article on the subject.[68]

Beneath this affront to citizens' rights and public well-being is a still-deeper injustice. It lies in how our society determines who becomes a felon in the first place. When our laws—notably those initiated in the infamous war on drugs—unfairly target communities of color and incarcerate them at disproportional rates, our democracy is failing. To grasp why broader criminal-justice reform is critical to an effective democracy movement, we recommend Michelle Alexander's *The New Jim Crow.*

No to Voting Districts that Dilute Voters' Voice

"Prison gerrymandering" might sound obscure, but as noted in the previous chapter, it simply refers to the anti-democratic counting of incarcerated Americans as residents of the district in which they're imprisoned. The result is power-skewing: a few small towns with prisons gain disproportionate political power while the communities from which the prisoners hail lose political clout. The Democracy Movement is addressing this too.

New York had long been a state with egregiously distorted districts due to the disproportional number of prisons in the north. But in 2010 a strong coalition of civil rights activists, legal experts, good-government groups, and black and Latino legislative caucuses came together to right this shameful wrong. Following the census, the window opened for redrawing districts, recalls Susan Lerner, the head of Common Cause New York. The coalition pressured Democratic governor Andrew Cuomo to push a measure with this simple fix: the New York State Department of Corrections and Community Supervision provides prisoners' last known place of residence to the public body compiling demographic data. It then makes that address the official one for electoral purposes. After months of coalition pressure, the law passed.

So in the 2010 redistricting cycle, New York joined Maryland to become the first states to base new district lines on non-prison-gerrymandered metrics. California and Delaware followed, passing laws to end prison gerrymandering, starting after the 2020 census.[69] Since the beginning of 2010, seventeen states have introduced legislation to end prison gerrymandering, and more than 200 counties and municipalities have fixed the problem themselves.[70] Keeping pressure on these bills is critical to ending this democracy distortion once and for all.

Ending prison gerrymandering nationwide is hardly complicated, though. All it would require is the national census to count incarcerated individuals at their place of last residence. States could then draw the least-skewed district lines, not having to rely on their own agencies to correct the census.

New York democracy champions didn't stop with prison gerrymandering. They took on partisan gerrymandering reform more broadly.

As 2010 grew near, Common Cause New York was determined not to let the legislature again manipulate political mapmaking without a fight. It used publicly accepted criteria to draft its own version of competitive district lines. Underscoring how one victory can abet another, the task was possible because of improved data resulting from the just-passed prison-gerrymander reform bill.

Common Cause then took its fairly drawn, alternative maps to the people, partnering with *Newsday*, with a daily circulation of almost three-quarters of a million. An interactive mapping tool on the newspaper's website allowed residents to comment. After taking in public feedback, Common Cause released a final version and launched a public-education campaign. Virtually every major newspaper editorialized in favor, in effect saying, "we endorse fair and honest redistricting—we know it can be done, just look at the maps Common Cause came up with," Lerner recalls.

The contrast between the maps regular citizens came up with and those offered by Democratic and Republican players was striking, to say the least. When laid alongside one another, "the maps told the story," Lerner told us. The Common Cause maps simply made sense. They kept communities together and party considerations out of the equation. A picture is worth a thousand words, and this picture made plain both the problem and its more-than-feasible solution.

Then, when New York's legislature failed to agree on the new district lines and a federal court had to sort it out, Common Cause received what Lerner calls a "ringing endorsement." Ultimately, for specific districts the court adopted the Common Cause map, and also followed suggestions of civil rights groups that had drawn a "Unity Map" for New York City districts. By going directly to the people, these organizations had turned public knowledge into public action.

So too is reform alive elsewhere.

Thirteen states have handed the power to draw district lines to commissions independent of the legislature.[71] Of these, California is a particularly bright spot. It has fought hard and imaginatively to defeat partisan interests' corrupting the drawing of district lines. In a new process for 2010 redistricting, any adult Californian with no conflict of interest was invited to apply to join the commission charged with the task. "Independent auditors" narrowed the pool to 120, made up equally of Democrats, Republicans, and Independents. Through interviews, they cut the number in half. Of the remaining sixty, leaders in the state legislature were allowed to remove up to a total of twenty-four. Then, eight were picked from each of the "three hats." These eight then got to choose six more, balanced by party.[72] Needless to say, these folks take their democracy seriously!

Iowa also stands out. Republicans in the early 1980s tasked a nonpartisan agency of the legislature, the Legislative Services Agency (LSA), with proposing district lines every ten years. It's required to keep communities intact and to bar use of political data to manipulate lines. The LSA submits its maps to the legislature, which can accept or reject them. If rejected, the agency just tries again. Only twice were the LSA's maps rejected, and in both cases, the legislature ultimately adopted the agency's "do-over."[73]

How well has Iowa's system worked? Since 2000, according to journalist David Daley, the state could boast "more competitive congressional races than California, Texas, and Florida combined."[74] As Ed Cook, LSA's senior legal counsel, explained to us, "The legislature could at any point change the redistricting process, but they don't. Over the past thirty years we've been doing it this way and everyone is very satisfied." The LSA has earned the trust of citizens and lawmakers alike, Cook continued.

For inspiration on redistricting fairness, America might also look north. During the second half of the twentieth century, Canadian provinces adopted independent redistricting commissions, rejecting a highly political district-drawing process. Nonelected, independent judges serve as chairs, and members include "academics and respected local attorneys, not partisan officeholders," among others.[75] Proof of success? The greater turnover of Canada's officeholders, especially compared with the United States, where incumbent members of the House of Representatives win reelection over 90 percent of the time.[76]

LESSER EVIL NO MORE, CHEERS FOR DEMOCRACY!

Have you ever agonized over whether to vote your head (what you believe is possible) or your heart (what you really want)?

Many Americans have. Voting for a third party can be a powerful voice of discontent in our two-party system. At the same time, a third-party vote can end up contributing to an outcome the voter abhors. In 2016, for example, more than six million Americans voted for a third-party presidential candidate. In Wisconsin, Michigan, and Pennsylvania—the three states that gave Donald Trump the presidency—Green Party candidate Jill Stein won more votes than the margin between Clinton and Trump. Yet few Stein voters, we feel certain, would have chosen Trump over Clinton.

What's the answer? How can voters register minority views without risk of being a "spoiler"? Again, the democracy champions of Maine may have an answer for us.

In the summer of 2016 hundreds of Mainers showed up at their state's famed microbreweries to participate in a novel political-learning moment. Each was invited to taste five beers, then rank their preferences one to five. Votes were collected and tallied, with the score displayed on a board. If no beer had more than half of the first-place votes, then the beer with the fewest first-place choices was eliminated. Votes of those who selected the defeated beer as their first choice were redistributed according to their second choice; and, so on, until one beer had the majority and was declared the winner.

It's called ranked-choice voting, and in 2016 Mainers approved a ballot initiative for its use in all political races except presidential and municipal. Proponents argued that voting for the "lesser of two evils" makes little sense when there's a candidate you really like. In Maine, this point resonated with voters because often three candidates run for governor, and in nine of the past eleven gubernatorial elections, no candidate had received a majority of the vote. In five of those races, the winning candidate received less than 40 percent.[77] Ranked-choice voting was a great solution.

Ranked-choice voting is used for national elections in Ireland and in some form in Australia, New Zealand, Scotland, and elsewhere.[78] At the time of the 2016 campaign ranked-choice voting had never been implemented on a state level in the United States—only in about a dozen cities.[79]

Sampling beer was just one way Mainers simulated ranked-choice voting. "One woman was having people rank her homemade brownies and cookies, and another guy was having people rank the art on his walls," ranked-choice voting campaign director Kyle Bailey recalls. "People were coming up with these ideas on their own," he stresses. Bailey recalls seeing one woman's eyes light up after a ranked-choice voting demonstration. "I've been registered Green for my entire life," she explained to him. "But I've never voted Green." Now, she seemed to be saying, this new system would mean she wouldn't have to fear voting her conscience.

In early 2017, opponents of ranked-choice voting asked the state's Supreme Judicial Court to declare it unconstitutional, and the court's subsequent advisory opinion put the measure at risk. But given Mainers' determination to strengthen their democracy, we feel confident that whatever happens next will not be the end of the story.

Imagine the difference ranked-choice voting could make. In 2000, George W. Bush won the state of Florida by 537 votes and independent candidate Ralph Nader received almost 100,000. Conceivably, if only a small share of Nader voters had marked Al Gore as their second choice in a ranked-choice process, Gore would have emerged the winner.

Regardless, Maine proves that states need not wait for Congress. They can develop innovative schemes for making this reform's advantages real for voters, and then act on citizens' common sense.

A POSITIVE END-RUN AROUND THE ELECTORAL COLLEGE

With Donald Trump's victory despite losing the popular vote, many Americans have suddenly awakened to what few of us like to admit: the way we elect our president is ridiculous. We ourselves recall being glued to the TV watching 2016 election returns. Knowing much of the world was also watching, we felt embarrassed that our elections are not decided by winning a majority of votes.

In presidential elections since 1824, the year in which the popular vote was first recorded, the highest vote-getter has failed to win five times—with two of those failures occurring just since 2000.

In addition to denying majority will, the Electoral College also encourages presidential races to focus on a handful of "swing states." Since some states are safe, there is no reason to devote resources to them. Of all 2016 campaign events, *94 percent took place in just twelve states.*[80] The result? Many voters feel they don't really count. Plus, candidates and media disproportionately register and amplify the views of swing-state Americans, who may not represent the views of the majority.

Most of us just swallow this affront to democracy, assuming only a constitutional amendment could solve it by abolishing the Electoral College. But some clever Americans came up with a simple work-around that would render the Electoral College irrelevant. Steve Silberstein, cofounder of a California software company serving libraries worldwide, tells us that "a few simple fixes" could be made to the system to make every vote count. The strategy and campaign, called the National Popular Vote, was first laid out in the 2006 book *Every Vote Equal.* It entails state legislators passing laws that require their states' Electoral College electors to assign their votes to the presidential candidate winning the national popular vote, which is perfectly constitutional.

The system would then go into effect as soon as enough states had voted to follow this rule to make their combined votes add up to a majority of Electoral College votes. That's 270. Once the national popular vote goes into effect, presidential candidates would feel compelled to adopt a fifty-state strategy and to spend money and time even deep in the heart of their opponent's territory. All Americans, even if they knew their party was unpopular in their state, would have a reason to vote.

More than 70 percent of Americans polled support the approach, even some hard-line Republicans.[81] Starting with Maryland, the national popular vote has already passed in eleven states, including two big ones, New York and California. Together these states represent a total of 165 electoral votes—so we're about 60 percent of the way to the goal.[82]

Success of the National Popular Vote campaign is eminently achievable, says Silberstein, who serves on the campaign's board, and its realization throughout the country would be an important step in restoring confidence in American democracy.

MOBILIZING FOR DEMOCRACY'S MEDIA

Democracy lives or dies on the quality of public conversation. "Were it left to me to decide whether we should have a government without newspapers or newspapers without a government," Thomas Jefferson wrote, "I should not hesitate a moment to prefer the latter."

Analyzing how to fix our broken news system, from corporate control of media to fake news, is far beyond the scope of our book. Nonetheless, we want to offer a few paths that democracy defenders are pursuing, starting with net neutrality.

If you've heard the term "net neutrality," is it something you imagine only Internet fanatics can grasp? Not at all. It simply refers to baseline protection ensuring that no Internet service provider can "interfere with or block web traffic, or favor their own services at the expense of smaller rivals."[83] As such, it is integral to democratic dialogue. And net neutrality's recent history offers an encouraging story of the power of the people to protect the core democratic principle of free exchange.

In December 2010 the Federal Communications Commission (FCC) passed what those most concerned considered "pretty weak half measures" prohibiting Internet service providers from blocking websites or imposing limits on users, says Craig Aaron, president and CEO of Free Press. And by 2014, a federal lawsuit brought by Verizon succeeded in striking down even this half measure.[84] Verizon's hubris ignited a massive call for the FCC to fight back. Protests demanded even stronger rules to reclassify Internet service providers as "common carriers," requiring them to act as neutral gatekeepers to the Internet and to protect access for all.[85]

By May 2014, inspired by the Occupy Wall Street protests, concerned citizens had set up camp in Washington at the FCC headquarters.[86] It had all started with a protest organized by Margaret Flowers and Kevin Zeese. Margaret, a pediatrician who cut her teeth in the fight for universal health care, and Kevin, a lawyer who fought injustices in the 1980s War on Drugs, announced at the protest's end that they were not going to leave. The duo rolled out their sleeping bags on the grass, stayed the night, and before they knew it, the occupation grew drastically. Fellow concerned citizens flooded in with tents and banners. One day followed the next, each to the tune of passing cars honking in solidarity. Not only did employees of the FCC come out to thank the occupiers, but three of the five FCC commissioners came to meet Flowers and Zeese.

A week later, FCC Chairman Tom Wheeler put out a "notice of proposed rule-making" that asked the public, "What is the right public policy to ensure that the Internet remains open?"[87] The preferred solution put forward by the FCC, outlined in the notice, would have left the door ajar for a "two-tiered Internet" plan wherein Internet service providers could sell content providers priority access to their subscribers at rates only big companies could afford.[88] Citizen reformers couldn't and wouldn't get behind this proposal.

But the notice also sought public comment on whether the FCC should "reclassify" the Internet as a common carrier under the law.[89] Doing so would give the FCC greater legal authority over providers to fully and truly keep the Internet open. This request for comments gave citizens, especially those emboldened by the FCC occupation, an opening.

For months citizens continued protesting and spreading awareness about the importance of net neutrality. Leading up to the closing of the comment period in September 2014, the activist group Fight for the Future parked a Jumbotron outside FCC headquarters.[90] The giant video billboard played videos of fellow citizens explaining why net neutrality mattered to them.[91] Later, reformers performed a skit outside the FCC, a "Save the Internet Musical Action." The musical's chorus—"Which side are you on, Tom? Which side are you on?"— would soon be answered.

These courageous public actions built on the momentum sparked by the FCC occupiers. Together, they galvanized citizens to submit four million comments to the FCC.[92] The FCC chairman reversed his position, endorsed strong rules, and moved to restore the agency's authority. In February 2015 the FCC announced it would reclassify Internet service providers as common carriers.[93] Wheeler called it "the proudest day of my public policy life."[94] Another FCC commissioner called it "democracy in action."[95]

The victory taught one very important lesson. As Margaret Flowers put it, "It showed we don't have to compromise. We can actually stay true to what we are fighting for and win." For that win, a broad coalition of citizen power united folks from the tech industry, such as Netflix and Tumblr, to the Black Lives Matter movement. They all understood the democratic value of a free Internet on which independent media is kept accessible and online grassroots organizing is made possible. "This cross-generational and multi-issue movement was critical in pressuring the FCC commissioners and lawmakers to support net neutrality," Aaron says.

By mid-2017, the Trump administration's FCC had put net neutrality on the chopping block, and already democracy stalwarts are stepping up to fight back.

The Trump administration has also threatened to cut the pittance the federal government contributes to public media. Democracy reformers can now weigh in to defend public broadcasting networks, such as PBS and NPR, as well as community media and independent nonprofit startups, and fight to increase their budgets—especially those supporting investigative journalism.

Moreover, given that media consolidation has played a major role in the degradation of news, fending off future mergers is imperative. Groups such as Free Press are leading the way with lawsuits to challenge unfair rules and by organizing town halls and providing activists with the research and policy proposals needed to fight back.

Finally, as Tim Berners-Lee explains, regulating online political advertising and data gathering is essential.[96] We can achieve a functioning democracy as we understand the nature of the work of data communications companies such as Cambridge Analytica, discussed in chapter 3, and set rules to make sure we're not unknowingly being manipulated and can therefore effectively participate in democracy deliberation.

DEMOCRACY, IT'S MORE THAN ELECTIONS

Before closing this chapter, we want to underscore that democracy is not just about elections. It's a way of life with many channels for engaging in issues that matter to us.

Take community safety. According to a Gallup poll, almost half of Americans lack "a great deal" or "quite a lot" of confidence in our police. So about two hundred localities now have citizen-police review commissions to encourage communication between the community and law enforcement and to ensure that police are accountable to the community.[97]

Since 1984, Richmond, California's citizen-police commission has handled citizen complaints and helped establish "community policing" that weaves law enforcement into the fabric of a community. In 2014, when tragedy struck and an unarmed man, Richard "Pedie" Perez, died at police hands, the commission took action. It came up with key reforms for improved investigative procedures that the city council then passed.[98] Confidence in Richmond police rose to 59 percent in 2015, up from just 38 percent eight years earlier.[99]

"Participatory budgeting" is another channel for citizens to be heard beyond the ballot box. In it, a municipality welcomes citizens into a multistage, deliberative process for allocating a portion of its budget. Beginning in Brazil in 1989, it has spread worldwide, including to at least seventeen US cities.[100]

Teaching active "civics," including hands-on opportunities to make a difference, is also key to building a culture of democracy in which we grow into adults competent in our many roles as citizens. As kids, it is easy to see democracy as for somebody else and boring—unless we're shown how it can be a thrilling part of our lives.

Thanks to the KIDS Consortium, serving Maine and neighboring New England schools, what's called "apprentice citizenship" enables young people from the earliest grades to know they count. We spoke with a fifth grader who'd helped teach kids about the importance of wearing helmets while biking and buckling seat belts. With glee, he told us, "I realized I was saving lives. Now that's the shocking part." Such excitement about making one's community stronger can't be "put back in the bottle." It lasts a lifetime.

DEMOCRACY'S CALLING

The stories in this chapter suggest that democracy is calling us and offering great rewards.

But why haven't we made more progress? Certainly a major answer is the mighty anti-democracy forces fighting to kill reform. But another explanation is *us*, or rather the lack of us. America has back-tracked on democracy in large measure because we haven't yet created a strong enough citizens' movement fighting for it. (We, of course, are writing this book to make the case that this is changing!)

In identifying this final force explaining our pain, an ecological worldview helps. It reminds us that, since we're all connected, we're all implicated. Thus we all play a role in the blows to our democracy, which may be an uncomfortable truth to take in. But assuming responsibility for our contributions also means acknowledging something very positive: *that we have real power.*

A little history here. Franklin D. Roosevelt was "in many ways a cautious, even conservative" president before being pushed, Occidental College professor Peter Dreier explains. Maybe that's how Roosevelt saw himself too, so to a group of reformers during the 1930s, he famously declared, "You've convinced me, now go out and make me do it."[101] And so they did, resulting in decades of advancement for all classes.

Or, consider Lyndon B. Johnson. During his first two decades in Congress, Johnson voted against every piece of civil rights legislation. Yet, upon becoming Senate majority leader and then president, he pushed through the most important civil rights laws since Reconstruction. Johnson understood that only citizen pressure could give him the muscle to overcome southern opposition. As journalist Bill Moyers recounts, Johnson told Martin Luther King, "Okay. You go out there, Dr. King, and keep doing what you're doing, and make it possible for me to do the right thing."[102] It was only after King, John Lewis, and thousands more marched in Birmingham and Selma and met brutal repression—attracting national attention—that LBJ was able to act.

What we citizens do matters a lot. And when we don't do much, what happens? Nothing. Consider that more than four decades ago, 72 percent of Americans supported public financing for all congressional campaigns.[103] And, as we've already noted, in 2015 it had precisely the same broad-based support. Yet, because there was no citizens' movement strong enough to push it through, nothing passed.

So now that we've proven public financing and other reforms work, what we need is a Democracy Movement strong enough to make them happen. In our next chapter we introduce you to such a movement. It carries a deeply unifying force for democracy within its astonishing diversity. As North Carolina's courageous democracy champion, the Reverend Dr. William J. Barber II, explains, by coalescing together we "create the opportunity to fundamentally redirect America."[104]

MEET THE
DEMOCRACY MOVEMENT

IT'S MARCH 25, 2016, and the house is glaring pink. It's two stories, on the outskirts of Washington, DC, and inside about twenty people from far-flung corners of America are preparing for what will be one of the biggest acts of civil disobedience at the US Capitol ever.

While the building's façade screams 1970s, inside it is a throwback to the 1960s. The living room is lined with couches and chairs making a large concentric circle, perfect for meetings. On the back wall hangs a huge, hand-drawn map of the mid-Atlantic coast, with scratchy lines tracking the 140-mile route from Philadelphia to DC that more than a hundred people would soon march.

Organizers move through the house in musical-chair fashion. As one person leaves a room, two more enter. Noise from meetings and phone calls enlivens the halls, creating a vibrant atmosphere. Everyone moves and talks so quickly they seem engaged in three conversations at once. Near the patio, one of the organizers chats on the phone with a woman in Colorado. He tells her about his own childhood, which he spent in Boulder, and the two bond over memories of the drive to the East Coast.

In many ways, this group, Democracy Spring, is the scrappy underdog compared with Democracy Awakening, its larger, sister mobilization of about three hundred organizations also planning public actions at the Capitol. Democracy Spring is less funded, has fewer mainstream organizations on board and fewer staff, yet what it lacks in resources it makes up in its organizers.

One week before the march, they are focusing like crazy on last-minute details, but the goal is huge: to spark and sustain a democracy movement that fundamentally reforms our democratic system.

And that unforgettable April, these two distinct but cooperating coalitions, Democracy Spring and Democracy Awakening—supported by hundreds of organizations in areas from labor to the environment to civil rights—did succeed in gathering thousands of people in Washington, DC, for an array of dynamic speakers, a march, and a rally. They sat in at the Capitol building nearly every day for a week. By the end, more than 1,300 people had been arrested.

Many of the organizations backing these April mobilizations were new to the Democracy Movement. In preparing and participating, countless staff and members of these new groups suddenly became players in the world of citizen agitation over money in politics and voter disenfranchisement.

On the final evening, we were exhausted but elated when Democratic congressman from Maryland John Sarbanes announced at the Capitol Visitor Center that he was making a formal request to relevant congressional committees for hearings on all four of Democracy Spring's demands, from public financing to restoration of voting rights. Almost a hundred fellow members of Congress soon signed on.[1]

CREATING A DEMOCRACY MOVEMENT

Heading home the next day, we knew something big had changed for us.

These April 2016 actions had convinced us that, *yes*, a Democracy Movement is under way. Americans can unite their issue passions so that together we can dissolve the mounting barriers in the path of true democracy, barriers preventing progress on issues ranging from racial justice and a fair economy to a healthy environment. More personally, we knew that we were part of a Democracy Movement for the first time. And as many Americans feel the very foundations of

America's democracy rattling, we see the continued building of this unprecedented movement as the clear and exhilarating task ahead.

As we jump in, here are two orienting questions: how must our Democracy Movement be quite unlike the forces opposing us, laid bare in chapters 3 and 4? At the same time, what can we learn from them to be more effective? Keeping both in mind, our Democracy Movement grows strong as we:

> *Make our visibility a conscious tool.* Secrecy is the weapon of the Anti-Democracy Movement—whether it's the Ohio Republican Party operatives holed up in the secret "bunker" in Columbus while they manipulate district lines or the secretive gatherings of Koch donors. But a democracy movement thrives on the opposite—on the widest visibility. We can proudly claim our identities, making it easy for worried Americans to find new friends, allies, and a sense of purpose in energizing learning in action.

> *Decentralize leadership under a common canopy.* The Anti-Democracy Movement is run by the super wealthy via "command and control." The Democracy Movement is the opposite. From neighborhoods to the national level, its leaders are creating, both geographically and by their focus and tactics, decentralized activism.

> *Draw on the energy of hope.* While the Anti-Democracy Movement uses fear of "the other" (especially of immigrants and people of color) to gain allies, the Democracy Movement draws on the power of hope. Hope opens people emotionally, making us more eager to meet others and learn together. It enables the experience of joy in taking risks together for a high calling. Hope even affects our brains, scientists tell us, helping us envision solutions.[2]

> *Become actively inclusive.* The Anti-Democracy Movement seems fine with its white, wealthy base, and with leveraging racism to defeat opponents. The Democracy Movement knows its success depends on embracing differences of race and culture within a common commitment to justice and love of democracy itself.

The Democracy Movement is already beginning to embody these qualities in sustained campaigns, making reform demands at all levels of government, as we saw in chapter 5.

ONE TREE, MANY STRONG BRANCHES

The Anti-Democracy Movement is working on many fronts simultaneously. So how can we also tackle the varied and essential reforms while also developing a sharply focused movement?

We see the answer as a "movement of movements" in which everyone working on democracy becomes generally familiar with the range of fronts in the anti-democracy assault—from big money in elections to our flawed redistricting process to attacks on the right to vote. With that awareness, the realization grows that concentrating on only one democracy reform at a time cannot work. Getting money out of politics means little, for example, if you don't have the right to vote.

In parallel fashion, those focused on specific "issues" come to grasp that without democracy there's almost no chance of tackling distinct environmental, racial justice, labor, poverty, or food justice problems. They then discover that each of us can maintain an issue-passion focus *and* at the same time devote resources and energy to building the Democracy Movement.

Years ago, Represent.Us founder, Josh Silver, who opened the previous chapter, grinned as he reminded us that "you can love two children at once." His common sense stuck with us. And this insight is spreading to many issue groups. Another metaphor that works for us is to imagine one's own specific issue passion as the branch of a single majestic tree. Our branch is beautiful and needed, but its flourishing depends on a healthy trunk and root system. Democracy—real, living democracy—*is* that trunk and root system without which all our branches wither.

A movement of movements requires more than just coalition building, however. Here's what we mean. Imagine a group we'll call Get Money Out. Its staff is trained in following the money in our political system. It's most valued for researching and advocating for public financing of elections. But a movement of movements means that when another group needs help—let's say, in its work to stop a voter-ID law—Get Money Out puts its name, resources, and people power into the fight. From social media campaigns to calling members to donating resources, when the call to action comes, Get Money Out will treat voting rights *as its own*.

If all this sounds like we are dreaming, below are four groups already embodying a movement-of-movements approach.

MOVEMENT OF MOVEMENTS, ALREADY IN MOTION

A movement of movements has many faces—in personality, strategy, geography, and focus. Here are elements that inspire us.

Democracy Spring. As you now know, Democracy Spring's march and actions in 2016 profoundly shaped our paths. It's what made this book possible. Democracy Spring's origins lie in the Occupy Movement that birthed 99Rise, whose leaders Kai Newkirk and Curt Ries lit the Democracy Spring flame in late 2015.

When they called for a 140-mile march for democracy, "people thought we were crazy," remembers Curt, who not long ago had spent two years in the Peace Corps in Paraguay. "I worked with poor farmers during the day, and during the long nights in my one-room shack I read eighty books," Curt told us. "I returned knowing I had to be part of something that could fundamentally change the systems of industrial capitalism and political corruption that are destroying the planet."

In total, more than one hundred organizations, from labor to student-based, endorsed Democracy Spring. And now, it lives on as a national network, committed to using the power of escalating nonviolent civil disobedience for democracy reforms, joining in solidarity wherever they are needed.

Moral Mondays. Since 2006, Reverend Dr. William J. Barber II, then president of North Carolina's NAACP, with key actors across the state has been creating what he calls "fusion politics." It's what we mean by "movement of movements."

As part of the fusion-politics approach, a coalition today embraces two hundred organizations with more than two million members. They all work together to champion a fourteen-point agenda against racism, poverty, and war, and for real democracy.[3] Each year the coalition publicly reaffirms its agenda and commitment to hold state lawmakers accountable to the people. Movement successes include playing a key role in passing same-day voter registration and other policy reforms.

Today "Moral Mondays" have become the coalition's signature public action. Shortly after Republicans won a majority of the legislature and elected Governor Pat McCrory in 2012, the GOP introduced multipronged assaults on democracy. Since 2013, Moral Mondays have been one way the coalition has fought back. Members meet frequently on Mondays, and at other crucial times, at the North Carolina legislature, and enter the building. A number are peacefully arrested. These acts of civil disobedience have been wildly successful in turning out hundreds of people for a range of causes.

Rev. Dr. Barber explains how this "fusion politics" works:

"Because our agenda . . . [covers] fourteen issue areas where we could move forward together with specific action steps, many asked us in the weeks following our [first] assembly . . . 'Which issues are your priorities for this session?'...We explained that, for us, every issue was equally important. In a fusion coalition, our most directly affected members would always speak to the issue closest to their own hearts. But they would never speak alone."[4]

The whole idea of a movement of movements is that everyone accepts that there is no "first issue." They fight for fair and democratic policies and take part, in solidarity, when any member in the coalition needs help. Rev. Dr. Barber and his allies embody their slogan: "Forward together, not one step back."

Moral Mondays have inspired actions in twelve states, not only in the South but in New York and Wisconsin, as well, and more recently in Illinois and New Mexico.[5] Moral Mondays and the broader struggle for democracy in North Carolina have so much to teach us that we devote chapter 7 to them.

Movement for Black Lives. In July of 2015, more than two thousand racial-justice activists gathered in Cleveland, Ohio, for the first ever national convening of the Movement for Black Lives (M4BL). In just a few days jam-packed with powerful speeches and transformative conversations, the Cleveland conference gave rise to a Movement for Black Lives Policy Table. Its mandate? To create a coalition known as the United Front formulating one common, bold, and unifying platform.[6] The United Front, and the multiple movements represented within it, reflect one bedrock truth, as illustrated on its website:

> State violence . . . includes the systemic underinvestment in our communities, the caging of our people, predatory state and corporate practices targeting our neighborhoods, government policies that result in the poisoning of our water and the theft of our land, failing schools that criminalize rather than educate our children, economic practices that extract our labor, and wars on our Trans and Queer family that deny them their humanity.

The Movement for Black Lives, through its platform, focuses on concrete ways to reverse this devastation. "We felt that it was important not to just have policy ideas," said Janae Bonsu, the national public policy chair of the Black Youth Project 100, "but also provide examples of model legislation and something that you can tangibly take to your elected official, whether it be at the federal level in Congress or at your state legislatures or your city council." [7]

The platform included the recognition of democracy reform as a key tenet in the struggle for black liberation, as well. The coalition recognizes that to truly advance the black community, progress must be made on all of the above fronts. One is not enough. Such multidimensional understanding of state violence is emotionally powerful and perfectly embodies a movement-of-movements approach.

Democracy Initiative. In late 2012, Sierra Club executive director Mike Brune—whose political awakening began as a teen when he discovered he could fight the pollution despoiling his beloved New Jersey beach—had an epiphany: "I thought, if I can get Sierra Club members to stand shoulder to shoulder with members of the NAACP and labor unions and those working for justice for refugees and immigrants, we could put together a really powerful coalition. We concluded that we could counterbalance all these billions of dollars coming from the Koch brothers and other oil and coal executives and people."

Turns out, leaders across many issue groups were having similar aha moments.

They came up with the idea of a new kind of organization—one in which each member retains its specific focus while committing a portion of its organization to the common goal of achieving real democracy. Formed in 2013, Democracy Initiative now boasts sixty partner organizations representing thirty million Americans from the labor, environmental, and civil rights communities.

Democracy Initiative's founders are powerful players indeed, including the Sierra Club, the Communication Workers of America, the NAACP, and Greenpeace.

Executive director Wendy Fields recounts, "These founders shared a simple premise—if we're going to build power, we can't just let the good-government groups go to the mat against *Citizens United*. Nor could we let voting rights be a black/Latino issue. And we can't have the environmental movement be a white issue, since black people and Latino people are also severely impacted."

In Democracy Initiative's convening circle, each board member has a representative from its staff, who runs its own organization's democracy program, aligning it with the coalition's work.

"We are a catalyst for change. We have the potential to be transformative," says Wendy, who was brought up by a gutsy single mom, cut her teeth in the labor movement, and then rose to become chief of staff and administrative assistant for United Auto Workers president Bob King, who's now retired. "We should be coming together to be more powerful, taking strong collective action in a way that you can't do at a home organization. We need to be edgy, and stay on the cusp, and push for big solutions to big challenges."

Democracy Initiative does not campaign for candidates but supports electoral reform. The goal is an "outside strategy," Wendy says, one that mobilizes millions of Americans to push government and elected officials.

One of the organization's first fights was the Fix the Senate campaign in 2014. The GOP-held Senate was abusing the filibuster, blocking all of President Obama's judicial nominees. The "fix" changed the rule so that only a majority vote was needed to confirm a nominee.

"Those rules can be used for you and against you, and we were willing to take that risk," Wendy explains. "You can't be partisan on everything—you have to build a movement."

Wendy's no stranger to risk. Her first job was in a public facility in Connecticut caring for people with mental disabilities, and her union asked her to join the fight against turning management over to a private company. "I was twenty-six. I was terrified, and after months of negotiating, we called a demonstration. I thought hardly anyone would show up, but hundreds came out, even on their off time. It was about the safety and care of their clients." Wendy was never the same again. That was when, she told us, it hit her: "There's something to this idea of 'the people being heard!'"

So you might not be surprised that in 2015 Democracy Initiative was a key force behind the one-thousand-mile America's Journey for Justice march led by the NAACP, and in 2016 showed up to help move public financing to victory in a Maryland county. While these were major successes, Wendy believes being a part of Democracy Awakening was a "pivotal point" for Democracy Initiative. She explains, "It was really powerful to watch the civil rights groups make the connection with money in politics and embrace the convergence. Democracy Awakening made it possible for good-government groups to get out of the box of lobbying people and engage in civil disobedience."

Ultimately, Democracy Initiative is about pushing boundaries, Wendy said. "Its role is to lift up and create a vision that is bolder and that creates unity. Tension to me suggests change," she told us with conviction.

YOUTH ON THE FRONT LINES

Democracy Matters is a totally different animal, but it too is all about movement building—in this case among those casting their first votes: students.

Former NBA player Adonal Foyle, determined to do something meaningful with the rewards of his basketball career, founded the organization in 2001. Foyle recalled his college professors' claiming that students were apathetic, and he wanted to prove that students do care. He believed they just needed to see a way to make a difference.

From that impulse, what took shape was an ingenious linking of student energy with experienced coaches. Starting on the Colgate University campus, it grew quickly into a national network. In Democracy Matters, students learn democracy by doing it both on their campuses and in surrounding communities. With hard work by Foyle's adoptive parents, Jay and Joan Mandle—now Colgate professors emeritus—Democracy Matters chapters are on more than forty college campuses. To create chapters for democracy reforms, Democracy Matters' interns receive a modest stipend, along with mentoring and support through regular communication with the group's staff.

On their campuses, Democracy Matters chapters carry out voter registration drives and petition campaigns, write newspaper op-eds, screen films, and put on concerts—all reaching thousands of students annually. They also work off-campus, personally lobbying their elected representatives and speaking at local civic organizations. Democracy Matters chapters have created strong coalitions with environmental, labor, social justice, and civil and human rights organizations. Working with these allies, students connect money in politics and voting rights to dozens of other concerns in their communities, helping to foment a movement of movements.

Each winter, Democracy Matters gathers for a summit. But in early 2017, at the sixteenth annual summit, the Mandles felt something new in the air. Beyond a record turnout, for the first time high school students joined in—ten of them. The summit convened soon after Trump's election, and Joan notes that "many of these younger activists contacted us, wanting to know what they could do to fight back. They asked if we could help, and of course we agreed."

"We value democratic discussion above all else at these summits," Jay tells us. He recalls the 2003 summit, right before the US invasion of Iraq:

> Then an economics professor, I started giving a talk about why the impending invasion was a terrible decision. I felt a restlessness in the room and knew some of the students disagreed with me. I stopped my lecture. What followed was a passionate debate—one of the most remarkable displays of democratic deliberation among young people I've ever seen. The students debated without name-calling or insults. Every year since, we've tried to emulate this.

At the summits students attend lectures about money in politics, lectures about lobbying, and messaging workshops. In breakout groups they discuss their role in the Democracy Movement with others they are meeting for the first time. "It's amazing how students' eyes light up when they interact and plan with one another," reports Joan, the executive director. "The energy in the room is inspiring."

After the 2017 summit we talked with student Kat Cline, originally from an Oregon logging town and president of her Simmons College Democracy Matters chapter. We asked the most basic question: why work for democracy?

"I realized that all the interests I had, all these things that I saw going wrong in politics, had an underlying similarity: big money in politics," she said. Kat went on, explaining that in this political climate, without her Democracy Matters community, "I'd feel adrift right now—if I didn't know I'm invested in something bigger that's trying to do good work."

Another sign of change? When Democracy Matters students were asked how many had hopes of someday running for office, for the first time almost half raised their hands. And even more surprising, a few had already filed the necessary papers.

In all, through Democracy Matters, students gain a political voice, and—as students of past generations had done—play a critical role in jump-starting a grassroots movement for political equality. "I do my best to help students realize that we stand on the shoulders of those in our history, each having paved the way for us to have a voice in democracy, and that gives us strength," field director Anita Kinney explains.

In the summer of 2015 Democracy Matters launched a new program, "Restore Democracy." Interns spent the summer in Iowa and New Hampshire organizing to turn money in politics into a central issue in the 2016 presidential primaries. These young people were the first to get Hillary Clinton on record supporting public financing of elections, and Donald Trump to offer mild support as well. Bernie Sanders issued a congratulatory statement to the organization for its efforts.

Candidates used the group's "Restore Democracy" language throughout the campaign, and it even found its way into the Democratic Party platform, says Max Stahl, the group's former political director.

NOT JUST A "PROGRESSIVE" ISSUE

All of this is great, you might be thinking, but America is a big country and progressives can't make change alone—so these reforms will never pass. What this view misses is that the Democracy Movement extends far beyond self-identifying "progressives." The vast majority of Americans across party lines believes our system for financing campaigns is broken and desperately wants reform. Remember, 85 percent of those polled want either fundamental changes or a complete rebuild.

One of the stars on the conservative side of the movement is Take Back Our Republic, a campaign-finance group founded by John Pudner, the chief strategist for Congressman David Brat, the Tea Partier who unseated the former Republican majority leader, Eric Cantor. His organization played a big role in passing the Anti-Corruption Act in South Dakota.

"Conservatives overwhelmingly feel like they need campaign finance reform," Pudner tells us. "We can disagree about how to go about reform—whether through matching funds or tax credits," he says, but he emphasizes that "Americans of all political beliefs are giving up on the system," which should concern us all. We were delighted Pudner walked with us for part of the Democracy Spring march.

For decades many leaders on the right have shared Pudner's analysis. In 2006, Fox News host Lou Dobbs lamented in his book *War on the Middle Class*, "What was for almost two hundred years a government of the people has become a government of corporations."[8] In July 2015, former GOP senator Bob Dole of Kansas, who ran against Bill Clinton for president in 1996, said, "It's unreal. We need to do something to stop all this money in politics. I've always believed when people give big money, they—maybe silently—expect something in return."[9] Also in 2015, former senator Alan Simpson, a Republican from Wyoming, railed, "Money's dominance over politics isn't merely one problem of many our country faces. It is *the* problem!"[10]

SOME INVISIBLE ADVANCES

Not only are people ready, but the movement of movements approach is already yielding successes. In 2016, among seventeen ballot initiatives across the country for democracy reforms, fourteen passed. In large part their successes derived from the vast support of multi-issue coalitions. Some highlights are:

South Dakota. This conservative state moved into the vanguard of the Democracy Movement by approving the Anti-Corruption Act, creating a voucher-based public-financing system for elections and other reforms. In early 2017 the governor used an emergency measure to block enactment, but reformers are determined to keep fighting, as explained in the previous chapter.

Maine. Already a leader in Clean Elections, Maine approved ranked-choice voting, explained in chapter 5. It applies to US Senate and House races, as well as to elections for governor and the state Senate and Assembly.

Missouri. With 70 percent voting in favor, Missouri passed a ballot measure amending the state's constitution to reinstate campaign contribution limits for state offices, lifted eight years earlier. (A 2017 legal challenge jeopardized part of the measure.)

California and Washington. Both states passed measures instructing their representatives in Washington to support efforts for a constitutional amendment to reverse the *Citizens United* decision.

Howard County, Maryland. A ballot initiative mandating the development of a public financing system passed. (Since 1974, the state had already offered this option to candidates for governor and lieutenant governor.)[11]

San Francisco. Represent.Us members helped to pass Proposition T to rein in the power of lobbyists. The ballot initiative, which was supported by almost 90 percent of voters, places "serious handcuffs on the pay-to-play world," the *San Francisco Chronicle* reported.[12] It strictly limits lobbyists' campaign contributions and gifts to city officials.

Berkeley, California. With two-thirds of the vote, democracy defenders in Berkeley created a public-financing system for mayoral and city council races without raising taxes.

Additionally, voters in Rhode Island passed major ethics reform. And numerous counties have stepped up to strengthen democracy. Boone and McHenry counties in Illinois are two: each passed a resolution endorsing the Anti-Corruption Act. Multnomah County, Oregon, passed major limits on the amount of money that can be donated in county elections, and nearby in Benton County, Oregon, voters approved ranked-choice voting for their elections.

These were the victories on election day 2016, but a lot had happened in the previous year, including:

Seattle. After an inclusive citizens' mobilization, the city passed Honest Elections, in which voters each receive four $25 vouchers to allocate to candidates as they choose.

Maine. Voters approved a measure to strengthen its Clean Election Act against secret money and more.

Ohio. With a 70 percent majority, Ohio passed new redistricting procedures that make it harder to manipulate district lines for partisan ends.

Oregon. Citizens passed automatic voter registration. Seven other states and Washington, DC, have followed suit.

Arizona. The Supreme Court upheld a 2000 ballot initiative establishing an independent committee to lead the redistricting process.

Austin, Texas. The city council passed tough new disclosure provisions.

Moreover, the Democratic Party platform endorsed public financing of elections, as well as other critical democracy reforms. And because of grassroots pressure from Bernie Sanders supporters, the Democrats also began the process of overhauling their super-delegate system.[13]

In almost all of these victories, diverse coalitions are key to success. Organizations from the NAACP to civics groups to local businesses are joining forces. "Unlikely allies are coming together to fight for democracy reform," Joan Mandle, executive director of Democracy

Matters, tells us. "People are truly beginning to realize that until we fix our democracy, we cannot solve anything else."

"There is profound power in Tea Party patriots lining up next to progressive activists to fix the political system," observes Josh Silver, founder of Represent.Us. "This was the most potent ingredient in our successes in South Dakota, Tallahassee, Florida [in 2014], and elsewhere."

Congressman John Sarbanes echoed this sentiment to us. Describing the victory in Howard County, Maryland, he said, "The fact that so many organizations with different missions, goals, and guiding principles can all come together in support of empowering reforms, like citizen-owned elections, speaks volumes about the appeal."

DEEP ORGANIZING

In covering Democracy Spring, *Rolling Stone* noted that democracy reform efforts have been "dominated by older, white public interest lawyers."[14] Democracy Spring succeeded in breaking through those limits somewhat, "trending" on Facebook and Twitter nationally during the first few days of the sit-ins, and getting more than six million views on its social media pages, according to its digital coordinator, Justin Smith. Democracy Spring didn't, however, alter the perception that democracy reform is a white people's game. That is not to say organizers lacked the desire to build a racially diverse coalition for democracy. So why hasn't it happened? Here we share insights of those deep in the trenches of organizing.

We'll start with a moment of missed opportunity from our experience with Democracy Spring—not to scold but to learn. Our march passed through Baltimore to Washington, DC, both cities with people-of-color majorities. We might well have enlarged the march and subsequent civil disobedience by including local Black Lives Matter groups, yet we probably spent more time trying to get folks from across the country to participate than these neighbors.

No Democracy Movement worthy of its name can think of people of color as "diversity points"—a collect-as-many-as-you-can number to justify itself, though. As professor Angela Davis explains, "You can't simply invite people to join you and be immediately on board, particularly when they were not necessarily represented during the earlier organizing processes."[15]

Marginalized communities must be engaged *from the beginning*. And not just passively but in leadership positions. "It's about giving them the power to lead," explains Rosemary Rivera, organizing director of Citizen Action of New York. For many longtime organizers, this can be uncomfortable. But Rivera implores, "Let us make our own mistakes. Let us learn."

Moreover, the Democracy Movement must shout out ever louder that racial justice and our democracy crisis are inseparable. Big-money interests pushing an anti-government, anti-tax agenda disproportionately harm people of color. For example, facing frequent budget shortfalls, many municipalities and states resort to hiking fines for minor infractions, including fees for posting bail, debt collection fees, administrative fines, and parking tickets.[16] But they "amount to a 'race tax,'" Princeton professor Keeanga-Yamahtta Taylor argues, underscoring that "it is nonwhite populations who bear the disproportionate burden of being overpoliced." In a town such as Ferguson, Missouri, "monies derived from these fines were the second largest source of revenue" for the city.[17] And, as noted in chapter 4, ALEC has fostered legislation promoting policies that encourage mass incarceration and the use of private prisons.[18]

A movement of movements for democracy can join with other historically disenfranchised groups too, whether it's native peoples at Standing Rock protesting the Dakota Access Pipeline, backed by big money, or immigration activists fighting against a border wall that would enrich contractors but do little to enhance security.

In all, a movement of movements means democracy activists show up when needed, even when the issue is not explicitly about political reforms—from attending rallies against Trump's anti-immigration orders to demonstrations against police brutality. Constitutionally protected human rights are foundational to democracy.

"It's not at all accurate to say, 'If we just pass public financing, then police will stop killing black people,'" explains Jodeen Olguin-Tayler, a fifteen-year veteran of the racial justice and immigrant rights movement and former vice president, policy and strategic partnerships at Demos, the New York–based think tank. "But if you do structural democracy reform—reform that changes who is able to build political and social power to influence our political and economic institutions—that will have an impact." This insight is grounds for coalition building.

The good news is that real efforts are moving us in this direction. "There were a lot of police shootings last summer," Democracy Initiative's Wendy Fields explains, "and we decided it was really important to take a position on racial profiling." She notes that she got "a little uneasiness" from some organizations, but when the leaders, who are committed to transformational movement building, focused together on the ultimate goal of a democracy that works for all, they took a stand.

In 2014, Demos also helped launch the Inclusive Democracy Project, convening seventeen organizations based in communities of color that work on economic, racial, and gender justice. Its purpose is to connect democracy and racial justice to actually begin to develop a power base to create deep democracy reform. According to Olguin-Tayler, who launched the program, some of these groups had previously been excluded, explicitly or implicitly, from coalitions that were working on democracy reforms.

Because of the Inclusive Democracy Project, "we're not just winning reform but actually running and doing campaigns differently," Olguin-Tayler explains. A great example was the 2015 passage of public financing in Seattle. A key to its appeal with low-income people is that providing vouchers, as opposed to matching funds, means that voters have an equal voice at election time without cutting into their family's limited budgets.

Other opportunities for alliances? Democracy reformers joining with living-wage campaigns, which since 1994 have raised the minimum wage in more than one hundred cities and counties. Ditto the Fight for 15 movement, which since 2012 has won raises for twenty-two million Americans.

In 2016, halfway along the Democracy Spring march, we experienced a moment of such solidarity. As we entered one of the central plazas of Baltimore, we learned that a memorial vigil for Freddie Gray—a young African American man who died in the custody of Baltimore police and whose death was ruled a homicide—was under way. So instead of ending the day with a celebration of our progress, organizers asked all of us to walk over to the vigil and stand in solidarity. Vigil goers expressed interest in what we were doing and Democracy Spring participants learned more about police brutality.

Of course, deep organizing does not end along racial lines. Inclusivity extends to gender, sexual orientation, religious preferences, and so on.

In reflecting on her work with the Inclusive Democracy Project, Olguin-Tayler reiterates that in this kind of organizing, "There's no shortcut." She continues: "It's showing up for fights that other people are prioritizing, and understanding why they see that issue as the most urgent one. It's about being willing to work on other people's stuff and do so with a curious mind . . . It's about being clear about what your own expertise is and what others' is."

Perhaps most important to consider, she suggests, is that "there's no circumstance where we can check racial justice at the door." Wendy Fields echoes this, saying, "When people cannot send their children out at night, you can't expect them to fight for money in politics and not have racial issues be at the center."

THE SPADEWORK OF DEMOCRACY

Though in many ways the "movement of movements" approach breaks new ground, four types of groups have long been laying the groundwork for a powerful Democracy Movement. To connect with their work, we and the Democracy Initiative welcome you to visit our online *Field Guide to the Democracy Movement*. Here's a quick rundown of some of the groups you'll find there:

First are *democracy reform crafters and campaigners*. For more than a hundred years, the NAACP has been fighting for voting rights, and since 1970, Common Cause has lobbied on behalf of citizens. Another early leader, describing itself as "the people's voice in the nation's capital," is Public Citizen, founded by Ralph Nader in 1971. And since 2012, Represent.Us has become a bipartisan champion of state-level democracy reforms. Other prominent crafters and campaigners include Every Voice, US PIRG, People for the American Way, and Issue One. Second are *democracy think tanks*. The Brennan Center for Justice, the Campaign Finance Institute, Demos, and FairVote equip democracy reformers with careful analyses. Third are *legal centers*. Providing arguments for reform and challenging injustices through the courts, they include the Lawyers' Committee on Civil Rights Under Law, Campaign Legal Center, Democracy 21, and Free Speech for People. Fourth are *centers providing essential data*. OpenSecrets, the Sunlight Foundation, MapLight, and the National Institute on Money in State Politics reveal funds going to politicians and from whom.

These organizations—and dozens more—have enriched the soil in which the Democracy Movement is growing.

MOVING THE DEMOCRACY AGENDA

The growth of these organizations and the spread of protests reveal increasing citizen anger. Yet, to differing degrees, both major parties remain trapped in the money system. In 2002, Republican John McCain co-led the passage of campaign-finance reform, but since then his party has all but abandoned the challenge. Democrats, too, are beholden to funders. In 2008, the finance, insurance, and real estate industries gave the party more money than did labor and liberal interest groups combined.[19]

Logically, the Democratic Party should be a reform champion. It was, after all, a Democratic president who signed the 1965 Voting Rights Act, and the party has been less ideologically committed to a wealth-concentrating market. Plus, most Democratic Party platforms have for almost a century advocated democracy reforms. Yet, even as outrage mounts, in 2016, Hillary Clinton failed to vigorously promote her own platform's call for public financing and voting rights' protection.

So how can a movement of movements move the agenda? The Democracy Movement must make it politically toxic for either party to ignore the changes required for a government of, by, and for the people. Recall FDR's admission that he could only act if the people pushed. Thus his command: "Now go out and make me do it."

In the next chapter, you'll meet gutsy Americans embodying precisely this spirit.

CHAPTER SEVEN

LISTEN UP, AMERICA! NORTH CAROLINA HAS A STORY TO TELL

RIGHT UNDER OUR NOSES is a battle for democracy uniquely intense and rich in lessons. In North Carolina we can see the worst and the best of our nation's ongoing struggle for democracy. No matter where we live, what's happening in this state can alert us, guide us, and profoundly inspire us.

Unlike in most of the South, for more than one hundred years Democrats held the majority in at least one house of the state legislature in North Carolina.[1] And during much of the past half-century, observed former state representative Larry Hall, the House Democratic leader from 2013 to 2016, North Carolina had pulled ahead of most other southern states in a variety of social measures.[2]

Yet, in voter turnout North Carolina still ranked consistently in the bottom fifteen states throughout the twentieth century. By the early 2000s, however, North Carolinians were ready for change and began mobilizing to improve voting rights. In 2003, with the leadership of Democracy North Carolina and others, the state launched a campaign to allow anyone wanting to vote during the early-voting period to register on the same day. It took a five-year battle to pass same-day registration but reformers got there in 2007, and just one year later it reaped major benefits. During the early-voting period leading up to the 2008 election, more than one hundred thousand people were able to vote because of same-day registration.[3]

In 2004 the North Carolina NAACP State Conference, Democracy North Carolina, and other groups pushed for polls to be open on the two Sundays within the early-voting period. Sundays are a critical opportunity for African American church communities to ensure that their members get to the polls. When the coalition won, churches organized "Souls to the Polls" outings, bringing people to the polls after Sunday-morning worship. In the 2008 election, voter turnout increased thanks in large part to this effort, as well as to same-day registration and the Obama campaign's ground game. Also, in 2005, North Carolinians ensured that those registered within the county but arriving at the wrong polling place could still vote, bringing tens of thousands of new voters into the fold.

By the 2008 presidential election, the state's turnout reached almost 70 percent, the highest in forty years, and North Carolina had the nation's biggest jump in turnout between 2004 and 2008.[4] Then, in 2009, with bipartisan support, the state approved preregistration for sixteen-year-olds. Three years later sixty thousand teenagers were able to vote by virtue of having preregistered.[5]

But in 2010 the game changed.

UNDOING DEMOCRACY

Anti-democracy forces converged on this state of ten million people dead set on rolling back these hard-won advances. *Citizens United* and related court rulings had just made their task even easier. Money to influence elections could now be easily funneled into super PACs and other entities operating independent of candidates and parties. And Republican donors seized the moment. They saw the once-in-a-decade chance to redraw district lines coming up, offering the possibility of ensuring safe Republican seats on the federal and state levels for at least a decade.

Art Pope, a former board member of the Koch-funded Americans for Prosperity and owner of a chain of southern discount stores, gladly took up the task of funding the campaign to take back the legislature.[6] Pope had served two stints as a state representative and had also built an astounding political machine in North Carolina, often providing massive funding in electoral races. To shape the political narrative in the state he had also created and funded a network of think tanks and university programs.[7] Staff from this network of groups often bounced between Republican campaigns and legislative offices, taking Pope's right-wing ideology with them.[8]

The roots of Pope's ideology run deep. During his adolescence, Pope attended a summer program run by the Cato Institute. He credits the program with immersing him in the writings of Friedrich August von Hayek and Ayn Rand, two shapers of the ideology of brutal capitalism (see chapter 2). Pope has since been a Cato donor.[9]

In 2010, a coalition of groups he put together spent more than $2 million on state-level races.[10] (This information was available only because of a disclosure law passed in North Carolina to fix reporting loopholes created by *Citizens United*.)[11] Of the twenty-seven races Pope and his network targeted, twenty-one of his candidates won. Several of these campaigns featured nasty ads with racist innuendos.[12] In the process, Republicans gained control of both houses of the legislature for the first time since 1870.[13]

But this shift to the right was not all about the money, Bob Hall, the longtime executive director of Democracy North Carolina, explains. At the time, cultural shifts occurred with which many white North Carolinians were uncomfortable—among them the election of an African American president and increasing acceptance of gay marriage. The discomfort, Hall argues, was easily exploitable by groups like Koch's Americans for Prosperity.

As in other states, the GOP's subsequent gerrymandering packed Democrats into "a small number of ultra-safe seats" and Republicans into "largely-safe seats that will be un-losable in anything but a wave election," according to the *Washington Post*.[14] After their redistricting handiwork, only five of fifty state Senate seats and ten of 120 state House seats were considered "swing."[15] Pope was himself involved in drawing the new district lines.[16] In all, many believed it would be virtually impossible for Democrats to take back the North Carolina legislature for at least a decade. At this writing the assessment seems sound.

In 2012, emboldened by its successes, the GOP was determined to win back the governor's mansion. Pope and his allies again stepped up with hundreds of thousands of dollars for Republican Pat McCrory's campaign.[17] It worked, and McCrory became the first Republican governor in more than twenty years. Soon, Pope would be rewarded. Governor McCrory chose him to lead his transition team and then appointed Pope to one of the state's most powerful positions: state budget director.

The newly GOP-controlled state government wasted no time. In 2013 it passed what many locals call a "monster" law with dozens of anti-democracy changes: a law with virtually every element proven to reduce voter turnout, especially among low-income people and people of color. It required voters to present IDs to vote—one of the strictest such laws in the nation—ended same-day voter registration, and cut a full week from early voting.[18]

The law also abolished preregistration for sixteen-year-olds and ended state-sponsored voter-registration drives. Plus, it increased secrecy—making it legal for campaign advertisements to exclude the candidate's statement of responsibility for an ad.[19]

"This North Carolina measure is the most sweeping antivoter law in at least decades," explained election-law expert and University of California, Irvine, political science professor Rick Hasen.[20] As we explore below, it would take years of courageous action by citizens and intervention by federal courts to begin to roll back some of the negative effects of this law.

Republicans eliminated public financing for state judicial elections too—even though it had enjoyed wide, bipartisan support since being implemented in 2004. Public financing, freeing candidates from dependence on private money, had helped more African Americans win election to the state Supreme Court, and had enabled the state's first-ever majority-female state Supreme Court.[21] Over five election cycles, 80 percent of candidates for NC Supreme Court and Court of Appeals had chosen to use public funds.[22]

Getting rid of this commonsense reform had been one of Pope's pet projects, and its repeal was in large part his doing. When Republican state representative Jonathan C. Jordan proposed an amendment to the 2013 budget to save the public funding mechanism, Pope pulled him aside. Following their private meeting, Jordan dropped his support for the amendment, and public financing in elections was doomed.[23] If you wonder why a big donor like Pope would bother to undo public financing for a state judicial race, here's what a study by three political-science professors reported: their "findings suggest that public financing reduced responsiveness to donors among participating justices."[24] Less influenced by donors, judges could focus entirely on the legal merits of a case. Imagine that.

It's worth noting how in pushing the anti-democratic agenda Art Pope moved Republican lawmakers with him. Take Phil Berger: in 2001, when the state legislature was debating public finance, Berger, then a freshman state senator, was a "key person" in passing judicial public finance, Bob Hall recalls. But after, when the GOP takeover of the state was complete, Berger voted to gut the program. "Berger was not going to fight Pope," Hall explains. The anti-democratic tide and the undercurrent of cultural tension also removed moderate Republicans from office. They were "squeezed, intimidated, and defeated," Hall recounts.

All of these changes—and we've only scratched the surface—brought about mass disenfranchisement. Repeal of early voting particularly affected the African American community, as more than seven out of ten of African Americans who voted in 2008 and 2012 had taken advantage of this time- and cost-saver.[25] In 2014 such voter disenfranchisement steps paid off for the GOP. In the US Senate race, speaker of the North Carolina Assembly, Thom Tillis—architect of the monster anti-voting bill—defeated Democratic incumbent Kay Hagan by a very slim margin.

DEMOCRACY–A MORAL CALLING THAT DEMANDS COURAGE

Given the GOP's multiple assaults on democracy, North Carolina's citizens faced a choice: continue to let Republican lawmakers wreak havoc or fight back in order to move forward. "It's very tough to see decades of democracy work torn down," Melissa Kromm, the director of NC Voters for Clean Elections Coalition, tells us. "But what's really great about North Carolina is that, yes, we're on the defense, but we are also still working on how to move this forward."

Many mark the last Monday of April 2013 as the day this choice was made visible for all to see. Then president of North Carolina's NAACP, the Reverend Dr. William J. Barber II, and a group of clergy, along with many determined citizens, blockaded the entrance to the

Senate chambers. It was an act of civil disobedience to place the assault on democracy front and center in the public's eye. The next Monday, they repeated the action, and more than one hundred determined citizens joined them.

And thus was born a movement—often called simply the Moral Mondays Movement or the Forward Together Movement. For the rest of the year, each week citizens gathered in front of the State Capitol demanding redress, from reinstating democracy reforms and eliminating the voter ID requirement, to creating a living wage and ensuring adequate health care for all North Carolinians. And each week the crowds grew, eventually drawing thousands. By July of its first year, approximately nine hundred active defenders of democracy had been arrested in acts of civil disobedience.[26]

But it didn't start that April. Melissa Kromm explains that the capacity to fight back against the anti-democracy forces had been building well before Moral Mondays. Pre-2010 deep-coalition work had created what she calls the "shakers and bakers"—those outside the political system, often protesting and holding rallies, were the "shakers," and those inside were the "bakers," lobbying, oftentimes spanning issue divides such as environmental and labor.

Many point to the formation of a new coalition as the pivotal moment. Since 2006, the NC NAACP has convened the more than two hundred organizations with more than two million members that now make up the Historic Thousands on Jones Street People's Assembly Coalition, known simply as the HKonJ Coalition. Named for its annual people's assembly show of strength at the statehouse on Jones Street in Raleigh, the HKonJ Coalition is the architect and force behind Moral Mondays.

The coalition champions a fourteen-point platform against racism, poverty, and war and for democracy, addressing concerns from health care to a living wage to voting rights.[27] Once a year, all the HKonJ groups convene to reaffirm their commitment to the platform and to network among one another. In coming together year after year and supporting one another in between, the groups have "learned to work together and trust each other on different campaigns," Hall explains. The personal relationships built through this work laid the foundation for Moral Mondays' sustained growth. "It's why the Moral Monday movement could jump off in such a dramatic way," Hall says, referring to actions in the spring of 2013.

The Reverend Dr. Barber, the national face of the movement, has served as pastor at the Greenleaf Christian Church (Disciples of Christ) in Goldsboro since 1993. And, from 2005 to 2017, Barber had also been president of the North Carolina State Conference of NAACP Branches—the nation's largest—with more than one hundred branches across the state.

Both of Barber's parents were active in desegregation efforts in the 1960s, and he's clearly taken their lessons to heart. He explains that in the sixties, civil rights leaders "first had to win the moral high ground" and "capture the attention and consciousness of the nation. When those two things came together, it gave space for people like Lyndon Baines Johnson, who was a segregationist, to step out of his normal pattern of politics into a new way."[28] Barber and his allies are trying to replicate this deep shift in North Carolina.

The strength of the HKonJ Coalition's mode of organizing, and its Moral Mondays Movement, is inclusivity—what Barber calls "fusion politics" and what we call a "movement of movements." All organizations in the HKonJ Coalition commit to support the fights of all other members—even if the fight is not directly within a given group's immediate purview. Everyone acts on each of the fourteen points in the platform and everyone moves forward together.

This "fusion" approach is powerful and appealing, remarks Clinton Wright, a former public school teacher and now an organizer with Repairers of the Breach, Barber's newest social justice organization. Excitedly, Wright shared with us the meaning of this approach:

> I remember the first time I went to HKonJ, which was my first time hearing Reverend Barber and the messaging of fusion politics. As a queer person going to a black, indigenously led, grassroots coalition, hearing a minister talk about the intersections of LGBTQ equality and mass incarceration, the fight for black lives, religious freedom, health care, inequality, food insecurity, and immigration reform, it was the first time I felt like all of my identities were represented and that the wholeness of my person as an activist and as a human were invited into a space.

And I've heard that story from many people . . . they went to HKonJ and realized everything about themselves that they were bringing to the table. And I think that is the true power of fusion politics. You don't have to let your identities go. All of yourself is welcome and has a place to fill in the moral movement. It's empowering in a way that is indescribable unless you've been there to be a part of it.

Wright goes further, describing joining the movement as a rebirth of sorts that has profoundly changed him.

Moral Mondays goes out of its way to invite all sides of political divides to attend protests. For Barber, we do not have "a left problem or a right problem or a conservative problem or a liberal problem. We've got a heart problem."[29]

One powerful example of normally unthinkable cross-partisan coalitions arose in Belhaven, North Carolina, after a huge conglomerate medical company came in and bought the only hospital in 2014. Because the town was small, the hospital didn't profit enough to justify its continued operation—so in less than three years the company closed it.[30] The people of Belhaven then had no hospital, and the closest was a forty-minute drive away. People "literally started dying because they had to drive to the next town," Wright angrily explains.

The mayor of Belhaven, Adam O'Neal—white, male, and Republican—was livid. He launched a campaign to try to get help, and even walked all the way to the White House—twice—to make his point. Soon he reached out to Barber, asking whether the NC NAACP would jump in. It did. For two whole years, a resistance camp was set up and people camped out to protect the hospital from closure. Court cases were filed and injunctions won. In the end, though, the campaign was defeated, and the hospital was demolished.

Despite the loss, organizers were not deterred. Wright explains, "One of our points in coalition building is this condition of building unlikely allies . . . the fight for health care in that town was driven by a black-led coalition *and* a white Republican mayor. I think that that says something about the power of this work."

More than four years in, the movement remains strong and has been remarkably effective in spreading information about the actions of the state legislature. "I'm still surprised when I go across the state and so many people know about these issues," Melissa Kromm told us.

VICTORIES FOR DEMOCRACY

Here we've tried to capture the multipronged assault on democracy in North Carolina and how it is being challenged by a powerful "movement of movements." Just before the 2016 election, this hard work was vindicated. A federal appeals court struck down parts of the GOP anti-voter law, declaring that it "target[ed] African Americans with almost surgical precision." Reversing much of the worst of existing voting-related law, the new ruling prohibited voter ID requirements and reinstated same-day registration, preregistration before turning eighteen, and early voting. [31]

Needless to say, Republican-controlled county election boards soon got busy figuring out ways around the verdict. Since they couldn't legally cut a full week off early voting, the state GOP instructed local boards to make "party line changes to early voting": cutting hours and locations.[32] Though the State Board of Elections blocked some of the most severe cutbacks, many remained in place through the 2016 election. Guilford County, for example, reduced the number of polling sites in the first week of early voting from sixteen in 2012 to just one in 2016.[33] And soon, the GOP sent out a news release that celebrated the inevitable results of the cutbacks—that African American turnout had dropped by nearly 9 percent during early voting.[34]

Nevertheless, despite the anti-democracy ploys that helped Donald Trump carry the state, in 2016 Moral Mondays and the HKonJ coalition could celebrate another major victory, the defeat of Governor Pat McCrory.

And how was this possible? Moral Mondays' "constant visibility" forced the controversial "issues to stay in the headlines," Public Policy Polling, a Democratic polling firm, noted. "Its efforts ensured that voters in the state were educated about what was going on in Raleigh, and . . . they got mad. All those people who had before seen McCrory as a moderate, as a different kind of Republican, had those views quickly changed."[35]

The new Democratic governor, Roy Cooper, as attorney general had fought to increase teacher pay and backed the state's children's health-insurance initiative. The coalition of community voices had also helped elect state Supreme Court judge Michael Morgan, making Democrats the majority on the Court. In just three years, the Moral Mondays coalition had moved two of the three branches of North Carolina's government in the direction of foundational democratic values—a remarkable demonstration of the power of fusion politics. Note that all this was accomplished despite the gerrymandering that kept the makeup of the state legislature largely unchanged.

The GOP was, of course, dead set against losing any more of the ground that it had taken during its four-year control of the state. So a sneak attack followed. Before leaving office in 2016, Governor Mc-Crory called a special legislative session to spearhead a bill covering relief for hurricane and flood victims. Soon after the special session was called, rumors of a GOP-led, secret plot leaked to the press. Republicans would use the special session to pack the state Supreme Court—adding two additional justices before the new governor took over, and thus retaining ideological control in conservative hands.[36]

Outraged, Moral Mondays stalwarts swarmed the Capitol to protest the power grab. At the time, Barber wasn't even in the state, but the culture of resistance had so deeply taken root that people snapped into action without him. Many in the movement are now accustomed, Wright explains, to calling their state representatives every day, when needed, to express their opinions. Resistance was now in their DNA.

In the end, the GOP did not introduce its revenge measure. But the outgoing GOP-majority legislature rushed through another "reform" bill gutting the incoming governor's powers to appoint a majority of members to the State Board of Elections, the body that decides the location and number of early-voting sites.[37] The rushed bill also made it more difficult to bring a case to the state Supreme Court, weakening the Court's power and thus thwarting its Democratic majority.[38]

This parting shot certainly hampers the new administration's ability to restore democracy in North Carolina. (At this writing, these "reforms" are being litigated.) Yet, for the next four years, the legislature—still with a veto-proof GOP majority—will at least have a slightly harder time causing additional damage to North Carolina's battered democracy. Unsurprisingly, early indications suggest they will indeed test their power, attempting more anti-democracy measures in the years ahead.

Just how much damage had the anti-democratic administration inflicted? Well, take this in: North Carolina can no longer be considered a "fully functioning democracy," according to professor Andrew Reynolds, whose conclusion draws on data from the Electoral Integrity Project.[39] Remarkably, "when it comes to the integrity of the voting district boundaries, no country has ever received as low a score as the 7 [out of] 100 North Carolina received. North Carolina is not only the worst state in the USA for unfair districting but the worst entity in the world ever analyzed by the Electoral Integrity Project."[40]

But Clinton Wright and his fellow fusion movement diehards are adamant. The movement will continue to build under a Democratic governor and beyond. There are many fights to win, and these engaged North Carolinians will indeed push on. As Barber wrote after the eleventh annual HKonJ gathering, in February 2017, "We march for political change in 2018 and 2020, yes. But we march for more than that. We march for a Third Reconstruction to revive the heart of democracy in America."[41]

Beyond North Carolina, Moral Mondays offers "a lesson for progressives in dealing with Trump. Push back hard from day one. Be visible. Capture the public's attention, no matter what you have to do to do it," Public Policy Polling declared. "By making news in their own right week after week after week," citizens in the fusion movement in North Carolina "forced sustained coverage of what was going on in Raleigh." The polling group then noted that theirs "was certainly a long game, with plenty more frustration in between, [but] those efforts led to change at the polls 42 months after they really started."[42] And that is remarkable.

Hats off to the Forward Together Movement in North Carolina. May the nation's Democracy Movement learn from you and be emboldened by your courage, your impact, and your determination never to give up.

CHAPTER EIGHT

|||||||||||||||||||

THE THRILL
OF DEMOCRACY

AT THREE IN THE MORNING, outside Washington, DC, juvenile holding, Angela Yarbrough anxiously awaited the release of her daughter, Tessa, who'd been arrested earlier in the day. The doors of the building opened, and an exhausted Tessa walked out. As she fell into the arms of her relieved mother, she couldn't help but wonder how she had gotten to this point. At fifteen, she would have quite the story to tell her friends when she got back to school next week.

A few months prior, Tessa's mother, the founder of a Represent .Us chapter in their hometown in central Virginia, casually mentioned to her family that she would be attending a 140-mile march for democracy reform and planned to risk arrest on the Capitol steps. Interested in politics and citizen activism, Tessa asked if she could tag along. With stellar grades, she felt she could afford to miss a week of classes. Her mother agreed, so long as she went home as soon as the march was finished—no getting arrested.

So on April 2, the mother-daughter team found themselves in front of the Liberty Bell in Philadelphia, about to embark on Democracy Spring's 140-mile march.

During the first couple of days, Tessa stayed near her mom, though slowly she struck up conversations with other marchers, held signs, and began to enjoy the experience. After nine days on the road, sleeping on floors and eating a lot of peanut butter and jelly sandwiches, they arrived in DC. Although Tessa promised her mother she wouldn't get arrested, something had changed. Feeling a part of Democracy Spring, she knew she wanted to stand in solidarity right up until the end. If she left before the arrests she'd feel as though she hadn't quite finished her mission.

After a sizable amount of convincing, the next day Tessa found herself walking to the Capitol steps with her mother and almost five hundred others. She sat down, waited for the police to arrive, and, far from being scared, reveled in the experience—chanting and singing with her new friends. As she was lined up with the other protesters to be handcuffed and arrested, she stood next to her mother.

The Capitol police, eventually making their way to her, stopped and looked befuddled. "The guy in charge tried really hard to convince my mom not to let me go through with it," Tessa recounts. "He told my mom that if she let me go to jail she would be an awful mother." They offered to release her.

A wave of connection to the other protesters came over her, and Tessa refused to take the officer's offer. As a juvenile, she was placed in a separate van and taken to a processing unit separate from the adults, including her mother. There she sat, alone in a transition cell, until being transferred to a holding cell, where she spent eight hours. She paced, sat down, braided her hair, and then took a nap.

When she awoke, she had two new cellmates, both of whom seemed younger than she. They were close friends and had been jumped by a small group of people whom they knew. At least one of the attackers had a knife. Apparently, there was also a Taser involved. "They only said a couple words to me; mostly they talked to each other. I just listened," Tessa recalls. They were with her for only an hour or so before being taken away.

Once out of jail, things looked different to Tessa. "I realized how deeply underprivileged many Americans are," she explains. "Children are growing up in what seem like completely foreign worlds. To think that twelve-year-olds have to worry about being attacked with knives was a little shocking, to say the least. They were all victims of circumstance, having been shaped by the violence and poverty they grew up in."

Far from acting as a deterrent, jail stoked Tessa's commitment to lifelong political activism. And no matter what would come in the future, she knew that things would now be different. To those who saw her the next day, Tessa's entire demeanor seemed changed. Her face, filled with vitality, greeted us; her hair, no longer tied tightly in a ponytail—because the officers had confiscated her hair tie—flowed freely. She gave us hugs and recounted her experience.

As word spread throughout the Democracy Spring family that she, as a fifteen-year-old, had risked arrest and even spent a total of twelve hours in jail, Tessa reveled in her new celebrity status. A mere twenty-four hours seemed to change this young activist completely.

EXPERIENCING THE THRILL OF DEMOCRACY

For many, politics is a spectator sport, and a dry and dull one at that. For others, an old adage captures the problem: making laws is like making sausage. You definitely do *not* want to watch that nasty process. If you are fortunate, though, a moment arrives in which politics is no longer abstract, impersonal, or nasty. It is real and oh-so personal. Politics is, after all, simply what we decide to do together. It is at the heart of everyday existence.

What drew us to write this book was a conversation—albeit a really long one—about these moments in our lives. What was it, in our own respective lives—in age, forty-nine years apart—that caused us to care so much about politics and, more specifically, democracy itself?

Over coffee and a lot of walking during the 2016 Democracy Spring march, our conversations drifted to our earliest, most vivid political memories. In those moments, our voices rose and fell with emotion and our hands waved emphatically with the retelling. What we discovered is that in these stories—what we would come to call our political-origin stories—we entered into situations as one person and left as another. As described in the opening note of this book, whether it was as a community organizer in Philadelphia in the 1960s' War on Poverty or in Occupy Wall Street in 2011, we experienced similar emotional shifts. It's not that we didn't care about making the world a better place prior to these events, but much like with Tessa, the biggest questions of the day suddenly became more real.

For some, such transformative moments occur during protest, which can be a high-stakes, scary process. For others, contentious or deliberative political engagement can not only be transformative but also liberating—as in those moments when you go beyond what you had thought yourself capable. On the power of pushing beyond our perceived limits, the Reverend Dr. William J. Barber II writes of his journey in North Carolina: "Resistance did more than confirm our purpose. . . . To move forward together, we would have to deal with unquestioned assumptions and internalized fears."[1]

In the months following Democracy Spring—both the one-hundred-plus-mile march and the civil disobedience—we spent a lot of time teasing out and giving words to what had changed inside us because of the experience and what had changed in others as well. From all of our talk emerged three emotionally transformative shifts that for us add up to the "thrill of democracy."

Choosing Civil Courage

First is *civil courage,* or *the power of choosing to walk with fear*—of protest and arrest or just looking foolish or being publicly criticized—in the service of one's deepest values.

Often people think of the sensation of fear as a stop sign. Isn't it just our body's way of putting us on notice that we aren't safe and should flee, fight, or freeze? We argue otherwise. Of course, it *can be* that simple, but fear can also be telling us that we are doing exactly what we should be doing for our own and our community's well-being—even survival. Our body's sensations are reminding us that, yes, we're stepping out beyond our comfort zones, and it is exciting and enlivening. From that frame, we can experience fear as exhilarating energy. A wildly pounding heart can become our inner applause. "Being able to speak out to power is very liberating," says Margaret Flowers, an Occupy FCC organizer, "and so is moving outside your comfort zone and recognizing that you can do that."

It was in Leipzig, Germany, that I, Frances, first heard the term "civil courage," when students described to me their families in 1989 marching to their churches with candles held high, protesting the East German police state. Soon, I learned, these simple actions of tens of thousands spread from city to city throughout the country, and within weeks the Berlin Wall would fall.

Walking with fear changes something inside us. Our hunch is that such experiences lead participants to stay engaged, increasing the likelihood of taking important risks. As Martin Luther King Jr. wrote shortly before he was assassinated, African Americans fighting for justice "have left the valley of despair; they have found strength in struggle."[2]

Civil courage, once experienced, changes how we see ourselves. We start thinking, "Well, if I could do one thing I didn't think I could, maybe I can take the next seemingly impossible step."

Bonding with Strangers

Second is *the power of discovering deep connections with strangers sharing a higher value.* Seventy-two percent of American adults reported loneliness in a 2016 Harris poll.[3] Even many of us with satisfying friendships rarely have opportunities for meaningful sharing with strangers.

Being shoulder to shoulder with complete strangers on behalf of deeply held principles can present such possibilities. On the Democracy Spring march, we spent evenings on church basement floors in group conversation and heard, for example, about lives as different as those of an Iraq War veteran and a former banker, both explaining why they care so much about our democracy. Afterward, we felt less alone, less like oddballs.

Most of us live in geographic and cultural "bubbles," sorted out by income, race, and so much more. Discovering that we share core values, even with folks in vastly different worlds, fortified us. We gained confidence in the near universality of sensitivity to democratic values that we see as expressions of the very best of our humanity. And these experiences satisfy as well the most basic human hunger for connection.

Public action for common purpose often means that total strangers quickly become friends—friends with an enhanced sense of their own power arising from sharing personal journeys. These feelings echo sensations that Kat Cline from Democracy Matters described as "energizing" and a "relief" in a scary time—sensations arising in organizing with people who share her commitment to democracy. Chris Grinley, a Democracy Matters campus coordinator at the University of New Hampshire, put it nicely: "Once you start organizing, it's really just socializing with a focus."

Richard Wilkinson, author of *The Impact of Inequality*, goes further, stressing that it is working together toward a goal in a community that's even more emancipatory than just being a member of a group: Working together, "People become more aware of themselves as not simply being used and exploited, but being part of a team. Their contribution being valued by the people with more of a sense of purpose . . . is absolutely fundamental to human wellbeing."[4]

Interacting within a new community can also alter preconceived notions. "I believe it in my core, if people are unified around the same fight, they forget their bias," explains Wendy Fields, executive director of Democracy Initiative. "I've seen white men who were once homophobic shift their views . . . When people understand the common goal, work together and act collectively, they get over bias."

Trust grows too through public action with strangers; and trust is one victim of brutal capitalism ruthlessly pitting us against each other. Returning from the Boston Women's March, we sat on the subway next to Tieren Adams, a family friend in the seventh grade. "You know," she said, "people aren't so bad after all. Did you see how everyone was looking out for everyone else?"

We smiled.

Realizing Our Power as Democracy's Guardians–as Holders of Solutions

Third is an inner shift from feeling like a protesting outsider to a powerful *"owner"* of our democracy. Standing up against plutocracy is great, but for us, Democracy Spring offered something more. Let us share a scene with you.

In the final moments of our march from Philly to DC, we approach the Capitol as cars honk and people wave from stoops. At full throat, all of us in unison are chanting our favorite call and response—*Whose democracy? Our democracy!* At that moment, suddenly ahead of us the Capitol dome comes into focus. First, we feel a chill, then tears begin to flow. We can almost feel the new synapses cracking in our brains: "Our Democracy"?—Really? *Yes, ours!*

For the first time in our lives, we feel our democracy is not "theirs"—belonging to those big shots in the imposing buildings, but ours, the citizens'. We feel like the "grown-ups" arriving with real answers. We'll probably never again see the Capitol without reliving that instant of recognition of ourselves as responsible for solutions. We never, ever want to forget.

And our fellow Americans agree with what Democracy Spring brought to Washington that morning. More than 70 percent of Americans polled favor small-money, public matching funds, for example. Feeling like the "adults in the room" with thought-out solutions to our society's biggest problems is a heady experience. As Carol Wyndham, an activist with New Hampshire Rebellion, told us, "If you want to live in a democracy, you have to take responsibility for it."

Taking responsibility helps unlock what we call the "democratic self," a way of interacting with society that prioritizes patience, learning, accepting discomfort with differences, and creativity in the face of ambiguity. Engagement enables us to cultivate these qualities of character essential to democracy. These values guide us toward taking ownership of a real democracy in which all voices are heard.

DEMOCRATIC VOICE

Experiencing the "thrill of democracy" we've described here meets the trio of needs we identified in chapter 1 as essential to human thriving—power, meaning, and connection. And in this process more people find their voices, the essence of democracy.

"To become a political subject is to be heard and seen," University of Warwick professor Oliver Davis writes.[5] Assembling together in public space and calling for reforms forces the government and fellow citizens to recognize that we exist and have ideas.

In 1999 many young Americans viewed Seattle's protest against global corporate power as their "coming-out party," recalls Jonathan Matthew Smucker. "We were 'coming out' not only to the nation and to the world, but also to ourselves—realizing our own existence as a *force*."[6] In 2011 in the Occupy movement many felt heard for the first time as well. Marine corporal Jason Washburn describes his experience in an encampment: "Being a veteran in America today is usually to be unheard, an unspoken voice that even if it is spoken is usually brushed off . . . [M]ore veterans have died by suicide than have died in the current wars in Iraq and Afghanistan . . . it breaks my heart. I feel like being a part of the Occupy Movement is bringing a voice to these veterans' cry for help."[7]

In North Carolina, Barber stresses that his coalition created space for "poor and hurting people's voices [to be] heard. They were our featured speakers, and we invited them to share their stories regardless of race, creed, or political affiliation."[8] In the stories of those participating in Democracy Spring, we heard similar feelings of being "seen and heard" for the first time.

Gaining a voice is so essential for human dignity that the experience can trigger deep emotion. "One of the most common comments I heard from people who went to the Women's March," the day after Trump's inauguration, "was joy," said Kevin Zeese, an organizer of Occupy FCC. "They felt really joyful," he continues, "that they were standing up to this bully and doing it all together and they weren't alone. And . . . at the airport protests regarding the immigration injustice, we see the same thing. The common look on everyone's face was joy." Even the wonky *Vox* recognizes the power of the internal shifts. "Not only have the resisters already markedly altered the trajectory of public policy," reporter Matthew Yglesias writes, "they have also begun to make a difference in each other's lives and their own conceptions of themselves. And this is the greatest threat to the [pro] Trump movement."[9]

Public protest has another consequence, one increasingly critical in the era of fake news that propelled Donald Trump to the presidency. As the *New York Times* explains, "Protesters can't easily be dismissed as 'fake news.' . . . Because they're people you know, they can't easily be maligned as biased or unfair."[10] News outlets that family and friends do not trust might not convince them, but seeing our passion taking us onto the streets might encourage them to think more critically.

LEARNING IN ACTION TOGETHER

Events like Democracy Spring also allow us to learn together in at least three ways, according to political theorist Janet Conway.

We learn the *informal nitty-gritty of organizing*—"the insights and know-how . . . [of] organizing meetings, planning campaigns, doing outreach for events, and so on," Conway writes.[11] In Democracy Spring, we participants learned how to Livestream, comport ourselves if arrested, deal with conflict, and more.

We engage in *self-education* too, as participants reflect alone or collectively on what's happened and why.[12] Before the march we imagined people walking along in their own world, with earbuds in place to make the time go faster. Were we wrong! As we trudged along, the sharing of stories, impressions, and knowledge never stopped. Democracy Spring organizers dug into the theory of "momentum-based organizing," drawing on *This Is an Uprising*, by Paul and Mark Engler. And on the march, all of us were learning about the role of money in elections and voting rights.

Movements also ignite learning in the wider culture by *producing new narratives* through which we view the world.[13] Occupy Wall Street shaped our understanding of fast-worsening economic inequality: the "99% and 1%." Democracy Spring shined a bright light on political inequality and popularized social scientists' proof of the power of a tiny elite over our political choices. Both movements helped create a new frame, perfectly illustrated and advanced by the Women's March, that economic justice and democracy are not just for "activists."

In the Women's March in Boston, as 150,000 people moved from Boston Common into the streets chanting, "This is what democracy looks like!" we couldn't help but notice a small boy, no more than five years old, holding hands with his mother and father. As the crowd chanted, the little guy looked up at his parents and asked, "What's democracy?" His parents looked first at him, then each other, and smiled. His mother replied, "It's when people have the power to decide their own future." "It's a government of, by, and for the people," the father added. The boy replied with a simple "Okay" and picked up his pace.

Herein lies the key to the power of public voice and learning. Forever more, when this boy thinks about democracy, he will not think "boring duty to vote." He'll remember the excitement in the air that day and the feeling of being safe while surrounded by thousands—all chanting in unison for the America they want.

His conception of democracy will be a living one, filled with possibility.

CHAPTER NINE
|||||||||||||||||

DARE FOR DEMOCRACY

IN PART II we shared the really bad news that over the past four decades an Anti-Democracy Movement has gained ground in America relatively unchallenged. We showed how it has altered our laws, lives, and the public's mindset; and how it helped to bring about Donald Trump's presidency.

Yes, it is a frightening time.

But we've also shared our excitement about America's unprecedented movement for democracy. Now, in our final chapter we want to describe what most energizes us right now and to offer soul-satisfying action steps. In all, we're greatly encouraged to see more and more Americans acting on the realization that *to save the democracy we thought we had, we must take our democracy to where it's never been.*

MOMENTUM MAKING

In the previous chapter, we noted that after the inauguration of Donald Trump, on January 21, 2017, Americans took to the streets—many for the first time—under the banner of the Women's March. On every continent people joined in solidarity, even in Antarctica.

Such massive demonstrations are often "exercises in catharsis, the release of emotions," former George W. Bush speechwriter David Frum opined, and "rarely leave behind any enduring program of action or any organization to execute that program."[1] Obviously, Frum didn't register the often-lasting inner changes we emphasized in the previous chapter: the confidence and clarity arising when we join with strangers and walk into the unknown for a higher purpose. But Frum does raise the right question. How *do* we create an "enduring program of action" together?

We sustain risk-taking as we act not just against but *for* something. Even though the early-2017 marches were called "protests," many participants felt themselves standing strongly for a more fair and inclusive society.

Moreover, we're more likely to sustain attention on what we feel is *urgent*. And that feeling shouldn't be hard to maintain. Regardless of who occupies the White House, we feel confident a sense of urgency about our democracy in crisis will remain the tenor of our time. Keeping our eyes on opportunity as well as threats can stoke the desire to make ourselves heard in local and national elections, as well as in critical legislative decisions, all on behalf of a positive agenda addressing the betrayal so many Americans now feel.

Focus helps also to sustain action, so concrete and realizable goals are essential. A couple of suggestions here. You might return to chapters 5 and 6 to remind yourself of entry points for democratic-system fixes that especially light your fire. And please check out the online *Field Guide to the Democracy Movement* that we at Small Planet Institute and our partner Democracy Initiative offer. There, you can tour the opportunities and match your passions and aptitudes with a world of democracy initiatives and their rewarding actions.

But, ultimately, what most gives human efforts staying power?

The answer is simple: people do. While we humans get pegged as being too individualistic, we are actually profoundly social creatures—certainly the most social of primates. Our biggest challenge is doing anything that breaks with our "pack." Too often, therefore, we go along. But if our democracy is in big trouble because of the concerted efforts of the Anti-Democracy Movement, we can no longer just go along. So what do we do? While some of us feel comfortable taking big steps alone into the unknown, most of us don't. So to succeed, we find and create new tribes that will join us on our journey.

So *connection* is the final key to sustaining actions. But to make new connections, most of us need at least one buddy for support. Consider this intriguing study that positioned two groups of University of

Virginia students at the foot of a steep hill, each with a heavy back-pack. The only difference between the groups was that in one, a buddy stood by each subject's side. All were then asked to estimate how steep the hill ahead appeared. And maybe you've guessed it! Those with a friend by their side judged the challenge to be less daunting than those standing alone. And the longer they'd known the friend, the less steep the hill appeared.[2]

So, if you're not the lone-hero type—and we aren't, either—think of even one person in your life with whom to share your takeaways from this book and share why you must do something you've never done before. Keep looking till you find just one more schemer eager to dare for democracy with you.

The good news is that, because humans are such social beings, *courage is contagious.* As your friends and family see you take even one step, you might be surprised by who's at your side.

SIGNS OF CONTAGION

Soon after the Women's March, word quickly spread of an online effort called Indivisible, started by husband-and-wife team Ezra Levin and Leah Greenberg and their colleagues Jeremy Haile and Angel Padilla. Following Trump's election, these former congressional staffers and their friends prepared a thirty-four-page guide on "best practices for making Congress listen." They called it *Indivisible: A Practical Guide for Resisting the Trump Agenda* and posted it online. By March, a million people had downloaded the guide and 4,500 Indivisible groups had formed. Also, MomsRising.org, around since 2006 and now with more than a million members, continues to build on the Women's March with its #KeepMarching weekly actions.

Another story of citizens stepping up is Meetup.com. Founded in response to 9/11, it's grown into a huge online platform people use to find others with common interests. In early 2017 the company did what it had never done before. Only a few days after the president's travel-ban executive order affecting seven Muslim-majority countries, Meetup staff held an "all-hands-on-deck-2-day resist-a-thon." They came up with "Meetup to #Resist" to enable decentralized groups to fight against injustice and for democracy. Within two weeks, more than one hundred thousand people had joined in more than a thousand #Resist Meetups. "It seems the way for us to help now," Meetup founder Scott Heiferman stresses, "is to unify and support (and mobilize) the welcoming and inclusive majority. Meetup to #resist was our way to do that."

Indivisible, Meetup to #Resist, and MomsRising.org, as well as groups such as MoveOn and Our Revolution—born from Bernie Sanders's remarkable 2016 presidential campaign—all are helping Americans find or create a democracy team near them. By early 2017 newly engaged citizens, finding each other through these and other connectors, felt an exhilarating jolt of their unified power. In early 2017, citizen groundswell reached such heights that calls to some members of Congress opposing the Republicans' plan to repeal the Affordable Care Act outnumbered those supporting it by fifty to one.[3] The bill became so unpopular the Republicans in the House couldn't bring it up for a vote. (At the time of this writing, the GOP is pushing for a health-care bill taking away health care from millions. Nevertheless, the resistance has and will likely continue.)

These tools build upon momentum already being created by the national organizations we highlight in chapter 6. From Democracy Spring to Democracy Initiative, millions of Americans passionate about a wide range of concerns are uniting for democracy. As the growing number of local teams connects with these national groups, the Democracy Movement gains ever more power.

DEMOCRACY TEAMS PUSH THE EDGE

So let's keep asking, what are ways to keep increasing visibility and opportunities for engagement, drawing more and more Americans into the powerful, positive, and welcoming Democracy Movement?

The previous chapter featured big, dramatic public actions, often involving civil disobedience. We emphasized positive emotional shifts triggered when we take risks in public with strangers for a shared, higher calling. But many of us simply can't be away from home, family, and work. And in many places, for communities of color the stakes of risking arrest are high. So how do we create opportunities for edgy action right where we live, opportunities that are accessible to as many people as possible?

Here are a few ideas. Some will be fun, some will build knowledge and awareness, and others will be edgy enough to get the heart pounding. All can strengthen bonds with others we might not otherwise meet.

Celebrate democracy. Invite local musicians to a public park or library event room to share and teach songs related to freedom and democracy. And if you have the clout of an organization behind you, goad them to go for the spectacular. Imagine tens of thousands in a big-city stadium celebrating democracy. Wouldn't Bruce Springsteen be up for that? We love the idea of audiences honoring Leonard Cohen by chanting and swaying to his powerful "Democracy," with its refrain "Democracy is coming to the USA." Concerts with a message have an impressive history. Some will recall the 1980s' "We Are the World" concerts. And decades ago, singer Harry Chapin created concerts in part devoted to alleviating world hunger. Between sets, Joe Collins and I, Frances, jumped on stage with Harry to share our ideas to help the antihunger movement grow. What about a democracy version?

Become a hub for multiplying power and building community. The Indivisible website became an avenue for a dear friend, Janet Surrey, to participate in one of its 4,500 groups nationwide that sprouted after the 2016 election. In the Boston area, under the banner "Re-creating Democracy," Jan meets people with a range of issue passions. In monthly meetings she loves hearing their action updates. Members support each other in learning together and are also there to pitch in on each other's key passion when a big-leverage moment arises—a great example of what we mean by the budding "movement of movements." Hosts rotate, and once when a host forgot it was her turn, folks arriving for the meeting didn't just go home disappointed. They met on her porch and had a great time anyway. And, Jan tells us, it was a cold day!

Together, get voices of citizens heard. Submit letters to the editor and op-eds to news outlets. Here, we take inspiration from Citizens

Climate Lobby. Through its many local groups networked nationally via monthly conference calls, its members' total of published letters to the editor rose from thirty-six in 2010 to more than three thousand five years later; and op-eds published went from twenty-nine to 547. Incredible. (And remember, even if you don't get published, somebody at the news outlet has read what you have to say.)

Become a citizen lobbyist, both by phone and in personal visits. Just about everyone feels tongue-tied the first time. But don't worry, you can get ideas from "scripts" offered by groups such as MoveOn and adapt them to your voice and angle. Create your own citizen-lobbying day. Make an appointment with your legislators and bring friends and family. Take photos, write up your experience, and share it.

If you are an employer, offer your staff paid time to fulfill their roles as citizens. Since politicians' offices are open only during workdays, offering employees, say, fifteen minutes to call their representatives sends an important signal about community, responsibility, and citizens' power. Of course, it can be done in a way that no one ever feels judged or coerced.

Organize highly visible citizen deliberations to choose the best long-term strategies, priorities, and immediate actions. Why not host "democracy for dinner" evenings in homes, cafés, or schools, facilitated to encourage curiosity and sharing about solutions? More formally, approach your local high school principal, religious group, or library to volunteer to help organize a debate or "democracy dialogue" on solutions to problems of money in politics and voting rights suppression. For ideas, check out the resources of the National Coalition for Dialogue and Deliberation.

If you have clout in a local, state, or national civic body, why not encourage something on a bigger scale? Perhaps citizen panels with randomly selected participants, all asking: how do we get money out of politics and our voices in? A website could document which strategies turn out to be most appealing to participants and invite visitors to weigh in.

Create inviting, intimate spaces for sharing stories. In our homes, houses of worship, and community centers, we can create opportunities for people to share concerns and solutions, including stories about being heard or silenced. "[W]e had not known the extent of others' pain and suffering," writes the Reverend Dr. William J. Barber II, "until we came together to listen. We did not know how much we had in common until we told our stories of struggle to one another."[4]

Create new public spaces for community talk, "People's Corners." In well-traveled public spaces in towns and cities everywhere, imagine the "democracy buzz" generated by citizens creating a mash-up of street theater, London's Hyde Park Speakers' Corner, and facilitated exchange, along with opportunities for public commitments to act on behalf of democracy. (I, Frances, remember standing on a soapbox in Rittenhouse Square in Philly, sharing my feelings about the war in Vietnam. The power of that moment stirs me to this day.)

We can draw from the experience of Brazil's Theater of the Oppressed, which blurs the line between spectator and actor, encouraging audience members to jump in.[5] We can embolden participants to seek and propose answers together, even elevating the people's solutions to policy actions.[6] A People's Corner could stage a debate on our nation's democracy crisis; or, organizers could pose a question to everyone gathered, then invite folks to turn to a stranger nearest them to take turns responding, then reflecting on their differences.

Make a personal, shared pledge to act. Most of us find the first step the hardest. Here's an idea that can help: because stating one's commitment to a specific action, and doing so publicly, can be powerfully motivating, at a People's Corner or other gatherings, organizers could distribute pledge cards on which each person is invited to write down one commitment to act for democracy. Or cards could be prepared for elected officials, asking them to pledge support for nondiscriminatory policing, automatic voter registration, same-day registration, action on climate change, or public financing of elections.

All of the above could stimulate the three positive emotional shifts, shared in our previous chapter, that democratic action and connection can trigger. Plus, if several democracy groups worked together to create any of the above, not only would everyone experience the satisfaction of cooperating, but the events could double or triple in size.

ENTER THE RACE

Here's another idea: turn your democracy group into a "campaign team." Find a candidate standing for your own value passions and commit to victory. Knock on doors, gather petition signatures, make phone calls, and help out however you can. As part of a team, you'll feel more accountable to fulfill your commitments and you'll have support as challenges arise.

Once you've gained some serious skills, you could start a new initiative. So many democracy reforms, from Clean Elections to Ranked Choice Voting, started with one or two regular citizens who decided to step up. Or connect your team with leading organizations such as Represent.Us or Common Cause. Volunteers in their chapters across America have achieved wonders, as we've recounted.

And if you don't find any good, pro-democracy candidates to support, run yourself! Politics can't work if it's just a game for insiders. If you hesitate, thinking, "Well, I don't fit the mold of a typical politician," think again. While in high school, eighteen-year-old Dan Torres was elected to the school board in New Paltz, New York. Dan was inspired to run, he told us, because his school board seemed to lack a "diversity of ideas." While taking the leap was scary, Dan said, after three years on the board, he'd built a solid enough reputation to win a seat on the town council. "I was tired of posting on Facebook about stuff I didn't like seeing in my town," he recalls. "So, I figured out how many Democratic voters there were, and I met with every one of them."

Comments about his age used to bother Dan, but, he said, "After a while you just roll with it." The work is not "glorious," he acknowledged, "and if you are younger you have to be extra prepared and work that much harder." But behind Dan's caveats is the smile of someone who took a chance and is reaping the rewards.

CREATING THE STORY OF REAL DEMOCRACY—IT'S *OUR* STORY

Certainly, the Anti-Democracy Movement has been strikingly effective in spreading a simple story line that goes like this: "Government is our enemy. It takes our money and wastes it on the undeserving. Our freedom is in the marketplace that sorts out winners and losers." It's a message of fear and blame. In the Democracy Movement, ours is a message of unity and possibility. To counteract anti-democratic messaging, however, we have to boil it down and make it accessible. Here's one attempt: "Stronger together, we're the owners of our democracy, so we can create a government and a market serving us all." Try it out or create a better nutshell version.

Of course, all the actions, here and throughout our book, are together creating a new story of democracy as a thrilling, lived experience, which further enriches our messaging. But how do we get even better at spreading our story? We might start with "watching our words."

In telling the story of democracy, we can consciously reclaim words that anti-democracy forces have twisted. "Freedom" is one with special power in our culture, and it's been actively narrowed to mean opposition to government: freedom from interference. But let's work to reconceive freedom to include the *positive*—freedom as opportunity in education and employment, for example, and in having a real voice in governance.

Plus, many still use the term "free market" to describe the status quo. But since a "free market" is fiction, why not substitute "rigged market" for what is dominant today? Or use the term "one-rule market"? It allows us to explain something important: that the driver of our market is a single rule. Decisions get made by the narrow logic of what will bring the highest return to existing wealth, leading inevitably to ever-greater economic inequality.

Or take the word "regulation." It hasn't always been a near curse word. In the forty years before the 1971 Powell memo, the *New York Times* was twice as likely to use it in a positive context as a negative one. In the following decades, however, the ratio reversed. It began to convey only restraint to progress.[7] Nobody wants that. Oversight and rules, however, are needed to protect our health, safety, and the environment on which all life depends. So, let's drop "regulations" and instead use "protections" or "standards," terms suggesting a positive, life-enhancing purpose.

Ultimately the key to good storytelling is a story that keeps listeners wanting more. As Ginna Green, managing director of ReThink Media's Money in Politics and Fair Courts Collaborative, tells us, there is mounting evidence that positive, solutions-based messaging "energizes and creates responsiveness" among listeners. So in the Democracy Movement storytelling, let's encourage others to "want more" by showing how our movement meets widely felt needs for more power, meaning, and connection.

How do we better tell democracy's story through words, symbols, and pictures?

Social media. Following groups like Democracy Initiative, Represent .Us, and the Brennan Center on Twitter and Facebook is a good way to stay up to date. Every Voice also sends out daily newsletters to alert citizens about the most important democracy news articles, making it easy to share information about democracy reform effortless. Note that ReThink Media, the Democracy Movement's chief online messaging coordinator, is increasingly taking a "movement of movements" approach to communications, now integrating voting rights into its money-in-politics and fair-courts collaborative.

Slogans and bumper stickers. Years ago we created the bumper sticker "Democracy—Live It or Lose It." Imagine our thrill in seeing it on a car two thousand miles from home. A "civil courage" sign from Germany hangs in our office, reminding us of one key to living democracy. Share your favorites and invent new ones.

Visual art. Poster messages and images help bring us all together and to move emotions. People waited in line for hours to grab a Women's March poster, for example.

Personal and surprising YouTube stories. Imagine three-to-five-minute videos, spread widely, of regular people elected to office with public financing. As we see others like us in office, more of us will find the courage to jump in. As we shared earlier, a story we love is that of Mainer Deb Simpson, who went from small-town diner waitress to five-term, stellar legislator. Her video story can be seen on the media section of the Small Planet Institute's website.

A democracy logo? Recognizable images can spread the democracy story, so what about a democracy "brand"? The color pink is used to create breast cancer awareness, and the peace symbol is recognized the world over. So, for democracy, what about the letter "d" in American Sign Language? Point your index finger up and bring your other fingers to rest on your thumb. The effect is a gesture that calls out "One person, one vote!" or "I count!" It worked for us. On the Capitol steps chanting "Whose Democracy? Our Democracy!" during Democracy Spring using this democracy hand sign felt strong and positive. Another plus: "D" for democracy works in dozens of languages. Worn as sticker or badge, a democracy logo sparks conversation. It could help spread democracy awareness on T-shirts, backpacks, and bumper stickers, as well as on thousands of websites.

A LOT GOING FOR US

Despite all the bad news, in this historic struggle we have a whole lot going for us.

For one, we Americans are not fundamentally a "divided" people. Yes, some differences get ugly, but there's plenty of evidence that much of the ugliness is manufactured for political gain, not a reflection of differences so deep that common ground can't be found.

There's tremendous agreement on some really important points—for one, that plutocracy harms us. Though most of us aren't aware of the well-orchestrated, anti-government, pro-big-business agenda we've laid out in part II, many share in feelings of distress, even alarm, about America's increasingly extreme income inequality, which is even greater than among western European countries. You might be surprised to learn that in 2014, people in forty-four countries were asked by the Pew Research Center to rank five dangers that could be considered the "greatest threat to the world." Many put "religious and ethnic hatred" at the top of their lists, but among Americans "inequality" ranked first as a somewhat worse threat.[8] Given Americans' grasp that a tiny elite has undue, unfair, and ultimately harmful power over our government, it's no surprise that raw anger, disgust, and despair helped decide the 2016 election. But that widely shared grasp of the danger of extreme inequality is great news.

As for solutions, there is also much common ground.

Two-thirds of Americans polled believe "money and wealth . . . should be more evenly distributed."[9] As mentioned, almost nine in ten of us agree on the need for fundamental reform or a complete rebuild of America's system for financing elections. That's huge. And even on contentious, specific issues, there's more agreement than we've been led to believe. Fully 69 percent of us want our government to act to fight climate change by limiting greenhouse gas emissions.[10] Almost nine in ten of us want universal background checks for gun purchasers; and more than half want stricter gun-control laws.[11]

What else do we have going for us? Thanks to some of our gutsiest citizens, we can now point to what *is working* to create democracy "of, by, and for the people." The straightforward reforms that we've highlighted are addressing real problems: recall, for example, the citizens of Maine, whose push for Clean Elections revolutionized the financing of elections. Behind all we've covered in this book are citizens who are awakening to their capacities as active shapers of our common destiny, as "owners" of our democracy. Perhaps for the first time a citizens' movement for democracy is arising that is a true movement of movements across all issues. What is thrilling for us is the possibility of a movement facilitating real "living democracy," one that gives every American a real voice, progressively enabling us to satisfy deep, personal needs and, in the process, to address our shared and unprecedented social and environmental crises.

DARING TO IMAGINE

Among the many positive contributions this movement makes to our evolving culture is "political imagination," our capacity to imagine our future with new eyes, informed but not strictly constrained by present realities. It means tapping the hidden visionary in each of us.

Oddly, to grasp the importance of political imagination, it's useful to recall the 1971 Powell memo. In it, Justice Powell expressed a very constricted view. He seemed to believe that society has just two choices, writing: "[T]he only alternatives to free enterprise are varying degrees of bureaucratic regulation of individual freedom—ranging from that under moderate socialism to the iron heel of the leftist or rightist dictatorship." In other words, either we accept unfettered "freedom" of the economically powerful to make decisions *or* we move to a dictatorship. What a failure of imagination!

Fortunately, since 1971 many Americans have come to appreciate that we do not have to settle for either. Democratic governance makes possible a democratic economy: a market economy that is accountable and gives workers (through unions, workers' alliances, and worker-owned businesses) and consumers and citizens (via agencies empowered to create protective standards) a real voice.

So to imagine and to achieve a different tomorrow, we now must dare.

And that means taking risks—doing what we've never done before. But, we argue strongly, the much greater risk is failing to risk. If we dare, we might fail or be disappointed. True. But if we do nothing, we could face something so much worse: regret and shame that we did not try—and, of course, even more dire, real-world results.

Note that to risk we need not be optimists. That would be asking a lot in this moment. All we need is a sense of possibility, and surely, the stories in this book—from North Carolina to South Dakota to Maine—make that easy. The magnitude and urgency of our democracy crisis, far from paralyzing Americans, are prompting action everywhere.

For some time, our organization's informal motto has been "It's not possible to know what's possible." By this we mean that because we can't be certain of outcomes, nor even know much about our odds of success, we don't have to base our choice of actions on the likelihood of their fulfillment. In fact, that would be pretty unwise. For before they happened, what odds would anyone have given to . . .

. . . a president from Texas with prior antagonism toward civil rights, Lyndon B. Johnson, passing the historic 1965 Voting Rights Act?

. . . and fifty years later, a Jewish socialist from a tiny state getting 43 percent of the votes in the 2016 Democratic Party primaries? Especially since the party didn't want him there at all!

... citizens of South Dakota, where Republicans have won 80 percent of state-wide elections in its history, passing public financing of elections in 2016? (And the fact that self-interested legislators resorted to emergency measures to block it should only embolden us.)

... a retired attorney in Hawaii one night in late 2016 asking her Facebook friends what they thought about a march opposing Donald Trump the day after his inauguration, then waking up to find that ten thousand people had enthusiastically responded? (Not to mention her idea turning into a multimillion-person global protest!)

... or citizens' actions blocking (at least temporarily) the repeal of the Affordable Care Act in early 2017, despite majorities of both chambers of Congress and the president being dead set on destroying it?

Our point is that a little humility is in order. Until we try with all we've got—which is a lot, as our book catalogs and celebrates—we will never know what is possible. That's the spirit our country, our planet, and all those we love need in us now. That, we can muster. It is not superhuman. It is the essence of humanity.

In our opening chapter, we argue that humans thrive best when the communities we create enable each of us, not just a privileged few, to experience a sense of power (that is, agency or simply knowing that our voices count), a sense that our lives have meaning beyond our own survival, and that we have satisfying connection with others. Add those together and what do you have? The essence of democracy. So as we choose to act in this do-or-die moment, we can trust that our deepest needs as human beings are met in the very journey for democracy itself.

And every journey begins with a first step. So here's an idea. Remember our earlier case for the power of pledging to ensure action? Try it. Grab a notebook, write down one act, just one, that you pledge to take for democracy. Include a date by which you'll do it. Then share what you've pledged with one person close to you.

Now to our final thought for your journey. Every day seems to bring yet more worrisome, frightening news, putting millions on the edge of despair. At the same time, we've come to see that despair itself is ultimately our only enemy, and we've become ever-more clear that there's an effective antidote: meaningful action we take together.

But we realize that to take action—and more, to join with others you do not know—requires courage. So in this moment of extreme threat, we may come to see that the opposite of evil is no longer goodness. It is courage. Goodness without action isn't good enough.

That, dear readers, is the message we hope you will take from our book. It is what we have learned.

ACKNOWLEDGMENTS
|||||||||||||||||||||||||||||||||||||

THIS BOOK WOULD not have been possible without the superb schol-arship of many. The books and articles that influenced our writing are too numerous to name, but several deserve special mention. We humbly acknowledge our debt to Jane Mayer's *Dark Money*, Zachary Roth's *The Great Suppression*, David Daley's *Ratf**ked*, Ari Berman's *Give Us the Ballot*, Lee Drutman's *The Business of America Is Lobbying*, Michelle Alexander's *The New Jim Crow*, Theda Skocpol and Alexan-der Hertel-Fernandez's "The Koch Effect," and Jacob S. Hacker and Paul Pierson's *American Amnesia*.

We also want to express our deep appreciation to those who re-viewed our work, offering corrections and suggestions big and small: Craig Aaron, Jonathan Albright, Stephen Arellano, John Berg, Allie Boldt, Jonathan Brater, Ed Cook, David Daley, Lee Drutman, Nikki Fisher, Laura Friedenbach, Brendan Glavin, Ginna Green, Bob Hall, Kathy Kiely, Tim Koechlin, Melissa Kromm, Timothy Kuhner, Adam Lioz, Joan and Jay Mandle, Lawrence Norden, Nick Nyhart, Jodeen Olguin-Tayler, Miles Rapoport, John Rauh, and Zachary Roth. Of course, we assume full responsibility for remaining over-sights and errors.

We are also indebted to those who spoke with us and helped us to formulate our thinking on the many democracy reforms we address: Kyle Bailey, Andrew Bossie, Mike Brune, David Donnelly, Wendy Fields, Margaret Flowers, Susan Lerner, Curt Reis, Rosemary Rivera, Douglas Rushkoff, Pam Wilmot, Clinton Wright, and Kevin Zeese.

Our fond appreciation goes to the Democracy Spring team that welcomed Adam to live in the movement house and join the team and invited Frances to speak. We can unequivocally say that without their bold initiative, this book would not exist.

We are deeply grateful as well to the remarkable Small Planet Institute team. Our profound appreciation goes to Ashley Higgs Hammell, the managing director, whose thoughtfulness, intelligence, and willingness to play every role—from editor to sounding board to fact-checker—allowed us to keep our sanity. We were also fortunate to be joined by unparalleled researchers, Laura Brisbane and Zach "Mitch" Zeliff, both of whom, with their collective humor and brainpower, made our book a million times better than it would have been without them. So too are we grateful for the other members of the SPI team who made this book possible: Marisa Anderson, Jana Brown, Elizabeth DePentu, Ellen Donahue, Courtney Kramer, Pariza Lovos, Rebecca Lucas, Sam Newmark, Michael Nichols, Julie O'Neil, Tim A. Wise, and Dongjin Xu.

We would also like to recognize our colleagues at Beacon Press, who, on short notice, understood the importance of the story we wanted to tell and moved swiftly to publish it. Our special appreciation goes to Beacon Press director Helene Atwan, who responded wholeheartedly from our first call, and Will Myers, our editor, whose kindness, enthusiasm, and editing prowess helped make our book better than we could have anticipated. And thanks also to our meticulous managing editor, Susan Lumenello.

Adam would like to thank his mentors, who laid the foundation for this book: Andrew Bush, Andrew Davison, Katherine Hite, Timothy Koechlin, Joan and Jay Mandle, Himadeep Muppidi, and Sidney Plotkin. He also extends heartfelt appreciation to Peter James Callahan, Justin Smith, and Elise Whitaker for making Democracy Spring one of the best experiences of his life, and to Jake Adelgren, Sam Beckenhauer, Toni Benke, Max Bienstock, Carter Davis, Dayle Davison, Gabriel Dunsmith, Sophie Gonsalves-Brown, Casey Hancock, Casey Khan, Nazir Khan, Shafqat Khan, Erika Nakagaw, Erik Peale, Shannon, Peale, Tyler Peale, Zach Peale, Joe Regan, Jared Stern, Jessica Sullivan, and Harry Zieve-Cohen for their never-ending support of me and this project. And it is with the utmost love and gratitude that he recognizes his parents, George and

Kathy Eichen, for without them he would have neither the moral compass nor the courage to fight back.

Frances wishes to thank her family: Richard Rowe, for the daily dialogue greatly enriching this work as well as his countless, selfless acts of support enabling us to meet our short deadline; and her children, Anthony and Anna Lappé and their beloved spouses, Clarice Lappé and John Marshall, for their encouragement at every step. And to express gratitude to dear friends Lama Tsomo, Janet Surrey, Steve Bergman, Hathaway Barry, Susan Bumagin, Paul Korn, Anne Tate, Bob Massie, Mollie Katzen, Susan Kanaan, and Heather Booth for their encouragement, feedback, and belief in this project.

NOTES

PART I: RETHINKING THE CRISIS

Aldous Huxley, *The Perennial Philosophy* (New York: Perennial Library, 1970), 44.

CHAPTER 1: WHAT IT WILL TAKE

1. Dee Hock, *Birth of the Chaordic Age* (San Francisco: Berrett-Koehler, 1999), 3.
2. Benjamin I. Page, Larry M. Bartels, and Jason Seawright, "Democracy and the Policy Preferences of Wealthy Americans," *Perspectives on Politics* 11, no. 1 (March 2013), 51–73.
3. Bernadette D. Proctor, Jessica L. Semega, and Melissa A. Kollar, "Income and Poverty in the United States: 2015," US Census Bureau, P60–256 (RV), September 2016, 44, table B-1.
4. R. J. Rummel, *Power Kills: Democracy as a Method of Nonviolence* (London: Routledge, 2002).
5. World Health Organization, *WHO Report on the Global Tobacco Epidemic, 2008* (Geneva: World Health Organization, 2008).
6. Philip Zimbardo, *The Lucifer Effect: Understanding How Good People Turn Evil* (New York: Random House, 2007).
7. Kate E. Pickett and Richard G. Wilkinson, *The Spirit Level: Why More Equal Societies Almost Always Do Better* (London: Penguin Group, 2009), pt. 2.
8. Eric Dash, "What's Really Wrong with Wall Street Pay," *New York Times*, September 18, 2009.
9. J. Kiley Hamlin et al., "Not Like Me = Bad: Infants Prefer Those Who Harm Dissimilar Others," *Psychological Science* 5 (2013): 589–94, doi: 10.1177/0956797612457785.
10. Scott E. Page, *The Difference: How the Power of Diversity Creates Better Groups, Firms, Schools, and Societies* (Princeton, NJ: Princeton Univeristy Press, 2007).
11. William H. Hastie, quoted in *The Great Quotations*, George Seldes, ed. (New York: Pocketbooks, 1967), 265.
12. Allan Luks and Peggy Payne, *The Healing Power of Doing Good: The Health and Spiritual Benefits of Helping Others* (New York: Fawcett Columbine,

1992); Michael Tomasello, *Why We Cooperate* (Cambridge, MA: MIT Press, 2009); Sarah Blaffer Hrdy, *Mothers and Others: The Evolutionary Origins of Mutual Understanding* (Cambridge, MA: Belknap Press, 2009).

13. V. S. Ramachandran, *The Tell-Tale Brain: A Neuroscientist's Quest for What Makes Us Human* (New York: W. W. Norton, 2011), 126–27.

14. James K. Rilling et al., "A Neural Basis for Social Cooperation," *Neuron* 35, no. 2 (2002): 395–405, doi: 10.1016/S0896–6273(02)00755–9; Natalie Angier, "Why We're So Nice: Wired to Cooperate," *New York Times*, July 23, 2002.

15. Adam Smith, *The Theory of Moral Sentiments*, ed. D. D. Raphael and A. L. Macfie (1759; Indianapolis: Liberty Classics, 1982), pt. 1, sec. 2, ch. 1, p. 80.

16. Sarah F. Brosnan and Frans B. M. de Waal, "Monkeys Reject Unequal Pay," *Nature* 425 (2003): 297–99, doi: 10.1038/nature01963.

17. Robert Reich, *Supercapitalism: The Transformation of Business, Democracy, and Everyday Life* (New York: Vintage Books, 2008), 36–39.

18. George Lakey, *Viking Economics: How the Scandinavians Got It Right—and How We Can, Too* (New York: Melville House, 2016), 248.

19. Drew DeSilver, "U.S. Trails Most Developed Countries in Voter Turnout," Pew Research Center, May 15, 2017, http://www.pewresearch.org/fact-tank /2017/05/15/u-s-voter-turnout-trails-most-developed-countries/.

20. World Intellectual Property Organization, "Global Innovation Index 2016: Switzerland, Sweden, UK, U.S., Finland, Singapore Lead; China Joins Top 25," news release, August 15, 2016.

21. "Campaign Finance: Germany," Library of Congress, Law Library, www.loc .gov, accessed May 4, 2017; "Income Inequality," OECD Data, Organization for Economic Cooperation and Development, accessed May 4, 2017.

22. *New York Times*–CBS News Poll, "Americans' Views on Money in Politics," *New York Times*, June 2, 2015.

23. Voice of the People/Program for Public Consultation, *A Not So Divided America: Is the Public as Polarized as Congress, or Are Red and Blue Districts Pretty Much the Same?* (Washington, DC: Voice of the People, 2014), 6.

24. Coral Davenport and Marjorie Connelly, "Most Republicans Say They Back Climate Action, Poll Finds," *New York Times*, January 30, 2015.

CHAPTER 2: BRINGING DOWN THE THOUGHT BARRIERS

1. Nicholas Kristof, "Canada, Leading the Free World," *New York Times*, February 5, 2017.

2. Christopher Chabris and Daniel Simons, *The Invisible Gorilla: And Other Ways Our Intuitions Deceive Us* (New York: Crown, 2010), 6.

3. "Child Poverty," National Center for Children in Poverty, accessed May 8, 2017.

4. US Department of Health and Human Services, Centers for Disease Control and Prevention, "International Comparisons of Infant Mortality and Related Factors: United States and Europe, 2010," National Vital Statistics Reports 63, no. 5, September 24, 2014, 1.

5. Pippa Norris, "U.S. Elections Rank Last Among All Western Democracies," Electoral Integrity Project, January 7, 2017.

6. Milton Friedman, *Capitalism and Freedom* (Chicago: University of Chicago Press, 1982), 20–21.

7. Smith, *The Theory of Moral Sentiments.*

8. *Income Inequality Update: Income Inequality Remains High in the Face of Weak Recovery* (Paris: OECD, 2016), 6.

9. Emmanuel Saez, "Striking It Richer: The Evolution of Top Incomes in the United States (Updated with 2013 Preliminary Estimates)," University of California, Berkeley, January 25, 2015, 4.

10. Barry P. Bosworth, Gary Burtless, and Kan Zhang, "What Growing Life Expectancy Gaps Mean for the Promise of Social Security," Brookings Institution, February 12, 2016, https://www.brookings.edu/research/what-growing -life-expectancy-gaps-mean-for-the-promise-of-social-security/.

11. Paul R. Epstein et al., "Full Cost Accounting for the Life Cycle of Coal," *Ecological Economics Reviews, Annals of the New York Academy of Sciences* 1219 (2011): 73–98, doi: 10.1111/j.1749–6632.2010.05890.x.

12. Emily S. Cassidy et al., "Redefining Agricultural Yields: From Tonnes to People Nourished per Hectare," *Environmental Research Letters* 8, no. 3 (2013): 3, doi: 1088/1748–9326/8/3/034015.

13. Ezra Klein, "Romney's Theory of the 'Taker Class,' and Why It Matters," *Washington Post*, September 17, 2012.

14. Jacob S. Hacker and Paul Pierson, *American Amnesia: How the War on Government Led Us to Forget What Made America Prosper* (New York: Simon and Schuster, 2016), 65–66.

15. Environmental Protection Agency, Clean Air Act Overview, Benefits and Costs of the Clean Air Act 1990–2020, the Second Prospective Study, April 2011.

16. Hacker and Pierson, *American Amnesia*, 84; Centers for Disease Prevention and Control, National Center for Health Statistics, "All Homicides," 15, 809.

17. Hacker and Pierson, *American Amnesia*, 139; Harold Glickman, "Americans Think Their Income-Tax Share Is Fair, According to Polls," *Christian Science Monitor*, April 19, 2017.

18. Calculated from the World Bank, GDP Per Capita Growth (Annual %): Finland, Sweden, Norway, Denmark, and United States; Years: 1961–2015.

19. John Helliwell, Richard Layard, and Jeffrey Sachs, eds., *World Happiness Report 2016, Update*, vol. I (New York: Sustainable Development Solutions Network, 2016), 18–23; "The Nordic Countries: The Next Supermodel," *Economist*, February 2, 2013.

20. Thomas Hobbes, *Leviathan* (1651; London: Penguin House Classics, 1982), 77.

21. Adam Grant, "Does Studying Economics Breed Greed?," *Psychology Today*, October 22, 2013.

22. Calculated from GSS Data Explorer, "Can People Be Trusted, Years: 1975–2014."

23. Melissa Healy, "Sugary Drinks Linked to 25,000 Deaths in the U.S. Each Year," *Los Angeles Times*, June 29, 2015; Elizabeth Bast, *Empty Promises: G20*

Subsidies to Oil, Gas and Coal Production (London: Overseas Development Institute and Oil Change International, 2015), 12.

24. Eva Sierminska, Andrea Brandolini, and Timothy M. Smeeding, "Comparing Wealth Distribution Across Rich Countries: First Results from the Luxembourg Wealth Study," Luxembourg Wealth Study Working Paper Series, August 9, 2006, 32; Kathrin Brandmeir et al., *Global Wealth Report 2015* (Munich: Allianz SE, 2015), 15; Lakey, *Viking Economics*.

25. Lakey, *Viking Economics*, pt. II.

26. Hrdy, *Mothers and Others*, ch. 1; Tomasello, *Why We Cooperate*; Rilling et al., "A Neural Basis for Social Cooperation."

27. James Randerson, "The Path to Happiness: It Is Better to Give Than Receive," *Guardian*, March 20, 2008; "New Equation Reveals How Other People's Fortunes Affect Our Happiness," EurekaAlert!, June 14, 2016.

28. Roberto Foa and Yascha Mounk, "Across the Globe, a Growing Disillusionment with Democracy," *New York Times*, September 15, 2015.

29. Ibid.

30. Norman Doidge, *The Brain That Changes Itself: Stories of Personal Triumph from the Frontiers of Brain Science* (New York: Viking Press, 2007).

31. Srinivasan S. Pillay, MD, *Life Unlocked: 7 Revolutionary Lessons to Overcome Fear* (New York: Rodale, 2010), 51.

PART II: EXPOSING THE ROOTS

"Remarks of President Barack Obama," Weekly Address, August 21, 2010, https:// obamawhitehouse.archives.gov.

CHAPTER 3: MANIPULATING THE MINDSET

1. Gerald Mayer, "Union Membership Trends in the United States," Cornell University ILR School, August 31, 2004, appendix A, 22.

2. Lewis F. Powell Jr., "Confidential Memorandum: Attack on American Free Enterprise System," August 23, 1971, 9, 24, 34, http://law2.wlu.edu/deptimages /Powell%20Archives/PowellMemorandumTypescript.pdf.

3. Earl Johnson, *To Establish Justice for All: The Past and Future of Civil Legal Aid in the United States*, vol. 1 (Santa Barbara, CA: Praeger, 2013), 73–75.

4. Joan Biskupic and Fred Barbash, "Retired Justice Lewis Powell Dies at 90," *Washington Post*, August 26, 1998.

5. Sandra Day O'Connor, *The Majesty of the Law: Reflections of a Supreme Court Justice* (New York: Random House, 2004), 150.

6. Powell, "Confidential Memorandum."

7. Reich, *Supercapitalism*, 39.

8. Robert Brenner, *The Economics of Global Turbulence: The Advanced Capitalist Economies from Long Boom to Long Downturn, 1945–2005* (London: Verso, 2006), 99–101, 312, fig. 15.8; Doug Henwood, *After the New Economy* (New York: New Press, 2003).

9. Powell, "Confidential Memorandum," 4.

10. L. A. Kauffman, *Direct Action: Protest and the Reinvention of American Radicalism* (London: Verso, 2017), 1–3.
11. Powell, "Confidential Memorandum," 6.
12. Gallup, "Majority of Americans Dissatisfied with Corporate Influence," January 20, 2016.
13. "Private vs. Government Utilities," *New York Times*, Business Day, March 13, 2013.
14. John Restakis, *Humanizing the Economy: Co-operatives in the Age of Capital* (Gabriola, BC: New Society Publishers, 2010), ch. 3.
15. Powell, "Confidential Memorandum," 11.
16. Ari Berman, *Give Us the Ballot: Modern Voting Rights in America* (New York: Picador, 2015), 75.
17. Arlie Hochschild, *Strangers in Their Own Land: Anger and Mourning on the American Right* (New York: New Press, 2016).
18. David Vogel, *Fluctuating Fortunes: The Political Power of Business in America* (Washington, DC: Beard Books, 2003), 199. We also developed our own figure based on Vogel's work.
19. Sheryl Gay Stolberg, "Pugnacious Builder of the Business Lobby," *New York Times*, June 1, 2013.
20. OpenSecrets.org, Center for Responsive Politics, "Lobbying: Top Spenders," accessed April 26, 2017.
21. James Toedtman, "Full-Court Press for Business," *Newsday*, January 4, 1998.
22. Stolberg, "Pugnacious Builder of the Business Lobby."
23. OpenSecrets.org, Center for Responsive Politics, "US Chamber of Commerce: Outside Spending Summary 2016," accessed April 26, 2017.
24. David Brodwin, "The Chamber's Secrets," *US News & World Report*, October 22, 2015.
25. Jim Tankersley, "U.S. Chamber of Commerce Seeks Trial on Global Warming," *Los Angeles Times*, August 25, 2009.
26. *Poll Report: Small Business Owners' Views on Climate & Energy Policy Reform* (Washington, DC: American Sustainable Business Council, June 2014), 3.
27. Jane Mayer, *Dark Money: The Hidden History of the Billionaires Behind the Rise of the Radical Right* (New York: Doubleday, 2016), 4.
28. Ibid., 96.
29. Ibid., 97.
30. Ibid., 94.
31. Ibid., 105; Lizzy Ratner, "Olin Foundation, Right-Wing Tank, Snuffing Itself," *New York Observer*, May 9, 2005. Michel J. Crozier, Samuel P. Huntington, and Joji Watanuki, *The Crisis of Democracy*, Report on the Governability of Democracies to the Trilateral Commission (New York: New York University Press, 1975).
32. Ratner, "Olin Foundation"; Ian Milliser, "The Little-Noticed Conservative Plan to Permanently Lock Democrats Out Of Policymaking," *ThinkProgress*, November 16, 2015.

33. Jon Campbell, "Trump's Education Secretary Nominee Is the Godmother of *Citizens United*," *Village Voice,* January 15, 2017; Mayer, *Dark Money*, 234–37.

34. Zach Stanton, "How Betsy DeVos Used God and Amway to Take Over Michigan Politics," *Politico Magazine*, January 15, 2017.

35. Mayer, *Dark Money*, 87.

36. Ibid., 27–31.

37. Ibid., 53–54.

38. Jacob S. Hacker and Paul Pierson, *American Amnesia: How the War on Government Led us to Forget What Made America Prosper* (New York: Simon & Schuster, 2016), 230.

39. Mayer, *Dark Money*, 43–44.

40. Ibid., 4.

41. Jane Mayer, "The Reclusive Hedge-Fund Tycoon Behind the Trump Presidency: How Robert Mercer Exploited America's Populist Insurgency," *New Yorker*, March 27, 2017.

42. Matea Gold, "The Mercers and Stephen Bannon: How a Populist Power Base Was Funded and Built," *Washington Post*, March 17, 2017.

43. Kenneth P. Vogel, "The Heiress Quietly Shaping Trump's Operation," *Politico Magazine*, November 21, 2016.

44. Gold, "The Mercers and Stephen Bannon."

45. Mayer, "The Reclusive Hedge-Fund Tycoon."

46. Theda Skocpol and Alexander Hertel-Fernandez, "The Koch Effect: The Impact of a Cadre-Led Network on American Politics," Scholars Strategy Network, January 4, 2016, 56, https://www.scholarsstrategynetwork.org/sites/default/files/the_koch_effect_for_spsa_w_apps_skocpol_and_hertel-fernandez-corrected_1-4-16_1.pdf.

47. David Brock, *The Republican Noise Machine: Right-Wing Media and How It Corrupts Democracy* (New York: Crown, 2004), 43; Jacob S. Hacker and Paul Pierson, *Winner-Take-All Politics: How Washington Made the Rich Richer—and Turned Its Back on the Middle Class* (New York: Simon & Schuster, 2010), 123.

48. Mayer, *Dark Money*, 82–83.

49. Ibid., 77.

50. Ibid., 77–78.

51. Ibid., 77.

52. Ibid., 88.

53. David Brock, *Blinded by the Right: The Conscience of an Ex-Conservative* (New York: Three Rivers, 2002), 77.

54. Hacker and Pierson, *Winner-Take-All Politics*, 123.

55. Mayer, *Dark Money*, 90.

56. Hacker and Pierson, *Winner-Take-All*, 123.

57. Ibid., 209.

58. Mayer, *Dark Money*, 87.

59. Ibid., 88.

60. Ibid., 142.

61. Ibid.

62. Michael Dolny, "Right, Center Think Tanks Still Most Quoted," *Extra!*, June 1, 2005.

63. David Levinthal, "Koch Brothers' Higher-Ed Investments Advance Political Goals," Center for Public Integrity, October 30, 2015.

64. Ibid.

65. Ibid.

66. Friedrich August von Hayek, *The Road to Serfdom* (Abingdon, UK: Routledge, 1944), 158.

67. The Bridge, Harvard University, "Legal Theory Law and Economics: Criticisms of Economic Analysis—and Responses Thereto," accessed May 5, 2017.

68. Mayer, *Dark Money*, 107.

69. Jacob S. Hacker and Paul Pierson, *American Amnesia: How the War on Government Led Us to Forget What Made America Prosper* (New York: Simon & Schuster, 2016), 167–69.

70. David Randall, "Making Citizens: How American Universities Teach Civics," National Association of Scholars, January 2017; Sarah Scaife Foundation, *Annual Report*, 2013, 2014, 2015.

71. Pam Vogel, "The Conservative Dark-Money Groups Infiltrating Campus Politics," *Media Matters*, March 29, 2017.

72. Red Lion Broadcasting Co. v. Federal Communications Commission, 395 U.S. 367 (1969).

73. Robert F. Kennedy Jr., *Crimes Against Nature: Standing Up to Bush and the Kyoto Killers Who Are Cashing In on Our World* (New York: Harper Perennial, 2004), 176.

74. Stephen James Schultze, "The Business of Broadband and the Public Interest: Media Policy for the Network Society," master's thesis, Massachusetts Institute of Technology, September 2008.

75. "Cable Communications Act of 1984," Public Law 98-549, October 30, 1984, 98.

76. John Stat. 2780, Amendment of Communications Act of 1934.

77. Peter J. Boyer, "Syracuse Group Appeals Fairness Doctrine Ruling," *New York Times*, August 11, 1987.

78. *The Fallout from the Telecommunications Act of 1996: Unintended Consequences and Lessons Learned* (Washington, DC: Common Cause, 2005), 5.

79. H. R. Mahood and Ramona M. Mahood, "Think Tanks and Public Policy: The Politics of Expertise," National Social Science Association, February 28, 2007, http://www.nssa.us/journals/2007-28-2/2007-28-2-15.htm.

80. Robert W. McChesney, *The Problem of the Media: U.S. Communication Politics in the 21st Century* (New York: Monthly Review Press, 2004), 213.

81. Transcript of proceedings before the Federal Communications Commission, December 12, 1995.

82. Laura Miller, "Sound Bites Get Shorter," *PRWatch*, Center for Media and Democracy, November 11, 2000.

83. Eric Boehlert, "Study Confirms Network Evening Newscasts Have Abandoned Policy Coverage for 2016 Campaign," *Media Matters*, October 26, 2016.
84. Ibid.
85. Nicholas Confessore and Karen Yourish, "$2 Billion Worth of Free Media for Donald Trump," *New York Times*, March 15, 2016.
86. John Nichols and Robert W. McChesney, *Dollarocracy* (New York: Nation Books, 2013), 133.
87. Michael Barthel, "Newspapers: Fact Sheet," Pew Research Center, June 15, 2016.
88. Cass Sunstein, *Republic.com 2.0* (Princeton, NJ: Princeton University Press, 2009), 143.
89. Mostafa M. El-Bermawy, "Your Filter Bubble Is Destroying Democracy," *Wired*, November 18, 2016.
90. Kenneth Vogel and Mackenzie Weinger, "The Tea Party Radio Network," *Politico*, April 20th, 2014
91. Ibid.; Will Bunch, *The Backlash: Right-Wing Radicals, High-Def Hucksters, and Paranoid Politics in the Age of Obama* (New York: HarperCollins, 2011).
92. Craig Silverman, "This Analysis Shows How Viral Fake Election News Stories Outperformed Real News On Facebook," *BuzzFeed News*, November 16, 2016.
93. Ibid.
94. Carole Cadwalladr, "Robert Mercer: The Big Data Billionaire Waging War on Mainstream Media," *Guardian*, February 26, 2017.
95. Max Kutner, "Meet Robert Mercer, the Mysterious Billionaire Benefactor of Breitbart," *Newsweek*, November 21, 2016.
96. Richard Pérez-Peña, "Contrary to Trump's Claims, Immigrants Are Less Likely to Commit Crimes," *New York Times*, January 26, 2017.
97. Cadwalladr, "Robert Mercer"; Zachary Mider, "'Clinton Cash' Book Got Most of Its Funding from One Hedge Fund Star," *Bloomberg Businessweek*, January 18, 2017.
98. Matthew Mosk and Brian Ross, "Bill Clinton Cashed In When Hillary Became Secretary of State," *ABC News*, April 23, 2015.
99. Cadwalladr, "Robert Mercer."
100. Carole Cadwalladr, "Google, Democracy and the Truth About Internet Search," *Guardian*, December 4, 2016; Nicholas Confessore and Danny Hakim, "Data Firm Says 'Secret Sauce' Aided Trump; Many Scoff," *New York Times*, March 6, 2017.
101. Kendall Taggart, "The Truth About the Trump Data Team That People Are Freaking Out About," *Buzzfeed News*, February 16, 2017; Cadwalladr, "Google, Democracy and the Truth About Internet Search"; Confessore and Hakim, "Data Firm Says 'Secret Sauce' Aided Trump; Many Scoff."
102. Cadwalladr, "Robert Mercer."
103. Tim Berners-Lee, "Three Challenges for the Web, According to Its Inventor," World Wide Web Foundation, March 12, 2017, http://webfoundation.org/2017/03/web-turns-28-letter/.

104. Jacob S. Hacker and Paul Pierson, *American Amnesia: How the War on Government Led Us to Forget What Made America Prosper* (New York: Simon & Schuster, 2016), 164.
105. Thomas E. Mann and Norman J. Ornstein, *It's Even Worse Than It Looks: How the American Constitutional System Collided with the New Politics of Extremism* (New York: Basic Books, 2016), 42–43.
106. Sheryl Gay Stolberg, "Gingrich Stuck to Caustic Path in Ethics Battles," *New York Times*, January 26, 2012.
107. Brock, *The Republican Noise Machine*, 103.
108. Zachary Roth, *The Great Suppression: Voting Rights, Corporate Cash, and the Conservative Assault on Democracy* (New York: Crown, 2016), 110.
109. Mike Lofgren, "Goodbye to All That: Reflections of a GOP Operative Who Left the Cult," *Truthout*, September 3, 2011.
110. Roth, *The Great Suppression*, 91, 110.
111. Kirsten Appleton and Veronica Stracqualursi, "Here's What Happened the Last Time the Government Shut Down," *ABC News*, November 18, 2014.
112. Steven Perlberg, "S&P: The Shutdown Took $24 Billion Out of the US Economy," *Business Insider*, October 16, 2013.
113. Tal Kopan, "Polls: Shutdown Nightmare for GOP," *Politico*, October 22, 2013.
114. Dan Balz and Scott Clement, "Poll: Major Damage to GOP After Shutdown, and Broad Dissatisfaction with Government," *Politico*, October 22, 2013.
115. Lofgren, "Goodbye to All That."
116. Burgess Everett and Glenn Thrush, "McConnell Throws Down the Gauntlet: No Scalia Replacement Under Obama," *Politico*, February 13, 2016.
117. Benton Strong, "New Poll Shows Americans Overwhelmingly Support a Hearing and Vote on Merrick Garland's Nomination," press release, Center for American Progress, May 9, 2016.
118. "No Improvement in Congress Approval," Gallup, March 9, 2016.
119. Skocpol and Hertel-Fernandez, "The Koch Effect," 15.
120. Ibid., 12.
121. Ibid., 8.
122. Ibid., 8.
123. Kenneth P. Vogel, "How the Koch Network Rivals the GOP," *Politico*, December 30, 2015.
124. Skocpol and Hertel-Fernandez, "The Koch Effect," 31–32.
125. Ibid., 31.
126. Ibid., 28, 36.
127. Mayer, *Dark Money*, 182.
128. Ibid., 183.
129. Skocpol and Hertel-Fernandez, "The Koch Effect," 25–26.
130. Ibid., 8.
131. Ibid., 8–9.

132. Ibid., 34.
133. Ibid., 44.
134. Ibid., 21.
135. Alexander Hertel-Fernandez and Theda Skocpol, "Five Myths About the Koch Brothers—And Why It Matters to Set Them Straight," *Moyers & Company*, PBS, March 10, 2016.
136. Skocpol and Hertel-Fernandez, "The Koch Effect," 23.
137. Ibid.
138. Mayer, *Dark Money*, 1–23.
139. Ibid., 9.
140. Lawrence Mishel, Elise Gould, and Josh Bivens, "Wage Stagnation in Nine Charts," fig. 2, Economic Policy Institute, January 6, 2015.
141. Lawrence Mishel and Alyssa Davis, "Top CEOs Make 300 Times More than Typical Workers," Economic Policy Institute, issue brief 399, June 21, 2015, table 1.
142. Alan J. Auerbach and James M. Poterba, "Why Have Corporate Tax Revenues Declined?," *Tax Policy and the Economy* 1 (1987): 1, http://scholarship.law.berkeley.edu/facpubs/2512.
143. Hacker and Pierson, *American Amnesia*, 197.

CHAPTER 4: RIGGING THE RULES

1. New York Times–CBS News Poll, "Americans' Views on Money in Politics," *New York Times*, June 2, 2015.
2. Niv Sultan, "Election 2016: Trump's Free Media Helped Keep Cost Down, but Fewer Donors Provided More of the Cash," Center for Responsive Politics, April 13, 2017; Laura Olson, "How Much Did Pennsylvania's U.S. Senate Race Cost?," *Morning Call* (Allentown, PA), November 17, 2016.
3. OpenSecrets.org, Center for Responsive Politics, "Election: Cost of Election, View Totals by Party, Adjusted for Inflation," accessed April 26, 2017.
4. Louis Jacobson, "Jimmy Carter Says When He Ran Against Gerald Ford, He Didn't Raise Any Money," *PolitiFact*, February 23, 2013.
5. Allie Boldt, "The Gatekeeper Class," *Demos*, September 2, 2015.
6. Wesley Lowery, "91% of the Time the Better-Financed Candidate Wins. Don't Act Surprised," *Washington Post*, April 4, 2014.
7. Linda Casey, "2013 and 2014: Money and Incumbency in State Legislative Races," FollowTheMoney.org, March 9, 2016.
8. OpenSecrets.org, Center for Responsive Politics, "Donor Demographics: Election Cycle 2016," accessed April 26, 2017.
9. "House Receipts from Individuals, PACs, and Other, All General Election Candidates, 1999–2014," Campaign Finance Institute analysis of FEC records, accessed April 26, 2016, http://www.cfinst.org/pdf/historical/Donors_HouseCand_2000-2014.pdf.
10. Adam Lioz, *Stacked Deck: How the Racial Bias in Our Big Money Political System Undermines Our Democracy and Our Economy* (New York: Demos, 2014), 20.

11. Martin Gilens and Benjamin I. Page, "Testing Theories of American Politics: Elites, Interest Groups, and Average Citizens," *Perspectives on Politics* 12, no. 3 (2014): 575–76, doi: 10.1017/S1537592714001595.

12. Jay Costa, "What's the Cost of a Seat in Congress," *MapLight*, March 10, 2013.

13. Ryan Grim and Sabrina Siddiqui, "Call Time for Congress Shows How Fundraising Dominates Bleak Work Life," *Huffington Post*, January 9, 2013.

14. OpenSecrets.org, Center for Responsive Politics, "Total Outside Spending by Election Cycle, Excluding Party Committees," accessed April 26, 2017; Center for Responsive Politics, "Outside Spending for Disclosure, Excluding Part Committees," OpenSecrets.org, updated April 3, 2017; Liz Kennedy, "Citizens Actually United," Demos, based on CRC poll, October 25, 2012.

15. Mayer, *Dark Money*, 234–37.

16. Ibid., 235.

17. Jon Campbell, "James Bopp Jr. Gets Creative," *Slate*, October 5, 2012.

18. Ibid.

19. Mayer, *Dark Money*, 237.

20. David D. Kirkpatrick, "A Quest to End Spending Rules for Campaigns," *New York Times*, January 24, 2010.

21. Alex Altman, "Meet the Man Who Invented the Super PAC," *Time*, May 13, 2015.

22. Ian Vandewalker, "Silent Scandal of Big Money in Politics," *US News & World Report*, February 22, 2017.

23. Mayer, *Dark Money*, 234–35.

24. Greg Stohr, "Bloomberg Poll: Americans Want Supreme Court to Turn Off Political Spending Spigot," *Bloomberg Politics*, September 28, 2015.

25. OpenSecrets.org, Center for Responsive Politics, "Election Cost: Cost of Election," accessed April 26, 2017.

26. Adam Lioz, Juhem Navarro-Rivera, and Sean McElwee, *Court Cash: 2016 Election Money Resulting Directly From Supreme Court Rulings*, Demos, March 14, 2017, 5.

27. Lisa Graves, "WI Senate Race Tightens with Flood of Last Minute Ads Against Russ Feingold," *PR Watch*, Center for Media and Democracy, November 4, 2016.

28. Ibid.

29. OpenSecrets.org, Center for Responsive Politics, "2016 Outside Spending, by Race," updated April 3, 2017.

30. Ibid.

31. Ibid.; James Nani, "Money Increasing Stakes Between Teachout, Faso," *Times Herald-Record* (Middletown, NY), October 29, 2016.

32. Lee Drutman, *The Business of America Is Lobbying: How Corporations Became Politicized and Politics Became More Corporate* (New York: Oxford University Press, 2015), 51.

33. Ibid., 57–58, 71.

34. Ibid., 71.

35. Ibid., 12, 16.

36. Ibid., 8.

37. Ibid., 13, 14.

38. Ibid., 3.

39. US Government Accountability Office report, *Toxic Substances: EPA Has Increased Efforts to Assess and Control Chemicals but Could Strengthen Its Approach*, GAO-13–249 (Washington, DC, March 2013), 12–13; Rebecca Harrington, "The EPA Has Only Banned These 9 Chemicals—Out of Thousands," *Business Insider*, February 10, 2016; European Chemicals Agency, "Chemicals Added to Annex I Group Entries," downloaded May 5, 2017, from https://echa.europa.eu/regulations/prior-informed-consent /list-chemicals.

40. Drutman, *The Business of America Is Lobbying*, 31.

41. Ibid., 64.

42. Nichols and McChesney, *Dollarocracy*, 79.

43. Jennifer Calfas, "Trump's Cabinet Picks Have More Wealth Than Third of American Households Combined," *Hill*, December 15, 2016.

44. Greg Gordon, "How Hank Paulson's Inaction Helped Goldman Sachs," McClatchy, October 10, 2010.

45. Anthony Faiola, Ellen Nakashima, and Jill Drew, "What Went Wrong," *Washington Post*, October 15, 2008.

46. Stephen Gandel, "Robert Rubin Was Targeted for DOJ Investigation by Financial Crisis Commission," *Fortune*, March 13, 2016.

47. Bill Bishop, *The Big Sort: Why the Clustering of Like-Minded Americans Is Tearing Us Apart* (Boston: Houghton Mifflin, 2008), 223–24.

48. Mayer, *Dark Money*, 90, 346.

49. Ibid., 346.

50. Wang, *Democracy at a Crossroads*, 18.

51. Ibid., 18–19.

52. Mike McIntire, "Conservative Nonprofit Acts as a Stealth Business Lobbyist," *New York Times*, April 21, 2012.

53. Brendan Fischer, "Cashing In on Kids: 172 ALEC Education Bills Push Privatization in 2015," *PR Watch*, Center for Media and Democracy, March 8, 2016.

54. John Nichols, "How ALEC Took Florida's 'License to Kill' Law National," *Nation*, March 22, 2012; Chandler B. McClellan and Erdal Tekin, "Stand Your Ground Laws, Homicides, and Injuries," National Bureau of Economic Research, Working Paper 18187, June 2012, 7.

55. Berman, *Give Us the Ballot*, 261.

56. Miranda Blue, "Seven Times Conservatives Have Admitted They Don't Want People to Vote," *Right Wing Watch*, September 24, 2015.

57. Louis Jacobson, "Donald Trump's Pants on Fire Claim That Millions of Illegal Votes Cost Him Popular Vote Victory," *Politifact*, November 28, 2016.

58. Brennan Center for Justice, New York University Law School, "Debunking the Voter Fraud Myth," January 31, 2017, 3.

59. "Four in Five Americans Support Voter ID Laws, Early Voting," Gallup, August 22, 2016; "2016 Election and Voting Accuracy," Gallup News Service, downloaded data, 2, August 15–16, 2016.
60. Berman, *Give Us the Ballot*, 7–11, 60–63.
61. Wang, *Democracy at a Crossroads*, 15.
62. Brennan Center for Justice, New York University Law School, "Voting Laws Roundup 2017," May 10, 2017.
63. Wendy Underhill, "Voter Identification Requirements," "Voter ID Laws," National Conference of State Legislatures, March 28, 2017.
64. "Citizens Without Proof: A Survey of Americans' Possession of Documentary Proof of Citizenship and Photo Identification," Brennan Center for Justice, New York University Law School, November 2006.
65. Bob Cesca, "Republicans' 'Voter Fraud' False Flag: Voter ID Laws Offer Imaginary Solutions to Imaginary Problems," *Salon*, August, 23, 2016.
66. ACLU, "Oppose Voter ID Legislation—Fact Sheet," American Civil Liberties Union, accessed April 28, 2016.
67. *Providing Identification for Voting in Texas*, PowerPoint presentation (Austin: Texas Secretary of State, September 29, 2016), 6.
68. Zoltan Hajnal, Nazita Lajevardi, and Lindsay Nielson, "Voter Identification Laws and the Suppression of Minority Votes," *Journal of Politics* 79, no. 2 (2017): 368, http://dx.doi.org/10.1086/688343.
69. "When Politicians Tell the Truth on Voting Restrictions," Brennan Center for Justice, New York University Law School, August 10, 2016, https://www.brennancenter.org/analysis/when-politicians-tell-truth-voting-restrictions.
70. Hajnal, Lajevardi, and Nielson, "Voter Identification Laws," 377.
71. David A. Graham, "What's the Goal of Voter-ID Laws?," *Atlantic*, May 2, 2016.
72. Roth, *The Great Suppression*, 41.
73. Nina Totenberg, "Stricter Voter ID and Other Voting Laws Rolled Back in Slew of Court Decisions," *Morning Edition*, National Public Radio, August 5, 2016.
74. Wang, *Democracy at a Crossroads*, 9, 16.
75. Ari Berman, "There Are 868 Fewer Places to Vote in 2016 Because the Supreme Court Gutted the Voting Rights Act," *Nation*, November 4, 2016.
76. Ari Berman, "Texas's Voter-Registration Laws Are Straight Out of the Jim Crow Playbook," *Nation*, October 6, 2016.
77. Merrit Kennedy, "Court Blocks Proof-of-Citizenship Requirement for Voters in 3 States," *The Two-Way*, National Public Radio, September 10, 2016.
78. Ari Berman, "The GOP's Attack on Voting Rights Was the Most Under-Covered Story of 2016," *Nation*, November 9, 2016.
79. Ibid.
80. Ibid.
81. Lauren Etter, Janan Hanna, and Mark Niquette, "Poll Law Depresses North Carolina Black Vote Even After Suit," *Bloomberg*, November 3, 2016.
82. "State Felon Voting Laws," ProCon.org, May 11, 2017.

83. Michelle Alexander, *The New Jim Crow: Mass Incarceration in the Age of Colorblindness* (New York: New Press, 2012), 159.

84. "International Comparison of Felon Voting Laws," ProCon.org, updated May 27, 2014.

85. American Civil Liberties Union of Wisconsin, "Felony Disenfranchisement in Wisconsin," accessed May 1, 2015.

86. Alexander, *The New Jim Crow*, 6.

87. Ibid., 6.

88. Ibid., 60.

89. Ibid., 7.

90. Harry J. Enten, "Felon Voting Rights Have a Bigger Impact on Elections Than Voter ID Laws," *Guardian*, July 31, 2013.

91. Marisa J. Demeo and Steven A. Ochoa, *Diminished Voting Power in the Latino Community: The Impact of Felony Disenfranchisement Laws in Ten Targeted States* (Los Angeles: MALDEF, December 2003), 15.

92. Mike Elk and Bob Sloan, "The Hidden History of ALEC and Prison Labor," *Nation*, August 1, 2011.

93. "Number of People by State Who Cannot Vote Due to a Felony Conviction," Procon.org, updated November 7, 2012.

94. Erika L. Wood, "Florida. How Soon We Forget," *New York Times*, April 5, 2012.

95. "Number of People," Procon.org.

96. US Election Project, "2016 November General Election," https://docs .google.com/spreadsheets/d/1VAcFoeJo6y_8T402gvIL4YcyQy8pxb1zYkg XF76Uu1s/edit#gid=2030096602; "2016 Presidential Election Results," Politico, updated December 13, 2016.

97. Alexander, *The New Jim Crow*, 158.

98. David Daley, *Ratf**cked: The True Story Behind the Secret Plan to Steal America's Democracy* (New York: Liveright Publishing, 2016), 51, 54, 58.

99. Olga Pierce, Justin Elliott, and Theodoric Meyer, "How Dark Money Helped Republicans Hold the House and Hurt Voters," *ProPublica*, December 21, 2012.

100. Daley, *Ratf**cked*, xix, 1.

101. Ibid., 43.

102. Ibid., 23.

103. Ibid., 87.

104. Roth, *The Great Suppression*, 101.

105. Daley, *Ratf**cked*, 86.

106. Tom Perkins, "Once Again, Michigan Dems Receive More Votes in the State House, but Republicans Hold Onto Power," *Detroit Metro Times*, November 16, 2016.

107. Calculated from Karen L. Haas, clerk of the US House of Representatives, "Statistics of the Presidential and Congressional Election of November 6,

2012," February 28, 2013, 73–74, history.house.gov/Institution/Election
-Statistics/2012election/.

108. Campaign Legal Center, *Make Democracy Count: Ending Partisan Gerry-mandering* (Washington, DC: August 10, 2016), 5.

109. Daley, *Ratf**ked*, 44.

110. Ibid., 88.

111. Ibid., 129.

112. Roth, *The Great Suppression*, 99.

113. 113. "Vieth v. Jubelirer," Brennan Center for Justice, New York University Law School, April 28, 2004, https://www.brennancenter.org/legal-work /vieth-v-jubelirer.

114. "Landmark Partisan Gerrymandering Case Whitford v. Gill Heads to U.S. Supreme Court," Campaign Legal Center, February 24, 2017.

115. Peter Wagner, "Breaking the Census: Redistricting in an Era of Mass Incar-ceration," *William Mitchell Law Review* 38, no. 4, art. 9 (2012): 1245, http:// open.mitchellhamline.edu/wmlr/vol38/iss4/9.

116. Erika L. Wood, *Implementing Reform: How Maryland & New York Ended Prison Gerrymandering* (New York: Demos, 2014), 4.

117. Ibid.

118. Peter Wagner, "Momentum Builds to End Prison-Based Gerrymandering," *Prison Legal News*, December 15, 2012.

119. Roth, *The Great Suppression*, 73–78.

120. Arn Pearson, "Flint Is a Casualty in the Right Wing's War on Local Democ-racy," *PRWatch*, Center for Media and Democracy, March 31, 2016; Act No. 4, Public Acts of 2011, State of Michigan, 96th Legislature (passed March 16, 2011).

121. Act No. 4, Public Acts of 2011, State of Michigan, 96th Legislature, Sec. 19(1) (ee) (passed March 16, 2011); American Civil Liberties Union of Michigan, *Unelected & Unaccountable: Emergency Managers and Public Act 4's Threat to Representative Democracy* (Detroit: American Civil Liberties Union of Michigan, 2012), 1.

122. Pearson, "Flint Is a Casualty."

123. Bureau of Local Government and School Services, "Emergency Financial Manager/Emergency Manager Appointment History," Michigan Depart-ment of Treasury, updated March 15, 2017.

124. Jim Lynch, "Late Bid Failed to Avert Flint-Detroit Water Deal," *Detroit News*, February 2, 2016.

125. Siddhartha Roy, "Test Update: Flint River Water 19x More Corrosive Than Detroit Water for Lead Solder; Now What?" Flint Water Study Updates, September 11, 2015; "Flint Water Crisis Fast Facts," CNN, last modified Feb-ruary 22, 2017.

126. Roy, "Test Update"; "Lead Testing Results for Water Sampled by Resi-dents," Flint Water Study Updates, September 2015.

127. Ibid.; Jen Christensen, Sara Sidner, and Mallory Simon, "Flint and Lead Poisoning: Living with It and Uncertainty, Long-term," CNN, March 5, 2016.

128. Christensen, Sidner, and Simon, "Flint and Lead Poisoning."

129. Latha Chandran and Rosa Cataldo, "Lead Poisoning: Basics and New Developments," *Pediatrics in Review* 31 (2010): 401, doi:10.1542/pir.31–10–399.

130. Ron Fonger, "CDC Finds First Genetic Link Between Legionnaires' Outbreak, Flint Water," *Michigan Live*, February 16, 2017.

131. Merrit Kennedy, "Lead-Laced Water in Flint: A Step-by-Step Look at the Makings of a Crisis," NPR, April 20, 2016.

132. Steve Friess, "Former Flint Emergency Managers, Others Charged in Water Crisis," Reuters, December 20, 2016.

133. Roberto Acosta, "Lawsuit Seeks More Than $720M for 1,700 Flint Residents over Water Crisis," *Michigan Live*, January 30, 2017; "Flint Water," CNN.

134. Mark Stelzner, *Economic Inequality and Policy Control in the United States* (New York: Palgrave Macmillan, 2015), ch. 2.

135. National Conference of State Legislatures, Right to Work Resources, accessed May 7, 2017.

136. Neil Gross, "The Decline of Unions and the Rise of Trump," *New York Times*, August 8, 2016.

137. *2017 Infrastructure Report Card: Drinking Water* (Reston, VA: American Society of Civil Engineers, 2017); Erik Olson and Kristi Pullen Fedinick, *What's in Your Water? Flint and Beyond; Analysis of EPA Data Reveals Widespread Lead Crisis Potentially Affecting Millions of Americans* (New York: Natural Resources Defense Council, June 2016), 5.

138. Fabian T. Pfeffer, Sheldon Danziger, and Robert F. Schoeni, "Wealth Disparities Before and After the Great Recession," *ANNALS of the American Academy of Political and Social Science* 650 (2013): 98, doi: 10.1177/0002716213497452.

139. OpenSecrets.org, Center for Responsive Politics, "Finance/Insurance/Real Estate: Summary," accessed May 2, 2017.

140. Wendell Potter and Nick Penniman, *Nation on the Take: How Big Money Corrupts Our Democracy and What We Can Do About It* (New York: Bloomsbury Press, 2016), 120; Ashley Kirzinger, Bryan Wu, and Mollyann Brodie, "Kaiser Health Tracking Poll: September 2016," Henry J. Kaiser Family Foundation, September 29, 2016.

141. Monmouth University Poll, "Public Says Climate Change Is Real," January 5, 2016, 5.

142. Calculated from OpenSecrets.org, Center for Responsive Politics, "Oil & Gas: Long Term Contribution Trends," accessed May 2, 2015.

143. Stan Greenberg et al., "Voters Ready to Act against Big Money in Politics: Lessons from the 2014 Midterm Election," memo to Friends of Democracy Corps and Every Voice, November 10, 2014, 3.

144. Gallup, "Confidence in Institutions," accessed May 2, 2017.

PART III: CREATING SOLUTIONS TOGETHER

Howard Zinn, *Disobedience and Democracy: Nine Fallacies on Law and Order* (Chicago: Haymarket Books, 2013), 25.

CHAPTER 5: DEMOCRACY'S CALLING

1. Truck Safety Coalition, "Twenty Years Later—the Tragic Truck Crash That Led to P.A.T.T.," October 1, 2013.
2. PBS, "*Now* Transcript, Show 242," October 20, 2006.
3. Francis X. Clines, "Bipartisan Voter Rebellion Against Big Money in Maine Is Expected to Succeed," *New York Times*, November 2, 1996.
4. Calculated from Maine State Legislature, Law and Legislative Reference Library, Legislative History Collection, Maine Clean Election Act.
5. Legal and Veterans Affairs Committee, "Maine Clean Election Act Overview of Participation Rates and Payments 2000–2008," Maine.gov, January 14, 2009.
6. Mike Belliveau, "Flame Retardants: Maine Leads on Safer Products," Environmental Health Strategy Center, March 29, 2014; Environmental Working Group, "Fire Retardants in Toddlers and Their Mothers: Gov't. and Industry Actions to Phase Out PBDES," September 4, 2008.
7. Belliveau, "Flame Retardants: Maine"; Safer States, "States in the Lead: Maine," accessed May 4, 2017.
8. Electronics TakeBack Coalition, "States Legislation," accessed May 4, 2017.
9. Arizona Free Enterprise Club's Freedom Club PAC v. Bennett, 564 U.S. 2 (2011).
10. LD 848, Resolve, Directing the Commission on Governmental Ethics and Election Practices to Study Modifying the Maine Clean Election Act, State of Maine, 125th Legislature (passed July 6, 2011).
11. Money in Politics Project, *Report #13, Clean Election Participation Rates and Outcomes: 2014 Legislative Elections* (Portland, ME: Maine Citizens for Clean Elections), 3, accessed May 4, 2017.
12. Money in Politics Project, *Report #14, Clean Election Participation Rates and Outcomes: 2016 Legislative Elections* (Portland, ME: Maine Citizens for Clean Elections), 3, accessed May 4, 2017.
13. *New York Times*–CBS News Poll, "Americans' Views on Money in Politics," *New York Times*, June 2, 2015.
14. Magnus Ohman, *Political Finance Regulations Around the World: An Overview of the International IDEA Database* (Stockholm: International Institute for Democracy and Electoral Assistance, 2012), 10.
15. Larry L. Berg, Harlan Hahn, and John R. Schmidhauser, *Corruption in the American Political System* (Morristown, NJ: General Learning Press, 1976), 25.
16. Marilyn W. Thompson, "The Price of Public Money," *Atlantic*, May 27, 2016.
17. Adam Nagourney and Jeff Zeleny, "Obama Forgoes Public Funds in First for Major Candidate," *New York Times*, June 20, 2008.

18. Committee on House Administration, "Letter to House Administration Committee," Democracy 21, February 6, 2017; "To Reduce Federal Spending and the Deficit by Terminating Taxpayer Financing of Presidential Election Campaigns," H.R. 133, 115th Congress (2017), accessed May 4, 2017.

19. Lisa Jane Disch, *The Tyranny of the Two-Party System* (New York: Columbia University Press, 2002), 1–3.

20. Gregory Krieg, "South Dakota GOP Uses 'Emergency' Rules to Repeal Anti-Corruption Law," CNN, February 2, 2017.

21. Brian Cruikshank, "Overview of State Laws on Public Financing," National Conference of State Legislatures, accessed May 4, 2017.

22. Michael J. Malbin, *Citizen Funding for Elections* (Washington, DC: Campaign Finance Institute, 2015), 10.

23. Ava Mehta and DeNora Getachew, eds., *Breaking Down Barriers: The Faces of Small Donor Public Finance* (New York: Brennan Center for Justice, New York University School of Law, 2016), 12.

24. Connecticut Senate Democrats, "Bio & Committees: About Senator Winfield," accessed May 4, 2017.

25. Mehta and Getachew, *Breaking Down Barriers*, 12.

26. Michael G. Miller, *Subsidizing Democracy: How Public Funding Changes Elections and How It Can Work in the Future* (Ithaca, NY: Cornell University Press, 2014), 54–55, 61.

27. Miller, *Subsidizing Democracy*, 77–78.

28. Paul S. Ryan, *Investing in Democracy: Creating Public Financing of Elections in Your Community* (Los Angeles: Center for Governmental Studies, 2003), 8.

29. Center for Working Families, "Public Financing of Elections and Communities of Color," memo from Chloe Tribich, Center for Working Families, to Larry Parham, Citizen Action of New York, February 16, 2012, https://www.scribd.com/document/81949813/Public-financing-of-elections-and-communities-of-color.

30. Angela Migally and Susan Liss, *Small Donor Matching Funds: The NYC Election Experience* (New York: Brennan Center for Justice, 2010), 21.

31. *2007 Study Report: Has Public Funding Improved Maine Elections?* (Augusta: Maine Commission on Governmental Ethics and Election Practices, 2007), 17.

32. Lee Drutman, "Congress Has Very Few Working Class Members. Here's Why That Matters," Sunlight Foundation, June 3, 2014.

33. Adam Lioz, *Stacked Deck: How the Racial Bias in Our Big Money Political System Undermines Our Democracy and Our Economy* (New York: Demos, 2016), 36.

34. Elisabeth Genn et al., *Donor Diversity Through Public Matching Funds* (New York: Brennan Center for Justice, New York University Law School, 2012), 4.

35. Clean Elections Institute, *Reclaiming Democracy in Arizona: How Clean Elections Has Expanded the Universe of Campaign Contributors* (Phoenix: Clean Elections Institute), 3.
36. Michael J. Malbin, Peter W. Brusoe, and Brendan Glavin, *What Is and What Could Be: The Potential Impact of Small-Donor Matching Funds in New York State Elections* (Washington, DC: Campaign Finance Institute, 2012), 3–4.
37. Rachael Fauss, *Fair Elections for New York State: How Public Matching Creates Greater Voter Choice and Competition* (New York: Citizens Union of the City of New York, 2012), 2, 15–21.
38. Calculated from *2007 Study Report*, 18.
39. Fauss, *Fair Elections for New York State*, 3.
40. Greenberg Quinlan Rosner, "Democracy Corps National: Frequency Questionnaire," December 2015, 10.
41. Robert M. Stern, *Sunlight State by State after* Citizens United*: How State Legislation Has Responded to* Citizens United (Washington, DC: Corporate Reform Coalition, 2012), 4.
42. Ann M. Ravel, "Dysfunction and Deadlock at the Federal Election Commission," *New York Times*, February 20, 2017.
43. Lee Drutman, "Congress Needs More and Better-Paid Staff," *Roll Call*, March 21, 2016.
44. Drutman, *The Business of America Is Lobbying*, 233.
45. Jack Maskell, *Post Employment, "Revolving Door" Laws for Federal Personnel* (Washington, DC: Congressional Research Service, 2014), 1.
46. Isaac Arnsdorf, "Trump Lobbying Ban Weakens Obama Rules," *Politico*, January 28, 2017.
47. "5 Crazy Facts about Lobbyists," Represent.Us, accessed May 9, 2017.
48. Drutman, *The Business of America Is Lobbying*, 231–32.
49. Ibid., 230.
50. Blair Bowie and Adam Lioz, *Billion-Dollar Democracy: The Unprecedented Role of Money in the 2012 Election* (New York: Demos, 2013), 7.
51. *Shelby County v. Holder*, 570 U.S. (2013).
52. Diana Kasdan, *Early Voting: What Works* (New York: Brennan Center for Justice, 2013), 5–8.
53. John B. Holbein and D. Sunshine Hillygus, "Making Young Voters: The Impact of Preregistration on Youth Turnout," *American Journal of Political Science* 60 (2016): 364–82, 10.1111/ajps.12177.
54. Project Vote, "Same-Day Registration Fact Sheet," 2015, 1.
55. Wang, *Democracy at a Crossroads*, 11.
56. Vanessa Perez, *Representational Bias in the 2012 Electorate* (Washington, DC: Project Vote, 2015), 6.
57. Ari Berman, "Automatic Voter Registration in Oregon Is Revolutionizing American Democracy," *Nation*, May 16, 2016.

58. Rob Griffin et al., *Who Votes with Authomatic Voter Registration?* (Center for American Progress, June 7, 2017).

59. Ibid.

60. Liz Kennedy, Lew Daly, and Brenda Wright, *Automatic Voting Registration: Finding America's Missing Voters* (New York: Demos, 2015), 2.

61. Democracy Day Act of 2014, S. 2918, 113th Congress (2014).

62. Mann and Ornstein, *It's Even Worse Than It Looks*, 140.

63. Lindsay Fendt, "6 Things You Should Know about Sunday's Elections in Costa Rica," *Tico Times*, January 31, 2014; Christopher Howard, "Two Important Events This Sunday," *Live in Costa Rica* blog, February 1, 2014.

64. Laura Barrón-López, Amber Ferguson, and Sam Levine, "67,000 Virginia Ex-Felons Just Got Their Voting Rights Back. This Man Wants to Make Sure They Keep Them," *Huffington Post*, October 21, 2016.

65. Alexander, *The New Jim Crow*, 161.

66. Ibid.

67. American Civil Liberties Union of Wisconsin, "Felony Disenfranchisement in Wisconsin," accessed May 4, 2017.

68. "Remarks by the President at the NAACP Conference," The White House, Office of the Press Secretary, Pennsylvania Convention Center, Philadelphia, July 14, 2015; Barack Obama, "The President's Role in Advancing Criminal Justice Reform," *Harvard Law Review* 130, no. 3 (2017): 864.

69. Wood, *Implementing Reform*, 7.

70. Ibid.

71. National Conference of State Legislatures, "Redistricting Commissions: State Legislative Plans," December 7, 2015, http://www.ncsl.org/research/redistricting/2009-redistricting-commissions-table.aspx.

72. California Citizens Redistricting Commission, "About: FAQ."

73. Daley, *Ratf**ked*, 152–53.

74. Ibid., 149–50.

75. Anthony J. Gaughan, "To End Gerrymandering: The Canadian Model for Reforming the Congressional Redistricting Process in the United States," *Capital University Law Review* 41 (2013): 1054–55.

76. Ibid.; Amy Roberts, "By the Numbers: Longest-serving Members," *CNN*, June, 7, 2013.

77. *Maine Gubernatorial Races, 1974–2014* (Augusta: League of Women Voters of Maine).

78. Robert Fekete, "Rank the Vote: Comparing Voting in Ireland and the United States," *FairVote*, June 24, 2013.

79. "Maine Voters Adopt Ranked Choice Voting," *FairVote*, November 9, 2016.

80. National Popular Vote, "Two-Thirds of Presidential Campaign Is in Just 6 States," accessed May 4, 2017.

81. National Popular Vote, "Polls Show More Than 70% Support for a Nationwide Vote for President," accessed May 4, 2017.

82. National Popular Vote, "Maryland," "Status of National Popular Vote Bill in Each State," accessed May 4, 2017.
83. Sam Gustin, "FCC Passes Compromise Net Neutrality Rules," *Wired*, December 21, 2010.
84. Andrew Zajac and Todd Shields, "Verizon Wins Net Neutrality Court Ruling Against FCC," *Bloomberg*, January 14, 2014.
85. Kimberlee Morrison, "Net Neutrality: FCC Reclassifies ISPs as Common Carriers," *Adweek*, February 26, 2015.
86. Battle for the Net, "How We Won Net Neutrality," accessed May 4, 2017.
87. Federal Communications Commission, "Protecting and Promoting the Open Internet," GN Docket No. 14–28, Notice of Proposed Rulemaking, FCC 14–61, para. 2 (2014).
88. Leticia Miranda, "The FCC's Net Neutrality Proposal Explained," *Nation*, May 21, 2014.
89. FCC, "Protecting and Promoting the Open Internet," para. 153.
90. Fight for the Future, "Net Neutrality Activists Park Truck with Giant Video Billboard Directly Across From FCC Building in Washington, DC," news release, September 15, 2014.
91. Ibid.
92. Battle for the Net, "How We Won Net Neutrality."
93. Rebecca R. Ruiz, "F.C.C. Sets Net Neutrality Rules," *New York Times*, March 12, 2015.
94. Corinne Grinapol, "FCC Chair on Net Neutrality Vote: 'Today Is the Proudest Day of My Public Policy Life,'" *Adweek*, February 26, 2015.
95. Jim Puzzanghera, "Top GOP Lawmaker Calls Net Neutrality 'Politically Generated Populist Furor,'" *Los Angeles Times*, March 19, 2015.
96. Berners-Lee, "Three Challenges for the Web."
97. Gallup, "Americans' Confidence in Institutions Stays Low," June 13, 2016; Priyanka Boghani, "Is Civilian Oversight the Answer to Distrust of Police?," *Frontline*, PBS, July 13, 2016.
98. Sean Pyles, "Richmond Police Commission Proposes Sweeping Changes," Radio Free Richmond, January 21, 2016; Nick Chapman, "Council Approves Police Commission Reforms, Perez Investigation," *Radio Free Richmond*, February 3, 2016.
99. John Geluardi, "Too Much Police Oversight in Richmond?," *East Bay Express*, March 2, 2016.
100. Participatory Budgeting Project, "What Is PB: PB Gives Ordinary People Real Power Over Real Money," accessed May 2, 2017.
101. Peter Dreier, "We Need More Protest to Make Reform Possible," *Nation*, August 6, 2009.
102. Bill Moyers, "Moyers on Clinton, Obama, Kind, and Johnson: A Bill Moyers Essay," PBS, January 18, 2008.
103. Berg, Hahn, and Schmidhauser, *Corruption in the American Political System*, 200–201.

104. Rev. Dr. William J. Barber II and Jonathan Wilson-Hartgrove, *The Third Reconstruction: Moral Mondays, Fusion Politics, and the Rise of a New Justice Movement* (Boston: Beacon Press, 2016), 122.

CHAPTER 6: MEET THE DEMOCRACY MOVEMENT

1. Paul Blumenthal, "Lawmakers Respond to Democracy Spring Protests with Call for Democracy Hearings," *Huffington Post,* April 21, 2016.
2. Srinivasan S. Pillay, MD, *Life Unlocked: 7 Revolutionary Lessons to Overcome Fear* (New York: Rodale, 2010), 51.
3. Forward Together Moral Movement & HKONJ People's Assembly Coalition, "About: President"; NAACP, "Dr. William Barber."
4. Barber and Wilson-Hartgrove, *The Third Reconstruction*, 53.
5. Cathy Lynn Grossman, "'Moral Monday' Expands to a Week of Social Justice Action Across U.S.," *Washington Post,* August 19, 2014; "Legislative Roundup, Jan. 25, 2016," *Santa Fe New Mexican,* January 25, 2016; "Hundreds of Moral Mondays Activists Protest At Chicago Board of Trade, 41 Arrested," ABC, November 2, 2015.
6. The Movement for Black Lives, "About Us."
7. Vann R. Newkirk II, "The Permanence of Black Lives Matter," *Atlantic,* August 3, 2016.
8. Lou Dobbs, *War on the Middle Class: How the Government, Big Business, and Special Interest Groups Are Waging War on the American Dream and How to Fight Back* (New York: Viking Penguin, 2006), 1.
9. Mark Hensch, "Bob Dole: We Need to 'Stop All This Money in Politics,'" *Hill,* July 1, 2015.
10. Alan Simpson, "Former Sen. Alan Simpson: Restore the Balance of Money in Politics," *Time,* December 15, 2015.
11. Fatimah Wasseem, "Howard Voters Approve Measure to Use Taxpayer Dollars for Local Campaigns," *Baltimore Sun,* November 8, 2016; *Governor's Task Force to Study Campaign Financing 1st Report* (Annapolis, MD: Task Force to Study Campaign Financing, 1975).
12. "Chronicle Recommends: Yes on SF Proposition T," editorial, *San Francisco Chronicle,* October 4, 2016.
13. Evelyn Rupert, "Democrats Vote to Overhaul Super Delegate System," *Hill,* July 23, 2016.
14. Ben Wofford, "Why Thousands of Americans Are Lining Up to Get Arrested in D.C. This Week," *Rolling Stone,* April 13, 2016.
15. Angela Davis, *Freedom Is A Constant Struggle* (Chicago: Haymarket Books, 2016), 20.
16. Keeanga-Yamahtta Taylor, *From #BLACKLIVESMATTER to Black Liberation* (Chicago: Haymarket Books, 2016), 128–29.
17. Ibid., 127–29.

18. Bob Sloan and Mike Elk, "The Hidden History of ALEC and Prison Labor," *Nation,* August, 1, 2011.
19. Lance Selfa, *The Democrats: A Critical History* (Chicago: Haymarket Books, 2012), 26.

CHAPTER 7: LISTEN UP, AMERICA! NORTH CAROLINA HAS A STORY TO TELL

1. Seth Freed Wessler, "Is This the End of the Southern Strategy, or Its Entrenchment?," *Color Lines,* November 12, 2012.
2. Chris Kardish, "How North Carolina Turned So Red So Fast," *Governing,* July 2014; "US Poverty Level by State," *World Atlas,* updated February 21, 2017.
3. Gary O. Bartlett and Veronica W. Degraffenreid, *Report On Same-Day Registration: Experiences in the 2008 Primary & General Election* (Raleigh: North Carolina State Board of Elections, 2009), 1.
4. North Carolina State Board of Elections, "Election Information: General Election Voter Turnout," accessed May 2, 2017; Wang, *Democracy at a Crossroads,* 16.
5. Democracy North Carolina, "60,000+ Teenagers Added to Voter Rolls Thanks to Unique Law in North Carolina," news release, September 17, 2012, 1.
6. Andy Kroll, "This Is What a Multimillionaire Calling in His Chits Looks Like," *Mother Jones,* June 14, 2013.
7. Jane Mayer, "State for Sale," *New Yorker,* October 10, 2011.
8. Ibid.
9. Ibid.
10. Chris Kromm, "Investigative Series: How Pope Reigns," *Facing South,* January 14, 2011.
11. North Carolina Session Law 2010–170, Section 1 (amending G.S. 163–278.6) and Section 2 (amending G.S. 163–278.12).
12. Chris Kromm, "Explainer: How Much Did Art Pope's Network Really Spend on North Carolina's 2010 Legislative Elections?," *Facing South,* October 7, 2011.
13. Mayer, "State for Sale."
14. David Weigel, "Gerrymandering Denialists: Still Wrong, For New Reasons!," *Slate,* October 14, 2013.
15. North Carolina Center for Public Policy Research, "49 Legislators Already Not Returning, Could Set Turnover Record, Says N.C. Policy Center," May 12, 2012.
16. Chris Kromm and Alex Kotch, "Big Money's Map Mischief in North Carolina," *Facing South,* February 12, 2016.
17. Chris Kromm, "Art Pope Rides Again," *Facing South,* November 21, 2012.
18. Lisa Rab, "Meet the Preacher Behind Moral Mondays," *Mother Jones,* April 14, 2014.

19. Reid Wilson, "27 Other Things the North Carolina Voting Law Changes," *Washington Post*, September 8, 2013.

20. Rick Hasen, "NC Senate Approves GOP-Backed Election Changes," *Election Law Blog*, July 25, 2013.

21. Democracy North Carolina, "Special-Interest Funding Declines in State Court Elections as 77% of the Top Judges Qualify for Public Funds," news release, December 21, 2010.

22. North Carolina Voters for Clean Elections, "First in the Nation: NC's Judicial Public Financing Program," accessed May 4, 2017.

23. Chris Kromm, "How Art Pope Killed Clean Elections for Judges in North Carolina," *Facing South*, June 13, 2013.

24. Morgan L. W. Hazelton et al., "Does Public Financing Affect Judicial Behavior? Evidence from the North Carolina Supreme Court," *American Politics Research* 44 (2015): 4, doi: 10.1177/1532673X15599839.

25. Julie Ebenstein, "North Carolina's Step Backward for Democracy," American Civil Liberties Union, July 30, 2015.

26. Associated Press, "Almost 900 Arrested So Far at Moral Monday Protests in Raleigh," WITN, July 22, 2013.

27. Forward Together Moral Movement/HKONJ People's Assembly Coalition, "About: People's Agenda," accessed May 4, 2017.

28. Rab, "Meet the Preacher."

29. David Swerdlick, "Moral Mondays' Barber Says America's Political System Suffers from a Heart Problem," *Root*, February 15, 2015.

30. Max Blau, "A Mayor Fights to Save a Small-Town Hospital: 'It's Life or Death,'" *Stat News*, December 21, 2016.

31. Michael Wines and Alan Blinder, "Federal Appeals Court Strikes Down North Carolina Voter ID Requirement," *New York Times*, July 29, 2016.

32. Colin Campbell, "NC Republican Party Seeks 'Party Line Changes' to Limit Early Voting Hours," *News & Observer* (Raleigh, NC), August 17, 2016; Zachary Roth, "Analysis: North Carolina Counties That Cut Early Voting Sites See Lower Turnout," NBC News, October 22, 2016.

33. Roth, "Analysis: North Carolina."

34. Max J. Rosenthal, "North Carolina GOP Brags About How Few Black People Were Able to Vote Early," *Mother Jones*, November 7, 2016.

35. Public Policy Polling, "Why Pat McCrory Lost and What It Means in Trump's America," December 5, 2016.

36. Albert R. Hunt, "North Carolina Republicans Want to Rig the System," *Bloomberg*, December 6, 2016.

37. Richard Fausset, "North Carolina Governor Signs Law Limiting Successor's Power," *New York Times*, December 16, 2016.

38. Ibid.

39. Andrew Reynolds, "North Carolina Is No Longer Classified as a Democracy," *News & Observer*, December 22, 2016; Pippa Norris, "U.S. Elections Rank

Last Among All Western Democracies," Electoral Integrity Project, January 7, 2017.

40. Reynolds, "North Carolina Is No Longer Classified as a Democracy."

41. Rev. William J. Barber II, "In North Carolina, the March Against Extreme Policies Is Working," *Sojourners*, February 14, 2017.

42. Public Policy Polling, "Why Pat McCrory Lost."

CHAPTER 8: THE THRILL OF DEMOCRACY

1. Barber and Wilson-Hartgrove, *The Third Reconstruction*, 66.

2. Martin Luther King Jr., "A Testament of Hope," in *A Testament of Hope: The Essential Writings and Speeches of Martin Luther King, Jr.*, ed. James Washington (New York: HarperCollins, 1991), 328.

3. Harris Poll, "Survey Finds Nearly Three-Quarters (72 Percent) of Americans Feel Lonely," October 11, 2016.

4. *99%: The Occupy Wall Street Collaborative Film*, dir. Aaron Aites, Audrey Ewell, Nina Krstic, and Lucian Read (Los Angeles: Field Pictures, Gigantic Pictures, Verisimilitude, 2013), 16:22.

5. Oliver Davis, *Jacques Rancière* (Cambridge, UK: Polity Press, 2010).

6. Jonathan Matthew Smucker, *Hegemony How-To: A Roadmap for Radicals* (Chico, CA: AK Press, 2017), 23.

7. *99%*, Aites et al., 1:11:06.

8. Barber and Wilson-Hartgrove, *The Third Reconstruction*, 104.

9. Matthew Yglesias, "The Big Lessons of Trump's First 2 Weeks: Resistance Works," *Vox*, February 6, 2017.

10. Farhad Manjoo, "The Alt-Majority: How Social Networks Empowered Mass Protests Against Trump," *New York Times*, January 30, 2017.

11. Janet Conway, *Praxis and Politics: Knowledge Production in Social Movement* (New York: Routledge, 2006), 21–22.

12. Ibid., 22.

13. Ibid.

CHAPTER 9: DARE FOR DEMOCRACY

1. David Frum, "What Effective Protest Could Look Like," *The Atlantic*, February 6, 2017.

2. Simon Schnall, Kent D. Harber, Jeanine K. Stefanucci, and Dennis R. Proffitt, *Social Support and the Perception of Geographical Slant* (Bethesda, MD: National Institutes of Health, 2008).

3. Philip Bump, "Per House Members, Phone Calls on the GOP Health Bill Run 50-to-1 Against," *Washington Post*, March 24, 2017.

4. Barber and Wilson-Hartgrove, *The Third Reconstruction*, 52.

5. Brecht Forum Archive, "Augusto Boal & the Theater of the Oppressed."

6. Paul VanDeCarr, "The Power of 'Theatre of the Oppressed,'" *Chronicle of Philanthropy*, November 14, 2014.

7. Hacker and Pierson, *American Amnesia*, 170.

8. Pew Research Center, "Greatest Dangers in the World," October 16, 2014.

9. *New York Times*–CBS News Poll, "Americans' Views on Income Inequality and Workers' Rights," *New York Times*, June 3, 2015.

10. Bruce Stokes, Richard Wike, and Jill Carle, " Public Support for Action on Climate Change," Global Attitudes & Trends, Pew Research Center, November 5, 2015.

11. Gallup, "Guns: Gallup Historical Trends," October 7–11, 2015.

INDEX

Aaron, Craig, 43, 103
ABC News, on *Clinton Cash,* 45
action, importance of, 77, 155, 162, 163
Adams, Tieren, 144
Aegis Strategic, 50
Affordable Care Act (2010), 35, 48, 152, 162
African Americans, 67, 69, 70, 115, 132,
    143. *See also* people of color
Alabama, 67, 68
Alaska, 95
ALEC (American Legislative Exchange
    Council), 64–65, 70, 73, 75, 124
Alexander, Michelle, 69, 96, 97
Allbaugh, Todd, 67
American Bar Association, 29
American Enterprise Institute, 37–38
Americans for Prosperity, 44, 49, 50, 51,
    61, 129–30
Amway, 35, 58
anticorruption legislation, in South
    Dakota, 86, 120, 121
anti-democracy mindset, 27–53;
    anti-democracy uprising, origins
    of, 28; Chamber of Commerce and
    Powell memo, 33–34; conclusions
    on, 52–53; overview, 27–28; Powell
    memo, 29–33; wealthy families, ac-
    tivism of, 34–37; wealthy families,
    strategies of, 37–52
Anti-Democracy Movement: central
    goal of, 51; characteristics of, 111; ger-
    rymandering, use of, 71; government,

denigration of, 46–48, 63, 75; impact
    of, 75–76; leadership of, 34; narrative
    backed by, 157
Arellano, Stephen, 74
Arendt, Hannah, 48
Arizona, 68, 79–80, 83, 85, 88, 122
Asian Americans, impact of voter ID
    laws on, 67
Astroturf activism, 41, 50
Austin, Texas, 122
authoritarians, blame as primary strat-
    egy of, 53
automatic voter registration, 94–95, 122

Bailey, Kyle, 101
Baltimore, Democracy Spring march
    in, 125–26
banking industry, 33
Bank of America, 30
Bannon, Steve, 36–37, 45, 53
Barber, William J., II, 108, 113, 114,
    132–35, 137–38, 142, 146, 155
Beck, Glenn, 44, 50
Belhaven, North Carolina, 135
Benton County, Oregon, 122
Berger, Phil, 132
Berkeley, California, 121
Berman, Ari, 32, 65, 68
Berners-Lee, Tim, 46, 105
Bipartisan Campaign Reform Act
    (2002), 126
Bishop, Bill, 64

McHenry County, Illinois,
    anti-corruption measures in, 122
media: manipulation of, 41–46; news,
    sensationalization of, 17; Powell on,
    31; pro-democracy actions via, 153–54;
    think tanks' successes with, 39
Media Matters, 41
Media Research Center, 44
Meetup.com, 151–52
Mercatus Center, George Mason Uni-
    versity, 40
Mercer family, 36–37, 44, 45, 61
M4BL (Movement for Black Lives),
    113–15
Michigan, 71, 72, 73, 100
military rule, increasing belief in, 23
Miller, Michael, 87
Minnesota, 85
Mississippi, 66
Missouri, 121
Mnuchin, Steven, 63
model legislation, 64–65
momentum-based organizing, 147
momentum making, in Democracy
    Movement, 149–51
MomsRising.org, 151
money in politics, problem of, 54–61.
    See also campaign finance reform
money primaries, 56
Moral Mondays (Forward Together
    Movement), 112–13, 133–35, 136–38
Morgan, Michael, 137
Movement for Black Lives (M4BL),
    113–15
movement of movements (fusion poli-
    tics), 11, 113–14, 134–35, 136, 137, 153
MoveOn, 152, 154
Moyers, Bill, 107
Multnomah County, Oregon, 122
Murray, Charles, 38
Myrdal, Gunnar, 21

NAACP, 116, 129, 133, 135
Nader, Ralph, 28, 30, 101
narratives, producing new, 147

National Association of Scholars, 41
National Coalition for Dialogue and
    Deliberation, 154
National Popular Vote, 102
National Rifle Association, 58
National Traffic and Motor Vehicle
    Safety Act (1966), 28
Native Americans, public campaign
    financing and, 88
Nazi Germany, 6, 35, 48
NC Voters for Clean Elections Coali-
    tion, 132
net neutrality, 103–5
new civics, 41
New Hampshire, motto, 18
New Hampshire Rebellion, 145
Newkirk, Kai, 113
New Mexico, 114
Newsday, 33, 98
New York City, 86, 88–89
New York State, 73, 89, 97, 98, 102, 114
99Rise, 113
Nixon, Richard, 28, 32
Nordic countries, 11, 18
North Carolina, 68, 71, 72, 113–14, 128–38
North Carolina State Conference of
    NAACP Branches, 134
Nyhart, Nick, 61

Obama, Barack, 25, 36, 47, 52, 85, 96
Occupy Movement, ix, 113, 146, 147
O'Connor, Sandra Day, 29
Ohio, 68–69, 71–72, 122
Olguin-Tayler, Jodeen, 124–25, 126
Olin family, 34–35, 38, 40
Olin Foundation, 34, 40
O'Neal, Adam, 135
one-rule market, 14–17, 20, 157
OpenSecrets.org (Center for Responsive
    Politics), 61
Oregon, 95, 122
Ornstein, Norman, 46–47, 96
Orwell, George, 14
Our Revolution, 152
Owens, Marcus, 58

public-interest groups, lobbying expenditures, 62–63

public opinion: on *Citizens United*, 59; on climate change, 12, 76; on corporations, size and influence of, 30; Democracy Spring goals, agreement with, 145; on drug prices, 76; on economic inequality, 159–60; on election campaign financing, 12, 54, 84, 89, 107, 120; Kochs' opinions vs., 51; on national popular vote, 102; on taxes, 18; on voter fraud, 65

public policy, corporations' views on, 62

Public Policy Polling, 136, 138

public-service jobs, undervaluing of, 63

public utilities, 31

Pudner, John, 120

race and racism, 32–33, 52, 53, 69, 73, 123. *See also* people of color

Rand, Ayn, 130

ranked-choice voting, 100–101, 121, 122

Rapoport, Miles, 94

rational self-interest, 20

Ravel, Ann, 90

Reagan, Ronald, 15, 38, 42, 46, 85

real wages, 52

redistricting. *See* gerrymandering

Redistricting Majority Program (REDMAP), 71

regulations, 18, 157–58

Renaissance Technologies, 36

Repairers of the Breach, 134

Represent.Us, 80, 156

Republican Party: Americans for Prosperity and, 51; DeVos family and, 35; election spending, 55; filibuster, use of, 47; gerrymandering and, 71–72, 130; industry support for, 76; national popular vote, Republicans' support for, 102; in North Carolina, 128–38; ranked-choice voting and, 101; Republican National Committee, comparison with Koch network, 50–51; in South Dakota, 86; voter fraud, false claims of, 65, 93; voter ID laws, 67

Republican State Leadership Committee, 71

Research on the Shifting US Political Terrain (website), 49

resistance movements, 151–52

"Restore Democracy" (Democracy Matters program), 119

ReThink Media, 158

"revolving door," 63, 91

Reynolds, Andrew, 137

Rhoads, Mark, 64

Rhode Island, ethics reform in, 122

Richmond, California, citizen-police commission, 106

Ries, Curt, 113

rigged markets, 157

right to vote. *See* voting, voting rights

right-wing ideology, foundations' control of, 38

risk-taking, importance of, 161

Rivera, Rosemary, 124

Rodgers, Daniel, 41

Romney, Mitt, 17

Roosevelt, Franklin Delano, 18, 80, 107

Roosevelt, Theodore, 85

Roth, Zachary, 47

Rove, Karl, 49

Rubin, Robert, 64

rules, rigging of, 54–76; Anti-Democracy Movement, impact of, 75–76; big-money, increasing influence of, 54–61; lobbying, expansion of, 62–65; local democracy, preemption of, 73–75; voting power of anti-democracy opposition, reductions to, 65–73; workers rights, failure to protect, 75

Russia, 6, 69

Rust, John, 45

same-day voter registration, 94, 128–29, 131, 136

Samuelson, Paul, 41

Sanders, Bernie, 95, 119, 122, 152, 161

San Francisco, limits on lobbying, 121

Sarah Scaife Foundation, 41